GOD ENCOUNTERED

GOD ENCOUNTERED

A Contemporary
Catholic Systematic Theology

Volume Two/4:
The Revelation of the Glory

Part IVA:
The Genealogy of Depravity:
Morality and Immorality

FRANS JOZEF VAN BEECK, S. J.

A Michael Glazier Book
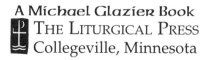
THE LITURGICAL PRESS
Collegeville, Minnesota

Grateful acknowledgment is made for the use of the following materials. Sizable portions of §137 and §139 appeared in article form as "Fantasy, the Capital Sins, the Enneagram, and Self-Acceptance: An Essay in Ascetical Theology," in *Pro Ecclesia* 3 (1994): 179–205. The illustration on the dust jacket, fol. 112*r* of *Codex Sanhippolytensis* N° 1 (15th cent.), is once again used by kind permission of the *Bischöfliche Alumnatsbibliothek*, Sankt Pölten, Austria.

Imprimi potest: Very Rev. Richard J. Baumann, S.J., Provincial, Chicago Province. March 29, 1999.

Nihil Obstat: Rev. Charles R. Meyer, S.T.D., *Censor Deputatus*. March 25, 1999.

Imprimatur: Most Reverend Raymond E. Goedert, M.A., S.T.L, J.C.L., Vicar General, Archdiocese of Chicago. March 25, 1999.

The *Nihil Obstat* and *Imprimatur* are official declarations that a book is free of doctrinal or moral error. No implication is contained therein that those who have granted the *Nihil Obstat* and *Imprimatur* agree with the content, opinions, or statements expressed.

FIRST EDITION

Cover design by Ann Blattner

Library of Congress Cataloging-in-Publication Data

Beeck, Frans Jozef van.
    The Revelation of the Glory. Part IVA. The Genealogy of Depravity: Morality and Immorality.

    (God Encountered; v. 2/4A)
    Bibliography: p.
    Includes index.
    1. Theology, Doctrinal. 2. Catholic Church—Doctrines.
    I. Title. II. Series: Beeck, Frans Jozef van.
    God Encountered; v. 2/4A
    BX1747.5.B4 vol. 2/4A
    ISBN 0-8146-5501-7

For Jim Walter

Παιδεύσει με δίκαιος ἐν ἐλέει καὶ ἐλέγξει με.[*]

(Psalm 140, 5 LXX)

---

[*] *The just man will rebuke me with compassion and so succeed in correcting me.*

O admirabile commercium!
Creator generis humani,
animatum corpus sumens,
de Virgine nasci dignatus est:
et procedens homo sine semine,
largitus est nobis suam deitatem.

What admirable exchange!
Humankind's Creator,
taking on body and soul,
in his kindness, is born from the Virgin:
and, coming forth as man, yet not from man's seed,
he has lavished on us his divinity.

(Antiphon at vespers, January 1,
Feast of the Holy Mother of God)

Contents

PART IVA. THE GENEALOGY OF DEPRAVITY:
Morality and Immorality

Preface

Another change of plans. Toward the end of 1993, after a productive summer and fall in Indonesia, supported by the grant of a paid
leave of absence from Loyola University Chicago, I had reached the
midpoint of what is now chapter 16 of volume II/4A; chapters 12,
13, and 14 looked acceptable and thus, ready for publication; they
became volume II/3, subtitled *Finitude and Fall*, published in 1995,
just over four years ago. On the other hand, chapters 15 and 16 had
begun to look more and more unsatisfactory. Small wonder that in
the preface to *Finitude and Fall*, I compared the magnitude of the
challenge involved in treating Creation and Fall in a dependably cos-
mological-anthropological-theological fashion to the sighting of a
dragon in the theological landscape.

At that point, lore of long standing should have reminded me that
dragons are a lot harder to either befriend or defeat than I imagined,
and that definitive victories and beautiful friendships are out of the
question. Thus, as I became more familiar with the dragon of my
choice, I found that he (she?) was far wilier than I had anticipated.
Worse, her (his?) tail was far longer than I had ever held to be possible. No wonder my *quarta secundæ* turned out to be a task of unexpected intellectual and emotional intensity, full of impasses and surprises. This is where a wonderful source of encouragement took pity
on me once again—I mean The Liturgical Press, capably represented
by managing editor Mark Twomey and marketing director Peter Dwy-
er. They ended up suggesting that volume II/4 be published in two
installments.

The subtitle of both installments, *The Genealogy of Depravity,* implies
a twofold bow (if there is such a thing) in the direction of two figures
who have helped mark the course of modern Western Christianity's
history: John Calvin and Friedrich Nietzsche. Calvin took up the theology implied in Brother Martin Luther's exemplary experience of
being a *peccator pessimus;* clear-headed lawyer that he was, he turned it
into cold fact. Humanity's permanent condition was simply one of

incapacity and immorality: human beings suffered from irremediable sinfulness—the bitter fruit of the human bent for self-enslavement, from Adam and Eve on. The biblical account of humanity's immemorial rebellion against God prohibited any softening of this position—not even on behalf of God's own elect.

Three hundred years later, Friedrich Nietzsche became persuaded, with a passion, that the opposite was the case. Humanity's condition was miserable indeed, and certainly no less permanent than Calvin had understood its condition of weakness and vice to be. But what Nietzsche saw as humanity's central problem was not sin but its opposite: *morality.* Morality, he thought, had been brought about by cowardice—the human penchant to recoil from humanity's glorious Will-To-Be-and-Accomplish all it could be and accomplish.

Both agreed that despair at humanity's self-induced misery was the obvious conclusion. They also agreed that there was only one way of salvation. John Calvin, caught in deep pessimism about the possibility of restoring humanity to its grandeur, rested his case by exhorting the Christian soul to desperate abandon to God's inscrutable and everlasting decrees; Friedrich Nietzsche rested his by daring humanity's most capable representatives to recover their souls at last, by desperate deeds of human strength and self-reliance. Just how serious either of them was in clinical terms it is hard to tell, given Calvin's interest in city government and Nietzsche's sad final years.

Predictably, the catholic theological tradition at once saw the *via media:* Christian humanism. The choice was sound, of course, but the *theological* account of it offered by the important Catholic thinkers was tainted by one of the great prejudices of modernity, *viz.* that definitions were both *objective* and *authoritative.* Objectivity, it was agreed in circles beholden to the "essentialism" of rationalist scholasticism, meant that whatever is defined must be conceived as a *separate reality.* In this way, Catholic theology began to understand "human nature" as a totally known quantity; accordingly, humanity got locked up in the prison of its "nature"; in this fashion, the orders of nature and grace came to be *separated* where the catholic tradition had understood them as *distinguished* (§§84, 86, 88).

Sin, so Catholics proceeded to explain, had never succeeded in corrupting human nature, which it had remained God-given and hence, good. Put differently, Catholic theologians felt that in taking the edge off the Reformation's seriousness about sin and sinfulness they were doing the right thing by both humanity and humanity's God.

Yet the only feat this Catholic move accomplished was: adding fuel to the Protestant suspicion that Catholics did not *really* believe grace was necessary for salvation; there was little or no room left between the darkness of arrogant humanism and that of arrogant Catholicism.

The present book, along with its companion, is written at least partly to help put an end to this unnecessary dispute. It will argue that catholic theology is capable of endorsing the Reformation's abhorrence of sin while not disavowing the catholic tradition's insistence on humanity's inalienable privilege: being created in God's Image.

This book, then, along with its sequel, is the *quarta secundæ* of *God Encountered*. Still, it is not the doctrinal heart of *God Encountered* any more than its earlier companion, subtitled *Finitude and Fall*. Let us phrase this differently. Together, the three installments, II/3, II/4A, and II/4B, are a lengthy in-between exercise in cosmology, anthropology, and theology as they occur in the lived Christian life—not only in its satisfactions, joys, rewards, and graces, but also in its setbacks, regrets, failures, and falls from grace. The full account of the Christian understanding of life in the gracious presence of God must wait till volume II/5, to be subtitled *The Glory of God in the Face of Christ*.

Why this long delay of the exploration of Christian theology's central and most sacred theme? The interpretation of a passage in the work of Irenaeus of Lyons offered earlier (§78, 3) has already stated the reason. It was worded as follows:

If humanity and the world are not accepted in their natural, material, carnal integrity, Christianity itself disintegrates; none of it survives. There is *concordance* between the divine life and the natural order; God's saving plan *intrinsically fits* the humanity and the world that are to be saved. If the natural world is rejected as irrelevant to salvation or if its natural capacity for the divine life is denied, then there is no divine creation either, no incarnation, no redemption by the shedding of Christ's blood, no restoration of humanity to the divine likeness, no Eucharist, no membership in the Body of Christ, no resurrection, no life eternal, no responsible Christian life now.

This thesis holds good even for a world infected by sin. Irenaeus insists that despite the Fall, the world and humanity, far from having become Satan's property, have remained the property of the divine *Logos*: "Into his own he came" (Jn 1, 11). In other words, Jesus Christ is not the new face Almighty God has put on a world irreparably lost, but the Revelation of the Countenance of the Ancient of Days to a world long gone astray yet indelibly made in the divine Image:

But surely, there is no justice in [Christ's] coming to a place that belongs to others, against their will? And he did not really redeem us with his blood if he did not really become man, and if he did not restore to the work of his hands that humanity which, we read, was made in the beginning, in the image and likeness of God [cf. Gen 1, 26]? But no, he did not deceitfully steal what belonged to another; rather, he regained what was his own, [and he did so] both justly and generously. He acted justly with regard to the Apostasy, for he redeemed us from it at the cost of his blood [cf. Col 1, 14. 20]. He acted generously with regard to us, the redeemed: for we did not give him anything in advance [cf. Rom 11, 35], and it was not as if he needed something from us—in fact, it is us that need communion with him. Hence it was out of generosity that he poured himself out, so that he might gather us in the bosom of the Father.

Thus, the two installments of volume II/4 are an effort to offer as realistic and recognizable a treatment of human life in the cosmos and before God as possible —realistic, that is, from the point of view both of the cosmos' natural promise and of the failure and degeneracy that *seems* to have become second nature to it, especially in the case of humanity. In the words of Blaise Pascal: what will be treated is the *grandeur de l'homme* and the *misère de l'homme,* and it will be done in such a way as to show that the two cannot be separated—not even by sin. Christians can make their own the words of that unforgettable and saintly Jewish genius, Rabbi Nahman of Bratslav: "Nothing is more whole than a broken heart."

The theological traditions that trace themselves back to the Reformation have shown how tempting it is to treat the gift of divine grace as the foil of the existential given of human sin *separately*—*i.e.,* without reference to created nature. But there *are* problems with this noble arrangement. For the big question is, in building Christian theology around the correlated themes of Sin and Grace, can we really be sure that our treatment will able to control our all-too-human fascination with evil? It has already been suggested (§113, 2) that

. . . not each and every instance of moral abhorrence is of God or unites with God. We have an inherent penchant for inauthenticity and self-absorption, by which we may lose touch with God, our true selves, and reality at large. One prominent form of this self-absorption is self-righteousness; consequently, not even righteous indignation at human sinfulness—our own and others'—is in every instance rooted in our deepest affinity with God; hence, it is not in every instance a reliable guide to God. Human beings will denounce the sins of the world they live in; they will even zealously confess their own part in them; known sinners are very capable of ardent self-reproach, and even more capable of it when found out. Yet no matter how sincere and conscientious such sentiments may be, and no matter how justified they may appear, they just may be, in cases, forms of the very inauthenticity and depravity they profess to detest—forms all the harder to detect for the robe of righteousness they wear.

In other words, any treatment of sin *as a theme in its own right* is liable to be guided by an all-too-human indignation at humanity's sinful ways or by a *ditto* frustration with the persistence of its sinful tendencies. That is to say, a properly *theological* treatment of sin may miscarry by that primal cause *and* consequence of sin: humanity's sinful absorption with both self and righteousness.

This is not to say that the option in favor of catholicity in the treatment of sin is without danger. The churches of the Reformation have long objected to what they view as the catholic theological tradition's systemic *naturalism*. And indeed, too often has catholicism displayed a facile confidence in humanity's ability to take its cues from the order of nature without realizing that the world in which we actually live is inconceivable apart from God's mercy. In fact, I just may be guiltier of this than I realize myself. Let me, in a departure from conventional wisdom, quote my wonderful, eagle-eyed ecclesiastical censor, the Rev. Charles R. Meyer. His report reminds me that "Christians generally believe that in all their struggles against adversity, both cosmic and psychological, individual as well as social, they are assisted by the grace of God." And he continues to suggest, with characteristic politeness and irony, that the treatment offered in this book "seems to lack little in the complexity of its parts," but "insofar as it presents itself as theological," it seems to lack "continuous insistence on this fact." I have checked this out, and I have indeed discovered that the word "grace" in the sense in which Father Meyer means it, actually occurs only five times—reason enough to revise this book, were it not for two facts. First, in my teaching and pastoral experience I have discovered that many Catholics regard "grace" as a quantifiable entity rather than as an intensity of encompassing divine *presence*. Secondly, in volume II/ 4B (§146, 1, b), I *will* elaborate this general Christian belief, which was already stated, albeit *sotto voce*, in an earlier volume (§122, 1, g):

... the Great Tradition has consistently held that wholly gracious and other-regarding love (*agapē*, or charity) *integrates* and *ennobles* natural love (*erōs*) just as grace presupposes nature and perfects it (§80, 2–4; cf. §26, 2, a; §23, 3). Or, to use an expression used earlier in this book, the Tradition has insisted that alienation, far from being identical with estrangement, "has a positive prognosis" (§122, 1, e and [*f*]).

My close friend and colleague James J. Walter, to whom I am offering this book, implicitly warned me of this years ago. Jim and I arrived at Loyola University Chicago in the summer of 1985. Newcomers to a large department, we both took our time getting to know one another, but one of my earliest recollections of Jim is the following. I was observing, in jest but certainly not *just* in jest, that my preference, in theology as in life, was the pursuit not of the good and the right but of the true and the elegant; in fact, I still cannot recall any resolution to do good things and do them right that I have kept for more than a day and a half. (In my own mind I added that truth and elegance—the former often in the shape of moments and times of constructive confusion or *ditto* embarrassment in the presence of others more accomplished than myself, and the latter mainly in the form of liturgy, music, and poetry, in that order—had proved far more effective than ethics in charming me into such moral probity as could reasonably be called my own.) Jim, smiling quietly, assured me that nobody can get away with doing systematic theology without facing the music of morality and immorality, sooner or later. He was right of course; but that is not my point; it is that in due time Jim's prophecy came home to me. Suddenly there it was, right in front of me: the question of the actual roots and the actual dynamics of Creation and Fall, of virtue and sin. Having never had much of a taste for moral theology of any kind, my only possible entry into these themes became: thinking them through for myself, from scratch, in the context of my own project. This is where Jim really came in.

While I was working on what is now volume II/3, I drew much profit from his advice and encouragement, but I was confident that I was still making theological sense pretty much on my own. Matters drastically changed once I had discovered the matters now contained in this book, and started to elaborate them. If Jim had not regularly reassured me that I was well within the ballpark, I fear I might have become so irresolute as to be incapable of sustaining any longer the unsettling climate of charm and ominousness, of *grandeur* and *misère*, of fascination and revulsion, of dazzling beauty and appalling degeneracy—the atmosphere which, as everyone knows, is so obvious in environments human beings have to share with a dragon or two.

Jim likes to say that he is a systematician who does ethics. That he is the former I have known since our earliest conversations at Loyola as well as from some of his writings. That he practices ethics of the fundamental and the applied kind is something I have known for a long time from some of his writings, and even more from meeting people whose judgment I respect. But only now that my foray into fundamental Christian ethics is done am I starting to realize what Jim must have had in mind when he first told me that I would have to face ethics before I would ever finish *God Encountered.* None of this implies, of course, that Jim is to be suspected, let alone accused, of complicity in the doubtlessly numerous passages in this book that bear witness to my continuing immaturity as an ethicist—a condition I am unlikely to change any time soon.

One feature—the most important—of my relationship with Jim is still missing in this account: deep, quiet mutual trust and friendship. This is also where my indebtedness to Jim very much begins to include his wife MaryAnn, as well as their children Jennifer and Robert. But these are blessings so exquisite that they are better enjoyed and cherished in moments of thankfulness than detailed in print. This is going to be all the more true by virtue of the fact that even as I am putting the finishing touch on this preface, the Walters are leaving Chicago and heading Westward, to California.

Once again, I owe much to friends and critics who helped shape sizable sections of this book, both by encouragement and criticism, and by their interest in, comments on, and conversation about, particular parts and specific issues. Among them, let me simply mention Marc Leclerc, S.J., George Schner, S.J., Michael Schuck (whose stimulating comments enabled me to improve large tracts of text in chapter 15), Dr. Jerome P. Wagner, and Michele Langowski.

Frans Jozef van Beeck, S.J.

Abbreviations

AristBWks	*The Basic Works of Aristotle.* Edited by Richard McKeon. New York: Random House, 1941.
CF	*The Christian Faith in the Doctrinal Documents of the Catholic Church.* Edited by J. Neuner and J. Dupuis. New York: Alba House, 1982.
DH	*Enchiridion Symbolorum Definitionum Declarationum de Rebus Fidei et Morum. Kompendium der Glaubensbekenntnisse und kirchlichen Lehrentscheidungen.* Edited by Heinrich Denzinger; revised by Peter Hünermann and Helmut Hoping. 37th edition, in Latin and German. Freiburg: Herder, 1991.
DictSpir	*Dictionnaire de Spiritualité,* Paris, Beauchesne, 1937–.
GS	*Gaudium et Spes:* The Pastoral Constitution on the Church in the Modern World (Vatican II).
Hall	Stuart George Hall, *Melito of Sardis: On Pascha, and Fragments. Oxford Early Christian Texts.* Oxford: Clarendon, 1979.
LG	*Lumen Gentium:* The Dogmatic Constitution on the Church (Vatican II).
LXX	The Septuagint version of the Jewish Scriptures.
MT	The Masoretic text of the Hebrew Scriptures.
NPNCF	*A Select Library of Nicene and Post-Nicene Fathers of the Christian Church.* New York: Christian Literature Company, 1887–1992. (Reprint. Grand Rapids, MI: Wm. B. Eerdmans, 1979–83.)
PG	*Patrologia Græca.* Edited by J. P. Migne. 162 vols. Paris: 1857–1866.
Philok	*The Philokalia.* Edited by G. E. H. Palmer, Philip Sherrard, and Kallistos Ware. 3 vols. London and Boston: Faber and Faber, 1979–86.
PL	*Patrologia Latina.* Edited by J. P. Migne. 221 vols. Paris: 1844–1864.
PlatoCDia	*The Collected Dialogues of Plato.* Edited by Edith Hamilton and Huntington Cairns. *Bollingen Series,* LXXI. Princeton: Princeton University Press, 1961.
Vg	The (Latin) Vulgate text of the Scriptures.

Part IV/A

THE GENEALOGY OF DEPRAVITY:
Morality and Immorality

Ambiguity, Self-Definition, "Misstatement"

[§126] ONCE AGAIN: POSITIONS

[1] In the previous parts of *God Encountered*, a theological understanding of sin—its origins, its progress, and its establishment as a system—was repeatedly promised (§12, 1, b; §79, 4, c and [*dd*]; §84, 4; §113, 3–4 and 5, b, [*s*]; §125, 7–8; cf. also §141, 1; §146, 13). The time has come to redeem these pledges.

By way of introduction, we return to previous discussions of "positions" (§108, 1–5; cf. §122, 2–4). Let us recall three points.

[a] First of all, what are the uses of alienation? In practice, alienation involves two things, distinguishable but not separable. Firstly, it involves going out of ourselves in the circumstances and situations in which we find ourselves, in such a way as to adopt positions, whether affirmatively or by default; in doing so, we both actualize and discover our native identity and further enhance it. Secondly, alienation involves engaging and appraising and testing and appreciating and further enhancing realities other than ourselves, of both the cosmic and the distinctively human kind; in doing so, we find ourselves summoned to turn some of the world of cosmic otherness to higher purpose, and (in the case of other persons and communities) to add to *their* advancement, by affirming their authentic identity and even enhancing it.

For the record (though not just for the record), let us recall that there are ominous alternatives to these possibilities. For, unfortunately, in adopting positions we may also turn alienation to dubious or evil purpose. Thus, in the very act of actualizing (or seeking to actualize) ourselves, we may compromise our identity; by abusing things cosmic, we may do an injustice to them, and through them, to others; and instead of enhancing other persons and communities, we may diminish them.

[b] Secondly, each and every manner of human engagement with otherness, whether involuntary or intentional, whether incidental

or relatively habitual, and at any level of ontological intensity whatsoever, involves taking positions [a]. Thus, the number of possible positions is *indefinite*—a multiplicity adding up to a profusion.

[c] Thirdly, it is precisely on account of this multiplicity that each and every position we take, including those we take in a deliberate, responsible fashion, are beset by *ambiguity*. This holds true even if we prescind from the fact that we are part of a *sinful* humanity and of a world marked by sin. For taking positions by engagement with otherness is *naturally* marked by ambivalence. No position, however attractive, persuasive, or defensible, is ever absolute.

[2] Having acknowledged that ambiguity is inherent in any and all positions we adopt, we are ready to take the first step toward a fundamental theological understanding of the genealogy of sin. This we do by raising a first question. *Where lies the root of this ambiguity?*

First of all, it lies *in ourselves*—human agents seeking to engage the otherness that is both different from us and integral to us. This, of course, does not imply that in the act of going out of ourselves we inevitably surrender or lose our deeper selves; that would reduce our every engagement to a wrong, and arguably even sinful, act. Rather, our engagement with otherness is frequently inspired by authentic, basic *freedom* to reach out to human persons and cosmic things as genuinely other. And even if some of our engagements should be less than genuinely free, they often lead to growth in authentic freedom. This is consistent with a claim already made: alienation has, at bottom, a positive prognosis (§122, 1, e).

Still, our engagement with otherness *also* bespeaks something rather different from freedom, *viz.*, a *necessary, inescapable condition*. It is this: we never entirely cease to *depend* on otherness, not only for our existence, but also for the actualization of our native potential for growth and development. Alienation is integral to our ontological makeup; it pulls us outside ourselves by virtue of our being involved in what we have called *the mutualities of cosmic process* (§115, 8; §122,

---

[a] "Positions," therefore, take not only the shape of personal, genuinely spiritual relationships and of profound, interpersonally shared intellectual, moral, and religious convictions and concerns. They also come in other, rather more cosmic forms of association with other human beings, be it at the more operational-con-sensual-rational level of "society" or at the largely indeliberate, functional-instinctual level of human life together having the properties of a "herd" (cf. §108, 1, d, [g]). Finally, positions occur in the form of patterns of engagement with the infra-human cosmos, such as moving about in our environment in pursuit of material objects like food, shelter, and attractive material things, and settling down permanently in order to use, cherish, enhance, and enjoy them.

1, b and e). On reflection, we realize this is perceptible. At the sentient level, we always remain open, *passively* (or on any case receptively), to the otherness that surrounds us; the life of the senses is something we can never entirely take our leave from; one way or another, we find ourselves affected by cosmic mutuality—the phenomenon Aquinas calls "natural immutation."[1] But this is not all. Even when we are most deliberate in adopting positions, we are still affected by a lack of definition, distinctiveness, completeness, and integration *within ourselves*; thus, taking positions is always a tacit acknowledgment of *need*. That is to say, elements of passivity and involuntariness (and hence, of confusion, mishap, and struggle) never cease to influence our every act of active engagement with otherness. Put differently: our engagement with otherness remains *at least partly involuntary* (cf. §111, 3). Eventually, the truth of this observation will become unmistakable: otherness will definitively catch up with us, in the form of the supervention of involuntary death (cf. §124, 3).

Our adoption of positions, therefore, no matter how freely and affirmatively we do it, never ceases to bespeak *our own finitude and inadequacy*. Let us put this differently. In our condition of alienation, we cannot help being affected by substantial elements of randomness and indeterminacy—the basic ingredients of cosmic process (§115, 5; cf. §115, 8; 10).[2] Hardly ever are we unconditionally assured in advance (nor even always in retrospect) that the positions we are about to adopt (or have adopted) are safe, productive, profitable, or right, either for ourselves or for others, or for the world outside us. The partial ways in which we shape, define, and identify ourselves in various degrees of intensity and permanence remain at least to some degree a matter of imprecision and irresolution—that is, of inadequacy and "weakness." Much as it may be true that we do not always adopt positions *out of* weakness, we always adopt them *in* weakness.

[3] These subjective sources of ambiguity have their counterparts in the world of objective otherness. Like ourselves, every cosmic reality we engage as we adopt positions is limited and particular. In that sense, all cosmic realities are *weak*—often more, often less than ourselves, yet never wholly unlike ourselves. The fact that we adopt positions in subjective weakness, therefore, is matched by the fact that the positions we adopt are *objectively* ambiguous, on two accounts.

Firstly, they are subject to inevitable (and often indeterminate) *extrinsic* involvements. All positions, being finite, have hidden affinities with and connote implicit counterpositions (cf. §108, 2 and a); that is to say, they resist complete definition. Secondly, just by reason of their being particular, all positions are *intrinsically* ambiguous as well. Nothing finite can fully satisfy us. And being finite, each and every position is less solid and stable than it looks. In sum, positions are liable to be either too vague or too restrictive for us; but either way, they are invariably inadequate to our native potential for authenticity and integrity. Both points deserve elaboration.

[a] Let us start with the lack of *extrinsic* demarcation and distinctness inherent in positions. If and when we adopt them, we find ourselves leaving at least some of their ambiguity and vagueness unattended to and unstated; that is, in adopting positions, we tend to treat things and persons as firmer, more free-standing, and more definite than they are. That is, we "misstate" our positions—in this case by overstatement. But in thus exaggerating their distinctiveness we implicitly underrate the fact that positions can draw us into involvements and commitments we do not intend, choose, or even care for. It is a matter of common experience that, in taking positions, we never quite know what they have in store for us further down the line. Not only do positions we have adopted have a way of disappointing us, going blank on us, or leaving us in the lurch; they also have a knack of mobbing us, of running away with us, of leading us by the nose, even of misleading us outright. That is to say, positions can defeat us by engulfing us in a wave of unintended and unwanted association and consequence. We have a tendency to overlook this, but this makes us even more susceptible to loss of self-discipline, self-definition, and self-possession.

[b] Analogous consequences attach to positions by virtue of their *intrinsic* instability. In taking positions, we find ourselves leaving at least some of their limitations and liabilities implicit. That is to say, in adopting and affirming positions, we will hide their weaknesses to ourselves and misjudge their inner strength; we will treat them as more reliable than they are. In that sense, too, we "misstate" them—again, by overstatement.

Yet in so doing we forget that *any* particular position is too tenuous a basis to bear the burden of our quest for authentic fulfillment, and too narrow and insignificant an aim to accommodate the intentionality of our entire being. We forget that "we cannot attach the width and spread of our feelings to so small a mark";[3] we disregard the fact that positions are capable of controlling us by dint of unwanted confinement and isolation. This, too, makes us vulnerable—in this case, susceptible to self-imprisonment and lack of freedom and self-abandon.

[c] Needless to say (and making allowances for differences in individual and communal temperament), most of us are naturally (though often only unthematically) *aware* of the indistinctness and the unreliability of everything around us. We are naturally wary of overstatement, too. Except for the truly impulsive among us, we tend to malinger. But this often results in our being hesitant in the adopting of positions. Thus, while it is true that we may misstate ourselves by committing ourselves to overstated positions, we tend to do so no less by being non-committal—by settling for ungenerous, cheerless understatement, and thus by passing up opportunities for growth.

We know, of course, that virtue lies in the middle, but genuine moderation often eludes us. The golden mean is hard to find, so we end up practicing mediocrity, by understatement (§123, 2–4).

[4] Now the question is, What makes us prone to misstatement? How is it that we fail to tailor our commitments realistically, prudently as well as courageously, in such a way as to suit the actual positions that we adopt, limited as they are? For answers to these questions we must search once again the human heart—that is, our "unstable ontological constitution" (§112, 5).

Basically, taking positions flows from humanity's native dynamism —our immanent, *unlimited* desire for growth and maturity, exercised in acts of engagement with the world of otherness. Yet there *is* a dark side to this. For the ambiguities attendant on otherness activate deep-seated ambiguities within ourselves—those that result from our unstable ontological constitution, which causes us to limp in our pursuit of authenticity (§112, 5). *Concupiscence* is with us (cf. §113, 3, b); the ways in which we take positions reflect the ways in which we handle ourselves at the most elementary level of our being.

By way of clarification, let us put this differently. Our experience of native transcendence is precarious; no wonder every encounter with otherness is a challenge to it. To grow in transcendence, we have no choice but to engage the other; yet the other is available to us only as conditioned by the contingencies of cosmic process, and cosmic process daunts us. After all, our participation in cosmic mutuality (cf. §115, 8) makes us not only familiar with otherness but also dependent on it; but the fact that we are dependent on otherness makes us apprehensive at the possibility of finding ourselves getting dissipated in it or captured by it. Either way, we feel we just might forfeit our transcendence. So, to cheer ourselves in the face of cosmic odds, we simplify, either by sharpening, exaggerating, idealizing, or by dulling, cutting down, and distrusting; we "misstate" our positions. But in doing so we not only fail to do justice to ourselves; we do an injustice to the other as well—we *distort* it. And in distorting the other, we also compromise our own integrity, identity, and freedom, whether quite grievously or ever so slightly, or (mostly) somewhere in between. But in so doing, we compromise that quality in ourselves by virtue of which we are natively attuned to God. We estrange ourselves from God. That is, we will falter and fail, pardonably. Not infrequently, we will sin. Quite often we will not sin very seriously, but then again, at times we will. In traditional catholic terminology, we will frequently sin "venially," and at times (or even often) "mortally" (cf. §121, 1, [*gg*]).

[5] Let us now make a key observation, to prevent ourselves from being a trifle too eager to plead not guilty by reason of insufficient deliberation. We may be absent-minded and irresolute, but not even the most ambivalent cosmic realities (or, for matter of that, the most forceful ones) can ever *force* a deliberately misstated (*i.e., strictly immoral*) position on us. Not even our own bodiliness can *force* misstated or immoral positions upon us, even though our bodies *are* the medium through which we experience, by dint of direct participation, the cosmos and its inherent penchant for what Emmanuel Lévinas has rightly called *violence:* purblind, undiscerning, unscrupulous sentient process along with its train of happenstance and natural evil. For the universe, "beautiful but morally unintelligible" as it is (§117, 2; cf. §115, 2), operates without *intentional* design; it neither misstates itself nor sins. Misstated positions, as well as genuinely sinful ones, come only out of us—human beings endowed with consciousness and free will:

All of you, listen to me, and try to understand this: nothing coming from outside people and going into them has the power to defile them. What really defiles people is what comes out of people. . . . Do you not realize that nothing that goes into people from outside can make them unclean, since it goes not into their hearts but into their bellies, and comes out and goes into the privy? . . . for from inside people's hearts come evil ways of thinking, acts of fornication, of theft, of homicide, of adultery, of cupidity, of wickedness; deception, debauchery, the evil eye, blasphemy, pride, lack of thoughtfulness: all these wicked things come from the inside, and they defile people.

(Mark 7, 14–15. 18–23)

It is true, of course, that all things cosmic, including our bodies, *lend themselves* to misstated positions. Quite often, too, they *tempt* us to adopt them without giving it too much thought. But *we ourselves,* free and capable of deliberation as we are, are the ones who give in to temptation: *we* are the ones who turn temptation into fall.

Let us put this differently. Misstated positions spring from *our integral selves* living in alienation and succumbing to its pressures as well as the pressure of concupiscence in ourselves (cf. Jas 1, 14–15). *We* are the ones who are unnerved by the precariousness of our identity. *We* tend to be mortally afraid of being invaded by otherness to the point where it may push us into the park of death. *We* are the ones who, defeated by the particular and the momentary, find ourselves ready to settle for mere survival here and now. Thus *we* are the ones who, in order to secure the particular, compromise the universal and the eternal; sometimes we even barter it away altogether. In this way, we fail to live judiciously and carefully with our precarious sense of transcendent self—how to accept it, endure it, embrace it, and cherish it in faith. And thus we will, under the combined pressure of outside otherness and inner trepidation, try to *compensate* for the precariousness of our true identity by forcing ourselves to project an inauthentic *persona* and to adopt postures to fit present, momentary situations rather than our authentic selves [*b*].

In doing so, we will, in various degrees of awareness and freedom, fail to strike, within our own selves and among one another, the balance between identity and alienation, between transcendent selfhood and participation in otherness, between soul and body. Vainly

---

[*b*] This picks up a theme treated long ago (§16, 6), where it was argued that faith is essentially open. But anxiety is inherent in the life of faith; hence, accepting anxiety is part of the Christian believer's life. But human beings, including believers, are always tempted not to *accept* anxiety in faith and so to *transform* it (cf. §16, 6; §137, 9; §146, 12, [*c*]), but to *suppress* anxiety by *compensating* for it, by forcibly creating inauthentic, mistaken forms of certainty and assurance. In due course, this is apt to lead to either integralism or modernism (cf. §§17–20)—to mention only one effect. The argument to be developed in the present volume will be analogous. None of us can live without somehow defining our ever-anxious moral and religious selves; we live under pressure to commit ourselves morally. In this situation, we find ourselves tempted to define ourselves hastily and forcibly, without patience or deliberation. Giving in to this temptation normally results in misdefinition of ourselves and in the adoption of misstated positions. In time, this leads to sin; in fact, at times it may already be sinful. Incidentally, what is being pointed out here prescinds from a key moral fact: unlike infra-human beings, *other human beings* do have the ability to *force* us into misdefining ourselves by adopting misstated positions. Such use of force is, of course, immoral. In fact, it will be argued later that the improper use of force is a tell-tale characteristic of immorality (§133, 2, [*v*]).

attempting to maintain ourselves, we will maladjust the very balance that gives us the prospect of true life and fulfillment.

To the extent we do so, both our identity and our participation in otherness will turn sour on us. In the end, we may even forfeit access to either of them. And as we lose touch with ourselves as well as with the reality of things other, we are apt to find, miserably, our access to God hindered or even simply obstructed. In a theology of sin, these *developmental* topics require careful elaboration and analysis.

[6] Our treatment of these issues will take the shape of a sequence of three lengthy chapters, increasing not only in complexity but also in theological and anthropological seriousness and intensity. Two of these are found in the present, first installment of Volume II/4, referred to as II/4A. For this reason, a brief preview is warranted, to help the reader not lose sight of the forest for the trees.

Let us start with the broadest possible outline. As promised, the chapters will follow Thomas Aquinas' order of basic goods—that is to say, the familiar, trichotomistic sequence *cosmology → anthropology → theology* (§116, 5, e and [s]; cf. §102, 10 and a–b).

[a] This has a twofold purpose. The first and more obvious is clarity of exposition: it makes the three chapters more manageable for the reader. However (and here we touch on a deeper, more substantive purpose) exposition must always remain "firmly subordinate to understanding—just as firmly as method is to be subordinated to truth, and the pursuit of scholarship to the quest for content" (§7, 2).

[7] This implies that we will engage in a treatment of *sin understood as a progressive miscarriage of human integrity*. In the next chapter, this will take the shape of an account of the genesis and development of of sin by studying failure, degeneration, and decay at the *cosmological* (*i.e.*, the sentient, psychophysical) level. What are the moral implications of the fact that humanity is a participant in cosmic process, as a living, sentient—*i.e.*, psychophysical—being?

Chapter 16 will take the harvest reaped in chapter 15 one step further. It will develop a theological conception of sin viewed as a miscarriage of growth and maturity in *responsibility*, at the distinctively *anthropological* level. That is, at issue will be the moral implications of the fact that humanity is characterized by *consciousness and freedom*—the two fundamental enablers of growth and development in the *deliberate* life. What will offer itself for treatment, therefore, are the failures and sins in which human beings can no longer appeal to passion and to the power of instinct in order to plead not guilty. Here, the degeneracy is properly a matter of intellect and will.

On this twofold basis, chapter 17, the opening gambit of Volume II/4B, titled "The Decisive Step," will issue a warning. Before venturing into the properly *theological* dimension of virtue and vice, we have to give ourselves an account of the fact that we are now part of a culture that resists what Robert Markus has elegantly called catholic theology's "totalising discourse." In his recent book *Gregory the Great and His World,* he writes:

For Gregory the Church had come to swallow up the world. He could think of *conversio* more easily as something undergone by the Christian soul on its way to perfection, than of a non-Christian to Christianity. The complexity of Augustine's world had lapsed into simplicity. Compared with Augustine, Gregory could take for granted the settled contours of his spiritual landscape. Christianity had come to give definitive shape to a 'totalising discourse'. The boundaries of Gregory's intellectual and imaginative worlds were thus the horizons of the scriptures. How to be a Christian, how to be the fullest Christian life: this was Gregory's central preoccupation in all his preaching; and this was the question into which the anxieties of his age had shaped themselves. Naturally, it helped to give his exegesis a predominantly moral direction.[4]

In the culture of our own day, we are closer to Augustine again. The unified vision of World, Humanity, and God, which matured during the two centuries that separated Gregory from Augustine, is hardly available to us any longer. There is no dearth of faith in God on cosmological terms, nor is there any dearth of faith in God based on humanity's own "spirituality"; but the same cannot be said for the availability of mystical experience understood as worshipful union with the Living God, whether of the contemplative or the sacramental kind. Awareness of God understood, professed, and encountered precisely *as the Living God* (*i.e.,* intuited, affirmed, and loved, without ever being nailed down or grasped) enjoys very little credibility among us. Thus, before venturing out into the "totalizing" style that has always animated the theological tradition of the undivided Christian Church, we must interrupt the flow of our exploration of virtue and its degeneracy, in order to meet contemporary demands for intellectual integrity. We must, in other words, interrupt ourselves in order to state in explicit terms the warrants for theological discourse of the genuinely (if never exclusively) *theo*-logical kind. Chapter 17 will be this interruption.

Having taken stock of what it takes nowadays to do Christian theology in the catholic tradition, we will be ready, in chapter 18, the center-piece of Volume II/4B, to ponder the fact that truly mature virtue is in the last resort a matter of *holiness and unconditional love,* just as vice is in the final analysis a matter of *refusal to worship rooted in habits of self-justification.*

[a] A warning. In the chapters 15, 16, and 18, the reader is apt to detect yet another element of complexity. Moral growth and development are processes as encompassing and as broad as the dynamics of influence, inclusion, and intimacy (cf. §98, 4). Issues of virtue and vice, therefore, occur on the widest conceivable range: they can be individual and/or familial, but they can also be social, societal, and even cultural. In the history of Roman Catholic moral theology, the individualized practice of the Sacrament of Penance, among other things, has favored a disproportionate emphasis on virtue and vice viewed as individual and personal issues. The recent consciousness of the social and societal dimensions of good and evil, encouraged so decisively by *Gaudium et spes,* the Pastoral Constitution on the Chuch in the Contemporary World promulgated by Vatican II, and carried forward in the teaching of Pope John Paul II, has caused a shift of emphasis both significant and welcome. In practice this means that the three principal chapters of Volume II/4A–B will treat the life of virtue and vice in a manner that tries to do justice not just to the *developmental* aspects of the moral life, but also to the *systemic.*

[8] Volume II/4B will achieve closure in chapter 20. It is not so much a chapter as a substantial epilogue to our treatment of sin as a whole. In it, we must reflect on what the Christian community has come to understand as "original sin," especially in the Latin West, deeply indebted to Augustine as always. It is also a theme of high ecumenical significance: the churches of the Reformation have been eloquent on it, though at some distance from the *Catholica.*

CHAPTER 15

Sense, Sensibility, Sensuality: Cosmic Forces and the Moral Life

DRAWN INTO SIN BY COSMIC FORCES

[§127] PASSION: DEPENDENCE, DESIRE, CONTEST, TEMPER

[1] Human beings cannot engage in self-maintenance or self-affirmation, let alone attain self-transcendence and identity, without accepting life in alienation (cf. §122, 1, a–f). Most fundamentally, this acceptance must occur *at the biophysical, sentient, instinctual level.*

At this level, the dynamics of cosmic mutuality provide human life at every stage of growth and development with its sustaining environment; that is to say, biophysical, sentient, and instinctual process becomes the fertile matrix that provides human beings with both the material conditions and the stimuli they need in order to grow in the direction of their distinctive, spiritual maturity. In other words, in order to be *who and what* we are we must accept as a basic given that we must learn how to live *as* we are—*i.e.,* significantly at the mercy of cosmic otherness. Growth in human maturity and freedom will never completely emancipate us from the mutuality inherent in sentient, biophysical life—its delights and its vexations. Death will, of course, but only at the expense of our biophysical life itself.

[2] Naturally, involvement in cosmic otherness looms larger in the more immature and incompetent stages of human life; it does so in the form of *dependence.* The less differentiated and focused our needs and appetites, the less self-reliant we are. It takes freedom of movement and of choice to be independent. To live and to become their true selves, therefore, the unborn, the newly born, and the immature that is, the almost-undifferentiated and the less differentiated—must begin by relying, willy-nilly, on other things and other persons and by taking their bearings from them. The same must be said of the feeble, the failing, and the dying; in the end, they are forced to take most of their cues from otherness and, willy-nilly, to depend on it.

This substantial dependence on otherness is a matter, not of deliberation, but of *direct, psychophysical, emotional perception*, known as *passion of desire*. Like it or not, we register our involvement in otherness, our reliance on it, and especially our craving for it (or, as the case may be, our abhorrence of it) with the felt intensity of our entire biophysical being. Otherness surrounds, embeds, and pervades us; it stirs us, setting off high-energy spurts of reaction (especially if we are healthy). These outbursts seem irrepressible; and, much as they may be gratifying, they can also be disturbing on account of their vehemence, sometimes to the point of having us transfixed and paralyzed or dispirited and languid. One measure—a negative one—of this vital vehemence is *fear:* we balk, panic, and faint at instances of otherness that startle or irritate us; we react to apparent threats to our survival by finding ourselves immobilized, frozen to the ground, instinctively hoping that the threat will pass if only we don't make a move.

One characteristic feature of the passionate gratifications and irritations set off by otherness is that they are as short-lived as they are immediate; hard on the heels of satisfaction or dissatisfaction, the desire for stimulation picks up again, hardly abated; lack of stimulation soon causes distress. Thus, being alive means being tossed about between stress and relief, between fear of death and pleasure in being alive, and the emotional intensity of both experiences is a measure of just how deep involvement with otherness runs in us. Swept along on the tides of either gratification and appetite or weariness and disgust, we find ourselves craving otherness or hating it with a passion; our entire being drives home to us the sense that we need and want the other. We simply cannot avoid dealing with it, even if we feel depressed or indifferent. Otherness is obviously part of being alive, of staying alive, and of being forced to stay alive.

[3] It does not take the young among us long to discover that otherness (and thus, access to survival) is *rationed*. From the outset life will give us a sharp taste, not only of the vehemence of our craving for such otherness as suits and serves our needs and likes, but also of the often painful necessity to make do with such pleasures and supports as otherness makes available to us. No gratification, we discover, is complete, let alone ours for the taking; there lurks a snub in every caress. Whenever our appetite is met, we find ourselves disappointed as well; the hands that feed us also discipline us; drawing life from otherness teems with threats (or at least reminders) of diminishment and death. We have little choice: as we find our critical need for oth-

erness both met and frustrated, we are forced to allow otherness to trim our libidinous appetite. Yet in this very process, something positive happens as well: our appetite is also molded and structured; willy-nilly we learn just what we can effectively crave and what not. We get what we want only by learning to want what there is to be gotten; we discover what is considered allowable out there; gratification, we learn, is contingent on adjustment to otherness; being (and staying) alive turns out to be a matter of acceptance and compromise. In the young, the appetite for life (or, the passion for self-maintenance) takes the shape of that lowly, characteristically animal form of *mimē-sis:* mimicry, *i.e.,* imitative behavior. Mimicry is induced, at least partly, by the instinctive sense that we start life at a disadvantage. Thus, to live is to mimic. To get along you have to start by going along.

[4] We do not very long persist in this adaptive (that is, largely passive, or at least receptive) mode. The reason for this is the following: the fact that we are alive and sentient means that we are energetically (or, as the case may be, wearisomely) *self-driven.* As we find that life-giving otherness is not unconditionally available, let alone in lavish supply, we instinctively discover, almost from the start, that we cannot resign ourselves to the happenstance of what is available. In this way, the very models we have been trained to imitate in the interest of our survival turn into rival forces for us. To live, we find, we must not only comply and imitate, but also contend. We must initiate, take advantage, struggle, fight for life. We cannot afford to let otherness push us around, let alone swallow us up. We must self-differentiate, even if only primitively. Compliance must frequently, even regularly, give way to *contest,* or at least to firm negotiation; to be effective, self-maintenance must resort to self-assertion, and even to attempts at downright controlling the other. Instead of complying with others and learning by imitation, we begin to feel, passionately and instinctively, like "teaching them" [a].

This primal, largely non-deliberate, involuntary step in the direction of self-enfranchisement and of the willful taking of positions is, once again, a matter of immediate experience. In the tradition, this

---

[a] In a fascinating monograph, entitled *Fighting for Life: Contest, Sexuality, and Consciousness,* Walter J. Ong has argued that consciousness (and specifically, consciousness insofar as it is shaped by accepted sex roles understood as individual, social, and cultural forces) is substantially conditioned by the experience of deep insecurity and the felt need for contest that results from this. This experience, Ong argues, occurs in the earliest biophysical and socio-biophysical phases of human development. He also persuasively shows that there are good reasons to think that even at these early stages there already are notable differences between the sexes.

is known as *passion of temper.* Whenever we encounter delays in gratification and self-maintenance, or (worse) obstacles to them, otherness begins to strike us not as a source of support and survival, but as a threat, or at least as a challenge—a resistant, alien object. With the self-serving immediacy of vital instinct, we respond (once again, if and when we are healthy) by asserting ourselves—that is to say, by *contest.* This spontaneous move is at least residually powered by fear of loss, extinction, and abandonment; no wonder we implicitly cast the other that resists our desire in the role of the *rival* that is liable to *diminish* us. With the keen (if shortsighted) vigor of passion we realize that this is not the moment for dependence, compliance, or adjustment. From our first tantrum on, we *react* by protesting instinctively, trying to prevail. We attempt to *reduce* the other in some fashion to something that will *enhance us* with as little cost to ourselves as possible. In this sense, too, we live by mimicry. We learn how to meet our match; we try to face down as we feel faced down.

[5] Instinctive desire and instinctive temper: we never wholly outgrow these two basic forms of passionate appetite. Not to acknowledge our passion for self-maintenance and self-assertion (for example, by claiming we have risen above them) is a serious illusion, even for the maturest and most spiritual among us. We may grow weary of depending on humanity and the world for sustenance, but this does not mean we are not being sustained. Our resolve to live may wane as we grow in contentment, or as we grow too weak to fight for life, but at least we hold on to what is left of it. For, as long as we are physically alive, the basic life process itself leaves us no choice but to stay alive. To stay alive is *in some way* to fight for life; failure to do so is the onset of death. Even more basically, to live is to get one's basic needs (no matter how residual) met *in some way.* To refuse life-support of some kind (or to accept it purely passively) is death's arrival.

[a] Readers familiar with the Greek fathers of the chuch will have recognized, in these few paragraphs, a retrieval of their philosophical anthropology, and specifically, of their account of the two basic human passions. Passions are the elementary resources for survival in us. The first is craving (Gk. *epithymia,* or to *epithymētikon;* Lat. *affectus concupiscibilis*): at the elemental level of our being, and indubitably from the moment we are born, we live and survive by a deep-seated yearning for pleasurable experience, as well as by its twin, the impulse to recoil from pain.[1] But almost right from the start of life, we also live and survive by another, no less deep-seated

passion: temper (Gk. *thymos,* or *to thymikon;* Lat. *affectus irascibilis*): the urge to overcome resistance, to contest, to compete [*b*]. Thus we react to apparent threats to our well-being by some form of self-assertion; we contend with obstacles to our cravings and desires; we even find sheer near-animal gratification in frolicking, cavorting, and romping, and in testing our mettle—our own and others' —or in having it tested; we even create obstacles: harmlessly as well as beneficially in play and competitive sports, and not so harmlessly when we enjoy creating enemies because we cannot live without picking fights with the purpose—often tacit—of proving our importance by defeating or at least provoking others (cf. §111, 5).

[*b*] Without further elaboration, let us simply observe at this point that the Christian West, and medieval scholasticism in particular, was to adopt this classical account of the passions eagerly and elaborate it energetically [*c*].

[§128] PASSION, POWER, AND THE MORAL LIFE

[1] What has just been proposed leads to corollaries for our understanding of the deliberate—*i.e.,* the moral—life. At the biophysical level, self-maintenance and self-assertion are involuntary—a matter not of deliberation and choice but of participation in sentient process. The goods and evils involved in the passionate life, therefore, are basically "natural," and *not in and of themselves moral.* Passionate

---

[*b*] Evagrius Ponticus' treatment of the ascetical and mystical life abounds with instances of this account of the passions. Cf. esp. *Praktikos,* 4, 15, and *Gnostikos,* 47. In the final analysis, Evagrius explains, mastery over these passions is accomplished by abstinence (*egkrateia*) in the case of craving, and in the case of temper by charity (*agapē*). Of the two basic kinds of passion, he adds, temper is the one that is harder to control, which is why charity is called "great" (*Praktikos,* 38; cf. 1 Cor 13, 13).

[*c*] An example is Aquinas' account of the passions (which is deeply indebted to Aristotle). Following contemporaries, Aquinas terms the two basic forms of passion "concupiscible" and "irascible," respectively. The concupiscible occur in three sets of two, such that in each set the one is the response to what attracts, the other to what repels. The first set lays out the concupiscent appetite's elementary, habitual emotions: like and dislike (*amor/odium*). The second describes its reactions to objects not actually experienced: desire and aversion (*desiderium* or *concupiscentia /fuga* or *abominatio*). The third set lists appetitive reactions to objects already possessed: delight and grief (*gaudium/dolor* or *tristitia*). The irascible passions are divided differently. The first set includes the reactions to good things yet to be secured: hope and despair (*spes/desperatio*). The second lays out the responses to undesirable things yet to be confronted: fear and valor (*timor/audacia*). The third set consists of only one passion, since good things we have secured do not arouse the irascible appetite; only things we reject as bad do; they provoke rage (*ira*). Cf. *S. Th.* I, 81, 2, *in c.;* I–II, 23, 4, *in c.*

activity is, obviously, an activity *of* human individuals and groups; but it does not *as such* qualify as *properly human* (cf. §115, 2, [*a*]).

However, while passions, and consequently, natural goodness and evil, are integral elements of "natural" human life, *human life in its totality* is very much a *moral* undertaking. Accordingly, while the passionate life is in and of itself "natural" and *in that sense* a-moral, it very much *lends itself* to both moral goodness and moral evil; for that reason it is aptly called *pre-moral* (cf. again §115, 2, [*a*])—a term indicating that *in the concrete actuality of human living* the passions and their objects cannot be presumed to be morally neutral [*d*]. Accordingly, in any moral deliberation the passions and their objects must always be taken into account. For they are never morally neutral, or at the very least not in every instance.

[2] It follows that weakness and (*a fortiori*, capitulation) in the face of passion can be (and often are) glaring forms of moral deficiency, irresponsibility, and degeneracy. As a matter of fact, we tend to find this "lower" kind of immorality all the more embarrassing for being so irrationally violent, so hard to manage and control, and thus, so hard to accept as genuinely our own, rational human beings that we are. For wherever and whenever human life is ruled by passion, the forces of cosmic mutuality (cf. §115, 8), rather than lending themselves to higher purpose, become the cause and the shape of an appalling disorder: by virtue of engulfment in biophysical and psychophysical dynamisms, the human spirit *effectively* forfeits its transcendence [*e*]. Whenever and wherever this occurs, bodiliness and the powerful sentient instincts associated with it become the human spirit's prison. Two forms of this moral degeneracy especially come to mind.

[*d*] This enables Augustine, with his keen awareness of the difference between the passionate and the spiritual, to discern even the roots of *sin* in the two elemental passions of craving and anger. Cf. his vivid, emblematic portrayals of a suckling infant's obviously pre-moral avidity, and of a small child's jealous but equally pre-moral resentment of an infant brother who is being suckled: *Confessions* I, vii, 11. Cf. also §153, 8, a.

[*e*] Immorality of the recklessly passionate kind will strike most persons and societies as the coarsest, most primitive kind of human outrage. No wonder they will regularly react in kind, by *deliberate* ferocity against perpetrators of such crimes, especially in the form of calls for inhumane confinement followed by the death penalty. Still, in practice this kind of response only aggravates the problem: it encourages citizens to seek retribution and revenge of the coarsest, most primitive kind available outside the penitentiary walls—*i.e.*, in "civil" society at large. Institutionalized, legalized inhumanity is, of course, little more than a thinly veiled form of instinctive revenge, and on that score, morally misguided. On this issue, cf. Joseph Card. Bernardin, *Consistent Ethic of Life*, pp. 59–65, esp. 64.

[a] The first is *passive* in nature, and frequently in practice irremediable. We all know there exists a kind of fundamental moral impotence that has its origins in *suffering*, often of the unjust kind. Miserably, countless human beings are forced to live in such idleness and abject poverty, and at such an elementary level of civilization, that they are incapable of meeting even the most rudimentary standards of decency and morality.[2] Scandalously, defenseless human beings, in particular the young and the vulnerable, are often deprived of the nurture and care required for basic psychophysical well-being and self-esteem. More scandalously, helpless human beings may find themselves subjected to such ruthlessness, violence, and abuse that their ability to maintain and assert themselves in appropriately disciplined, measured ways will be forever wounded. As a result, their lives turn grim. There is little or no room for that training-school of life in alienation, which is at the same time that delightful prelude to all culture: the give-and-take of *play*. Wretchedly, many victims of deprivation and abuse end up living, through no fault of their own, not humanly and morally, but by sheer instinct, and doing so not just incidentally, *while* they are suffering abuse, but habitually, as a way of life. And to compound their misery, the awkwardness or dullness or even depravity of their manners often make them the hapless objects, not only of general disapproval and discrimination, but also of executive and even judicial rigor: they are apt to find themselves officially treated as savages. All of this, of course, will only drive their humanity further into abeyance.

[b] The second form of degradation is rooted in *activity*, of the deliberately degenerative kind. Its customary shape is that caricature of play: heedless, mindless profligacy, whether of the overt or the covert kind. In the park of *craving*, profligacy will take the shape of willful, untrammeled self-indulgence: at the expense of their own integrity, human beings, alone or in packs, abandon themselves, not infrequently to the point of addiction, to the physical attractions of things, animals, and other human beings; gratification becomes *moral abdication.* Examples are enslavement to drugs or alcohol, habitual gluttony, and sexual licence practiced as a matter of course. In the area of *temper*, profligacy takes the form of effrontery in all its many guises: individually or collectively, human beings, instinctively and at times quite aggressively, try to use and exploit other persons and things for all they are worth, with no re-

gard for their integrity; gratification degenerates into *moral insolence.* Examples are rapaciousness, rioting for rioting's sake, wanton destruction, intentional cruelty, rape, and other forms of sexual abuse prompted by naked power.

But very often, too, the two—self-indulgence and abusive manipulation of the other—go together, spawning varieties of wanton violence so base that calling them "beastly" (as the second Letter of Peter equivalently does: 2 Pet 2, 12. 22) amounts an injustice done to the animal kingdom and its primal innocence (cf. §116, 1).

[3] It is time to sum up. It is also time to introduce a proposition that will dominate the remainder of this chapter, namely, that there prevails an intimate connection between passion and power. Put differently, capitulation to passion and instinct is the equivalent of letting oneself be dominated by the dynamics of *influence* (cf. §98, 4). In the realm of passion, might is taken to determine right; instead of living humanly (that is, considerately and in a disciplined manner), the citizens of this realm struggle for *survival at all costs.* They do so by instinctively trying to bend the cosmic forces of mutuality (or interdependence; cf. §115, 8) to their own advantage, by living on the strength of *vital, animal power.* That is, they will try either to *drain* others of their power, or to wield their own power in such a way as to *subdue* the power of others.

[a] This last paragraph may well sound a bit too forceful to be true, so let us make a brief *excursus* to clarify the point. First, let us recall that the dynamics of power and forcefulness can operate in ways that are not primitive or crude at all; force is no less force for being clever, subtle, sophisticated, shrewd. Secondly, as a case in point, let us take a modern artistic *genre* which features the themes of power, influence, forcefulness, victory, and defeat very prominently indeed. It is found in literature and in movies: *science fiction.*

[b] At its best, science fiction is a wonderful product of the creative and often the prophetic *imagination;* yet, unfortunately but not surprisingly, in many cases it is an exercise in mere *fantasy,* and so, of morally questionable value—an assessment to be argued later on (§137, 4–5, a). Fantasy is fantasy, of course. Still, it is not completely devoid of assumptions and prejudices about the real world. Science fiction is no different. As a *genre,* it relies to a significant extent on natural science and, specifically, on two postulates that lie at the basis of every form of natural science. The first is: force, power, and influence are the chief themes of intelligent life in the

cosmos is mainly about force. The second is: everything that exists in the cosmos exists *in quantity.* This requires explanation.

Let us start with the latter. Every scientist knows that research findings are valid only if verifiable *and verified.* One very important way in which verification occurs is when it is found that the test procedures that produced the first findings can be replicated again and again, with virtually identical results. *Demonstrated repeatability signifies predictability,* and thus, scientific truth. But this principle is apt to lead to an inference that is mostly unstated but logically unwarranted: if intelligent life exists on Planet Earth, it is so likely that other forms of intelligent life, whether the same or different, exist elsewhere in the cosmos is so high that their existence is virtually certain. This conclusion is, of course, purely hypothetical. However, this does not keep many science-fiction readers and movie-goers (and, in their wake, many others among us) from feeling confident about the existence of life, even intelligent life, elsewhere in the cosmos. Clearly, many among us are undeterred by the total absence of any "hard" data needed to validate the hypothesis. Quite consistently, too, those who postulate the existence of intelligent life in places other than planet Earth generally take it for granted that science and technology, *and science and technology*—our own or "theirs"—can be counted on to furnish us (or "them") with the tools that will one day enable both of us to communicate with each other, and thus to learn what our intelligence and will are all about—*i.e., what we, human beings, really are.* How will we learn this? Much science fiction suggests (and here we touch upon its first implicit postulate): *by forceful competition, if not outright war.*

In regard to all this, what is less well known is this: by statistical and scientific standards, it is far more probable that humanity is in fact the only instance of intelligent life in the cosmos.[3] And since, in the words of Bishop Joseph Butler, "to Us, probability is the very guide of life,"[4] it is distinctively human not to be too confident about encounters with extraterrestrials, let alone to get ready for the encounter at the expense of things and human beings we do know exist. And if it is wise to be extremely wary of speculations and fantasies about alternative forms of intelligence and morality, at least this much follows: we should not let the suggestive force of science fiction run away with us or keep us in suspense (except, of course, by way of recreation). It certainly should not impress us to such a degree that *in practice* we end up leading our *deliberate* lives on the basis of a pure hypothesis rather than on the basis of our understanding of, and responsibility for, humanity and the cosmos *inasmuch as we unquestionably know them from direct experience* [*f*].

Let us make the point more affirmatively. It is a sign of neither intelligence nor moral responsibility to act as if all forms of human understanding and commitment known to us, including human self-consciousness, are radically improbable and unreliable till confirmed in *imagined* encounters with extraterrestrials. For now, the intelligent and responsible thing to do, *both scientifically and morally*, is to treat humanity (not as ultimate but) as virtually unique [*g*].

[c] All of this, of course, has moral consequences. In the cosmos as we know it, it is characteristically human to transcend infrahuman cosmic processes. It is also virtually (*i.e.,* morally) certain that humanity is unparalleled in the cosmos. It follows that humanity must be taken to be virtually (*i.e.,* morally) alone in having the ability to understand *that the distinctively cosmic goods—i.e.,* physical, biophysical, and psychophysical power and forcefulness—*are relative goods* (cf. §132, 4, b).

This intuition is in and of itself a highly significant victory of human transcendence over cosmic process. As such, it is as inestimable an intellectual privilege as human transcendence itself. Yet *noblesse oblige:* privilege comes at a price: moral obligations.

At the cosmic level, these obligations are basic: minimally, human beings must protect or (as the case may be) bring about, at least within the sphere of the cosmic influence that is theirs, some sort of *balance of cosmic power.*

[*f*] The exact opposite of what this paragraph warns against was brilliantly accomplished by C.S.Lewis, in his "space trilogy" *Out of the Silent Planet* (1938), *Perelandra* (1943), and *That Hideous Strength* (1945). Lewis not only produced one of the earliest and most successful instances of science fiction; he also used the new *genre's* capacity for the marvelous and the affective not in order to call humanity's uniqueness into question, but in order to celebrate it. Interestingly from a theological point of view, he did so by evoking an exciting, delightful world—one in which humanity *could* very well be happily living, if only we were as kind and humane as the moral and religious imagination can imagine extraterrestrials to be. And very significantly, power, forcefulness, and war play a fittingly subordinate part in Lewis' space trilogy.

[*g*] An afterthought. In much popular science fiction, what is striking is the absence of art (especially painting, poetry, and song), of flowers, plants, and trees, not to mention simple charm and tenderness. What is no less striking is the prominence of fierce emotion, made only more fierce by dint of shows of cold self-control. The emotions are usually connected with "aliens," war, terror, cruelty, and unnamed "forces" (unnamed "*Forces*"?). Could it be that all this is far from accidental? Is it symptomatic? Could it be evidence of the real theme?

Let us put this differently. Doing everything we can in order to relate to otherness of any and every kind in a temperate, considerate, reasoned, deliberate, constructive manner is a basic, compelling moral duty. Vis-à-vis human beings, from innocent human life on up (cf. §116), this respect for "otherness" is obviously more vital; nevertheless, the two—*i.e.,* cosmos and humanity—require the same *fundamental moral disposition.* And thus, in practice, professions of ecological sensitivity can reasonably be called suspect when regarded as compatible with professions of indifference to, and tolerance of, activities inconsistent with the rights of innocent human life, and *vice versa.*

[d] We can now go back to our point of departure. There clearly are those who are in the habit of doing almost everything they can so as to take advantage of *imbalances of power;* they will even bring such imbalances about where none exist, whenever they feel like it and find no opposition. They act this way because their overriding interest in life is to establish *domination,* whether by manipulation or by *force majeure;* they will seek, whether by impulse or by design (though usually by both), either to sap otherness of its power or to overpower it. Or (as it was put earlier) they will either *drain* others of the power that is theirs, or wield their own power so as to *subdue* the power of others. Equivalently, the faith they profess is in power alone, and in the kind of tools that will enhance power. That is to say, for all the sophistication of their means, they live by sentient instinct, captives of their need for power and influence. As a result, their practice of power and forcefulness stays below the distinctively human level, especially when (heaven forbid) intentional and focused. To them, living seems to mean surviving, either by taking advantage of otherness (often by instinctive displays of passivity and subservience), or by intimidating otherness (often by impulsive displays of forcefulness and swagger). But whether they justify themselves by appeals to the lack of gentler alternatives or by pleas in favor of aggressive action, their high-strung manner betrays one and the same motivating force: psychophysical anxiety only very partly tempered by reason.

Where lies the root of this anxiety? It would appear that the root is sound enough: it is the trepidation, deep down inside us, where we live precariously, between hopes and fears—hopes of gaining our lives by hook or by crook, and of thus finding ourselves, and fears of losing our lives by caving in to otherness, and of thus forfeiting ourselves.

[§129] CLASS, PATTERNS OF POWER AND INFLUENCE, AND THE MORAL LIFE

[1] In the park of the dynamics of power and influence, a crucial issue remains. It is both *moral* and squarely *social.* To develop it, let us briefly retrieve what we have explored so far.

Up to this point, our approach to the dynamics of passion and power has frankly favored *developmental* themes. This may have created the impression that capitulation to passion is basically an individual or perhaps familial matter, or that it may be at most a matter of sizable communities finding themselves at the mercy of adverse environmental conditioning forces so overwhelming that in practice they are powerless, and thus can hardly be blamed for failing to lift themselves above the life of instinct and passion.

It is true, of course, that many underdeveloped and maldeveloped individuals and families live at the mercy of instinct and passion. The same can be said of larger segments of the human family. Quite often, this is attributable to debilitating biophysical and psychophysical impairments such as genetic mishaps of either the hereditary or the random kind. Frequently, too, it is the effect of the damaging impact of environmental, tribal, circumstantial, or familial forces. Individuals and communities thus afflicted frequently bear little or no moral responsibility for their actions; forced by natural misfortune to live in sub-human ways, they are, as the traditional expression goes, "invincibly ignorant." Put differently, what would normally have to be considered moral failures are in practice no more than unfortunate instances of natural, pre-moral evil (cf. §115, 1–2); the habitual immorality of such people, though often quite serious, is of the primitive, uncivilized, almost purely instinctive kind. While objectively regrettable, it strikes us as subjectively excusable; it has a way of looking pardonable. In our biologically, psychologically, and sociologically sophisticated culture it may even look interesting (and, more alarmingly, as worth preserving on that account, as if it were moral to confine human beings to nature preserves). Such are the odds of biophysical and psychophysical life, we will say; accidents of maldevelopment and circumstance will occur always and everywhere, and they will result in failure to live humanly and morally, at least on the part of some in the human family.

But even if we grant that human beings are apt to become self-indulgent and violent through no fault of their own, and that their subhuman acts and habits are therefore substantially attributable to adverse social, developmental, and environmental forces, it would be an act of egregious thoughtlessness to leave things at that, for two reasons.

The first is simple enough: in many cases, the immorality of the naively innocent, the unobservant, and the uncouth is due to the fact that they must suffer types of violence that are appreciably *deliberate*. The fact is that there *are* among us degenerate individuals and *ditto* ruling classes that are morally responsible for their own degenerate acts, just as there are familial and tribal and corporate environments where theft, malice, mistrust, licentiousness, or belligerence are not just condoned but positively commended as desirable ways of life.[5] How can anyone be expected to stay (let alone grow up) kind, honest, chaste, discerning, or peaceful in such settings? How can virtue be within reach of those who must live, as a matter of course, under the threat of abuse, violence, and discrimination at the hands of persons and groups of persons who systematically and largely deliberately abuse, degrade, misguide, or corrupt them? If this is not an issue of both individual and social morality, none are.

But secondly, and more importantly, it must be realized that the dynamics of power and influence usually operate *systemically*—*i.e.*, in the form of *authoritative social systems*. It is hard to discern, in regard to social systems, just where individual responsibility lies. Some of these systems are so immemorial, so traditional, and so stable as to *appear* only natural and moral, or at least a-moral; there simply are certain things you must do because they are "the done thing." Some other authoritative systems are more obviously the fruit of human artifice (a theme to which we must come back at some length: cf. §135; §137, 7–14); still, *de facto* they frequently enjoy the same authority. In either case (though in the latter rather more than in the former), we have questions of *social morality* on our hands.

For the time being, let us limit our exploration to the basic features of the issue of power and influence in human communities. All human communities aware of some sort of authoritative tradition; accordingly, in no community is the law of the jungle the favored operative norm. Typically, any human community's members enjoy at least some latitude for independent decision and action. This latitude is made possible (rather than prevented) by the fact that their freedom is limited, usually by rules that count as moral, sometimes written but very often unwritten. Taken together, such prevailing precepts embody the community's moral code; they shape its moral sense; they enable the community to count, at least in its own eyes, as a *moral community*. The authority to enforce the rules, or in cases to set or alter them, is usually invested in authoritative institutions of one kind or another.

Whatever other functions or capacities these institutions may or may not have, they invariably are *dominative*: they have a way of exercising power and influence. In characteristically cosmological fashion (as will be argued further down: §129, 2, a and e), they are apt to operate by virtue of *sheer presence*—whether of the quiet, imperturbable kind, or of the loud, ostentatious kind, or of the ominous or even sinister kind. They know how to intimidate; they also know how to punish transgression, often by forceful intervention. Such institutions are typically overt ("formal"). Quite often, though, they are surprisingly covert ("informal"), whether partly or even entirely; the latter was shown by a now famous study, undertaken in a small town somewhere in the United States in the late nineteen-fifties.[6]

The structure of these institutions may be monarchic, feudal, oligarchic, tyrannical, democratic, or a blend of two or more of these; they may maintain themselves in a variety of ways, dynastic or otherwise; in any case, these structures of power and influence are regarded as morally relevant, and thus they set the community up, at the most basic level of its functioning, as a moral community. Invariably, the structures are staffed by, and thus embodied in, authoritative and frequently very powerful individuals or groups of individuals—sometimes insiders, sometimes relative outsiders. If we leave aside for the moment cases of outright foreign repression or indigenous rebellion, it is safe to conclude that traditional communities handle the *moral* responsibility for their proper functioning by living, willingly, impassively, or reluctantly, by accepted systems of power and influence.

Such public systems of power and authority, though never perfect, are often beneficial. Early Christians could even regard them as entitled to respect and submission by reason of their divine mission "to punish wrongdoers and to commend those who do good" (cf. 1 Pet 2, 13–14); interestingly, Jesus seems to have taken dominative power for granted, though he did caution his disciples against making it normative "among you" (Mk 10, 42–44).

Systems of dominative power can indeed help shape and positively support the native human yearning for transcendence over the purely sentient; thus they often succeed in maintaining and enforcing a shared morality, at least at an elementary level. However, in many instances, the reverse is the case: systems of influence can encourage the reluctance or the downright refusal to transcend the biosphere and the passions associated with it. In these latter cases, glaring forms of both abdication and insolence at the expense of the weak and the powerless may be habitually condoned or even approved and encouraged, usually by default. To the extent that systems of influence have these effects they must be considered *cultures of violence* (cf. Gen 6, 11), and as such, immoral—*i.e.,* instances of *social sin.* Let us elaborate, carefully.

[a] By way of backdrop to the explorations that are to follow, let us begin by recalling two observations made long ago and combining them.

The first is very brief: human life is radically marked by alienation (§122, 1 and a–f); no human being can exist as a human being without engagement with otherness.

The second is more elaborate. At every level, and antecedently to any human deliberation, human life in alienation is marked by three basic dynamics: *influence, inclusion, and intimacy* (or forcefulness, association, and mutual attraction); they are radically bound up with, respectively, *class, race, and sexuality* (cf. §98, 4 and a). All three of them, along with their endless permutations, combinations, and interferences, assert themselves and demand attention in each and every human situation.

[b] Let us phrase this differently. If we make appropriate allowances for characteristic variations in emphases due to environmental, cultural, and incidental factors, we can safely maintain that issues of up/down, in/out, and intimate/distant will make themselves felt wherever and whenever human beings live and communicate. The Jewish and Christian traditions have recognized that these dynamics are both very stimulating and very perplexing, and thus quite treacherous; but unlike many polytheistic cultures, they have refused to regard them as unmanageable and thus insuperable, let alone as all-powerful or divine, or—at the other end of the range—as obstacles to transcendence or outright evils. Instead, by interpreting them in faith, they have positively accepted them as integral to the human condition. In the perspective of God's transcendent power, God's all-encompassing care, and God's faithful love, so Jews and Christians have insisted, the vicissitudes and vagaries of the human dynamics of power, care, and love serve to drive home the devout realization that humanity is like God, and that finitude is radically and permanently etched into it. The three may be pervasive, they are not ultimate (cf. also §137, 7–9; §154, 1–2).

[c] Life in alienation is not a stable state but a demanding, frequently spirited exercise. Its dynamics are those of influence, inclusion, and intimacy, which are naturally quite unpredictable and often utterly erratic. Yet they are never altogether free-floating. They exist and operate in recognizable and manageable patterns—that is to say, *in structures* (cf. §11). Obviously as well as painfully, all three of them—class, race, and sexuality—are running interference all the time; they have a way of constantly creating irritating differences and thus, of turning the human condition into the "region of dissimilarity" of which Augustine spoke (§113, 3, e, [k]). Nevertheless, we *can* face them, largely because we know and acknowledge the immemorial, "given" bio-social patterns that structure and regulate them. We *know*, of course, that these patterns must be at least partly the result of culture, and to that extent artificial. But they are commonly *experienced* as having existed prior to any *fully deliberate* socio-cultural arrangements (or "systems of justice": cf. §135); no wonder they are often regarded as "natural" and hence, as equivalently non-negotiable and hence, as definite and normative.

[d] Power, trust, and *erōs* are, in their several ways, life-and-death issues for *all* human beings, not only in relation to themselves, but also, and especially, in relation to others as well as to the infrahuman world. This is so because differentiation implies *relative limitation*. All human communities, along with all the individuals in them, are marked by the following fact: *actual access* to the advantages and satisfactions of power, trust, and *erōs* is always limited because *all communities are differentiated*. Consequently, no single human being or group of human beings enjoys *unlimited* access to them. Something follows from this: no human beings can ever be expected to ignore other human beings who, in the areas of power, belonging, and intimacy, enjoy advantages and comforts which they themselves do not enjoy. In these three domains, *all are vitally related to all,* whether they like it or not, and whether they find it reasonable or not.

This relatedness is intensified by the fact that the patterns of possession and enjoyment (as well as their opposites, want and deprivation) are limited. As a result, no matter how immemorial and established they may be, they remain ambiguous and hence, always slightly in flux, perceptibly or imperceptibly. This also implies they are always open to challenge. No *particular* form of limitation of access to the goods of power, belonging, and intimacy, therefore, is final or definitive, as any human community with even the slightest sense of history realizes. Yet whether human communities are historical conscious or not, they know from experience that *some* limitation of access to the goods of power, belonging, and intimacy is inescapable; it is inherent in the human condition, marked as it is by cosmic alienation and finitude.

Human life, we have concluded, is marked by *limitation of access to all that is other, coupled with an inescapable relatedness to it.* But this implies that all human beings (and, for that matter, all cosmic beings) must willy-nilly live, *as part of themselves,* with otherness, and most of all with other human beings. They cannot resign from living with otherness and others without renouncing their own existence. Such are the mutualities of cosmic existence; such, too, is finitude.

Moreover, not only *are* human beings finite, they also *register finitude.* This happens to them not only reflectively, say, in the privacy of personal, existential anguish, in the hushed dignity of a funeral procession, in the philosopher's study, or in the quiet of wordless prayer; people also (and far more often, and far more directly and intensely) register finitude in the psychophysical affections and passions stirred up by immediate contact with otherness, especially of the involuntary or sudden variety. The self-experience and self-consciousness of all human beings, both individually and communally, is marked by the direct experience of passion and (in the case of individuals and communities with a developed self-awareness) by the awareness of trepidation and anxiety (cf. §113, 1 and [e]).

Obviously, this is bound to influence the *relationships* which human beings and communities have with other human beings and communities, especially with those living at close quarters, if for no other reason than that they cannot (and indeed, from the moral point of view, must not: §95, 4) ignore each other.

[e] Patterns, or *structures* (cf. §11), are marks of *finitude.* Among other things, this means that any structure is apt to be both an asset and a liability. That is to say, structures are ambivalent, and the bio-social and psycho-social structures of human life are no different.

On the one hand, they make the engagement with otherness manageable and thus give shape to it; fences, borders, and other means of demarcation make neighbors easier to deal with, especially if appropriately equipped with gates, doorways, and other expedients to negotiate mutual access. By setting limits, they also guarantee for all parties involved, an elementary (if necessarily provisional) sense of identity, and hence, a basis for balance, contentment, and harmony. This considerably alleviates the pressure constantly exercised by the never entirely domesticated dynamics of power, trust, and *erōs*. All human beings find themselves anxious as they engage otherness; structures facilitate the engagement and often simply enable it. As a result, human beings can turn the dynamics inherent in alienation into the stepping-stones of development and growth in the direction of authentic selfhood and ultimately, of God (cf. §122, 1–2).

But there is a reverse side to this medal. What makes the engagement with otherness inevitable and thus causes the anxiety? The answer is: the simple givenness of otherness and the inexorable difference made by that givenness. This must drive home the realization that the only thing that structures can succeed in doing is *managing and regulating* the engagement; they *remove or cancel* neither the strangeness of the other, nor the anxiety on the part of all parties involved. Even where the structures work well, they only *attenuate the tension*; they never take it away. In fact, precisely because structures facilitate the engagement, they sometimes draw parties into engagements that become practically interminable, to the dismay of those involved. Thus even the most reliable structures have unforeseen consequences in store. Once those so engaged suddenly find themselves waded in too far to withdraw from the engagement, the very structures that once made the other's strangeness and the anxiety manageable, turn around to intensify them, as Macbeth found out.[7] Alienation has a positive prognosis (§122, 1, e); yet at the same time it offers no permanent solutions, no storm-free zones.

The dynamics of influence, inclusion, and intimacy are biophysically and psychophysically (*i.e.*, cosmically) based, and associated, respectively, with physical strength, racial characteristics, and sexual differentiation. Like everything cosmic, they are in ceaseless process; hence, they are forever active and never entirely settled. For this reason the play of influence, inclusion, and intimacy is an inherent feature of human life; as such, they are morally indifferent—*i.e.*, simply part of *natural* concupiscence (cf. §113, 3, b). Accordingly, the unavailability of permanent resolutions in matters of power, trust, and intimacy is a natural given, too; for that reason it, too, is simply pre-moral.

However, in humanity's actual, fallen condition, the unavailability of complete resolution is far from innocuous. The dynamics of influence, inclusion, and intimacy are apt to be employed, are always being employed, and often are even deliberately exploited and manipulated by sinful people. Some are sinful because they are frail; some are willfully sinful; all have in common that they will avail themselves of influence, inclusion, and intimacy to cause trouble, stalemates, and outright evils. Say, they will wield *power* to bring about undesirable imbalances of power. Or they will abuse *trust* in order to aggravate the touchy issues invariably raised by human life together, whether at close quarters or at appropriate distances. Worst of all, they will pervert *love*, either to thwart the dynamics—so delicate yet so engrossing—of mutual attraction and affection or to pander to them. In all of these ways, miserably, the central dynamics of humanity's growth and development (cf. §122, 1–2) are vigorously turned into the stuff of *sinful* concupiscence (again, cf. §113, 3, b).

[f] With these observations, the preliminaries of our treatment of the dynamics of alienation are complete. The dynamics of inclusion and intimacy will be treated, respectively, in chapters 16 and 18–19. From now on, we can concentrate on the proper topic of the present chapter: the dynamics of *influence*.

[2] Like the dynamics of inclusion and intimacy, those of influence are both tempered and regulated by social structures, whether of the more "natural" ("given") or the more artificial ("conventional") sort. These structures are, by definition, *structures of power and influence*. They shape and regulate dependence, interdependence, and independence. The prototype of human power structures is *class.* Class structures both embody the dynamics of influence and control them; they also shape their effects.

[a] Class exists in the shape of many structures of power and influence. We can think of royalty, ruling class, aristocracy, patricians, and elite; of dynasty ("our family"), syndicate (*"cosa nostra"* = "our business"); of caste, rank, station in life, status, and position; we can even think of idioms like "this great nation" and "my country right or wrong."

All these forms and analogues of the phenomenon of class have this in common, that they show an fascinating and (upon reflection) perplexing feature: their *quasi-cosmological* nature. This invites further explanation.

[b] In one regard, class most conspicuously differs from both race and sexuality. The latter two are unmistakably connected with *specific, readily observable anatomical and physiological features of the human body.* By contrast, the observable basis of influence and class is not so easy to locate. Nonetheless, surprisingly, superior influence and class are widely treated as if they were at least as obvious and physically manifest as race and sexuality. Even in our democratic world one can hear it confidently alleged that "class runs in the family." Class marries class, clout, clout, and money, money. Blue blood can tell blue blood. So can "people of quality," for no other reason than that "this is the way things *are.*" "Free men" and nobles and their contemporary equivalents "naturally" deal with free men and nobles; so (at least presumably) do slaves and villains and their contemporary equivalents [*h*].

It is precisely this kind of vehemence that allows us even today to get a sense of the forbidding barriers of class that once prevented commoners from thinking of themselves as natively honorable. Yet we realize that the demise of the *ancien régime,* now over two centuries ago, has hardly eliminated every established structure of power and influence. The sullen sense of inferiority, the indignant vehemence, and the impotent rage—all of them so characteristic of human beings controlled and browbeaten by class and its analogues—are hardly things of the past.

[c] Class and its ability to establish and maintain unquestioned relationships of influence is even frozen into the language—not just in some of its standard idioms, but even in its objective ("formal") structures. Thus most languages require its users to identify implicitly the class to which they belong (and hence, their influence

---

[*h*] Like so many of his young contemporaries, Wolfgang Amadeus Mozart disagreed. Barely twenty-five years old, on June 9, 1781, he can write a letter to his father, Leopold Mozart, in which he protests, with a vehemence that is liable to astound us, that his inner nobility is in no sense inferior (and probably superior) to the nobility of his nasty but blue-blooded employers and masters: "What makes a person noble is the heart. And while I may not be a count, I may have more integrity in my body than many a count. And whether man-servant or count, the minute he abuses me he is an arrant cur" [*Das Herz adelt den Menschen. Und wenn ich schon kein Graf bin, so habe ich vielleicht mehr Ehre im Leib als mancher Graf. Und Hausknecht oder Graf, sobald er mich beschimpft, so ist er ein Hundsfut*]." Quoted by Erich Schenk, *Mozart,* p. 383. The reference is to Hieronymus Colloredo, the Prince-Archbishop of Salzburg and Mozart's employer at the time.

or lack thereof), by means of language functions connoting relative stations in life. Fixed grammatical, syntactical, and lexical features, and even pronunciation patterns, permanently enable (and indeed "require") people of class to talk down to people of low class or no class, and even to intimidate them; corresponding low-class linguistic features require (and indeed "enable") people of low class or no class to tacitly acknowledge their lack of status in front of those of higher class, even to the point of self-abasement.[8] Some highly cultivated, ceremonious languages (like classical and present-day Central Javanese) compel their speakers to profess their status far more systemically and elaborately than others; this sharply contrasts with, say, everyday American English, with its preference for (often amounting to insistence on) egalitarian expression.[9]

[d] In these ways and many other implicit ways as well, the forceful, the powerful, the influential, and the upper classes will typically act as if superiority were a natural condition—an objective, inborn attribute. The social dynamics unleashed by this presumption of objective capability on the part of the influential convey, of course, that social subordination is an equally objective fact [i]. As a matter of fact, a depressing sense of inferiority is still found even today, among the lower classes, the marginal, and the ineffectual—a sense often tacitly reinforced by school systems tacitly designed to perpetuate class distinctions and fixed types of employment, for instance in a modern country like Great Britain. No wonder there is dismay among the social activists and idealists who try to help the oppressed raise themselves up to a consciousness of their native worth as human beings and of the rights connected with it.[10]

[e] Thus, paradoxically, of the three basic forms of human differentiation, the one whose *observable anatomical foundation* is hardest to locate and point to proves to be the most savagely *factual,* and in that sense *irrational* and *impersonal.* Class and related structures of power, forcefulness, and influence, so it appears, are simply *there*—givens all the more authoritative for being so enigmatic.

---

[i] Greco-Roman civilization is a case in point. It thought of slavery as a quasi-physical form of subhumanity (as have other "civilizations" since). Accordingly, slaves, even the most capable and sophisticated, had to live under the continual threat of punishment by the *servile supplicium*: crucifixion. This vilest form of execution was otherwise meted out only to those who offered an immediate threat to existing power structures: violent criminals and foreign insurgents or invaders. Cf. Martin Hengel, *Crucifixion,* pp. 46–63.

[f] In one sense, there is nothing intrinsically or fundamentally wrong with the visceral feeling of capacity on the part of the force-ful and the influential. In fact, there is a great deal right with it. From early childhood on, *all healthy human beings* feel—mostly un-consciously—the excitement and the sheer delight inherent in the experience of the vital forces at work within them, and in the sense of power inherent in psychophysical well-being. Enjoying power and influence—of "making a difference in the game of life"—is simply part of being psychophysically *alive*. Little wonder that a glorious, *animal* kind of gratification characterizes the self-experi-ence and demeanor of the young, the carefree (including the care-free poor, as anyone who has been at an old-fashioned peasant wedding in a small village knows), the healthy, the confident, the comfortable, the energetic, and the well-off; they naturally "enjoy themselves."

This is not said to belittle, let alone to deny, the sensuous, in-tensely soothing comfort available in the sensation of being ten-derly fondled and nourished, or in the experience of feeling one with nurturing nature, which is so apparent in moments of peace and of physical closeness with other human beings, animals, and scenes of great natural beauty; in fact, this kind of gratification of the passion of *craving* in us is integral for human well-being. Still, the no less sensuous gratification of the passion of *temper* affords a keener kind of pleasure. It occurs in the displaying and wielding of power, and in the thoughtless yet skillful releasing of energy. The latter tends to be manifest more in and among boys and men than in and among girls and women; in fact, there are good rea-sons to think that males are, right from the outset, more "agonis-tic" and ambitious than females.[11] But many forms of instinctive, energetic, competitive performance for its own sake are delightful to both male and female, albeit in different ways. In fact, energetic contest is an integral element of that primal form of dexterous psy-chophysical, sentient performance known as *play* (cf. §128, 2, a; §161). No wonder most forms of play depend for their enjoyment on obstacles deliberately created: authoritative lines drawn in chalk on pavement, complex rules of the game, and (as anyone knows who has ever attempted a sonnet or a haiku or finished one) pre-cise rules of meter and rhyme [j].

---

[j] When asked why he wrote no blank verse, the poet Robert Frost is reported to have replied: "It's like playing tennis without a net."

Still, we indulge our instinct for playful competition in more primal ways as well. We enjoy the sight of animals at play; many of us actually play with animals; some of the more warm-blooded, venturesome, and affluent among us will take to animals, not only for close companionship but also to win contests.

These examples show that the vigorous enjoyment of psychophysical well-being is simply a sign of good health and vitality. In children and young people, a sharp sensorium and energetic, increasingly well-coordinated movements hold the promise of sound personal and social development further down the line. Sigmund Freud, perceptive as usual, appreciated this and termed it *Funktionslust*: the gratification inherent in functioning well at the sentient level. He was right (even though he misinterpreted the gratification inherent in the less instinctive, more refined forms of psychophysical, kinesthetic exertion, such as play, games, musical performance, dance, and even poetry). There is (indeed, there remains) an elemental, intense pleasure as well as relief from tension, unparalleled by physical closeness and tenderness, in flexing one's muscles, throwing one's weight around, bantering and joshing at the top of one's lungs, sporting one's health or athletic skills without apparent effort, pulling rank, flaunting one's influence, being number one. Developmental psychologists have shown that things like these actually are an indispensable factor in the process of *self-definition*—a topic to which we will return (§131, 1; §160, 7).

[g] Still, all this is desirable and promising only as far as it goes. What has just been explained suggests that sentient gratification and animal power and forcefulness tend to function as if they were their own warrants. That is to say, in the park of power and influence, the difference between means and ends is unclear. This is consonant with the observation that it is by forcefulness and power that the influential will acquire and maintain forcefulness and power, as well as the pleasures associated with them. Analogously, class tends to present itself as an uncomplicated, self-evident fact— self-begotten and self-made. Influence, power, and class typically come across as matters of *elemental fact*, in no need of any justification. Small wonder so many of the rich and famous end up being famous for no reason other than their simply being rich and famous [k].

---

[k] The facticity of power and its deep irrationality are confirmed by a modern observation. When complete strangers meet, apparently as equals, in the setting of

Insofar as they are primal facts of sentient experience, *Funktionslust* and its more differentiated variants are no more than pre-moral. But this does not mean they are morally neutral. Since they are habit-forming, they can become quite troubling and intimidating; potentially, they are far from harmless. Whenever the healthy wealthy and the wealthy influential "play" with a vengeance, and when "playboys" are only too anxious to posture as "good sports," the considerate, the moral, and the humane may still be able to shrug it off as something only to be expected from the rich and famous. But when the mindless, heedless influential insist on chasing pleasure, pursuing power tactics, wielding force, and claiming influence as a matter of unquestionable fact, then the considerate, the moral, and the humane have reason to be concerned, especially when they hear it proclaimed that "power is the name of the game." And those who are compassionate and care about the poor and the marginal have reason to be scandalized as well.

[3] The distinctive phenomena of influence and class just discussed invite further philosophical interpretation. First of all, if the wielding of superior influence and power is experienced and presented as "only natural," this betrays an affinity with *cosmic process*. This in turn implies that both the wielding of superior power itself and its effects are apt to be, to a significant extent, a function of chance—that is to say, of the odds inherent in the play of large numbers. It is not for nothing that the influential are called "fortunate," just as it is typical of the life of forcefulness and influence that it is, at least partly, a matter of "good luck."

As a matter of fact, there are very good reasons to suspect that class and its analogues are biophysically—*i.e.,* cosmically—based. Physical strength, animal prowess, a knack for contest, family traditions of personal forcefulness, and similar traits have propelled whole tribes, clans, families, and even individuals to positions of systemic power and influence. This must at least partly be the outcome of the contingencies of genetic, hereditary, and early developmental factors. These factors are, of course, too numerous and especially too inde-

---

a human relations training group, the first and most pressing group issue tends to be *authority*. This is due to the fact that when strangers meet the first thing to be instinctively perceived is the *power vacuum*. This raises the anxious (and hence, unspoken) *projective* question, Somebody's bound to be in charge here—who is *it?* The issue is commonly felt to be a hot one; it is hazardous, therefore, to bring it out in the open. Cf. W. G. Bennis and H. A. Shepard, "A Theory of Group Development"; cf. also William C. Schutz, *The Interpersonal Underworld*.

terminate to map in any definite manner.[12] But it is precisely this
element of indeterminacy that supports the hypothesis that power
and influence are, at bottom, *cosmological* givens.

However, the hypothesis suggests something else as well: like everything cosmic, class and the forms of influence associated with it have
clay feet. Put differently, despite their clout, power and influence
are apt to be, at bottom, a fragile commodity. Not surprisingly, people of class are well aware of this. The influential instinctively feel
that their dominant position "forces" them to protect and systematically enhance the patterns of forcefulness that shore them up; they
"have no choice" but to encourage and require their allies and associates to do the same and flex their muscle. Occasionally, therefore,
and at least by way of a temporary measure, people of class will feel
they "have to" flaunt and overstate their influence, in the interest of
survival; they may even have to fake it outright, just to keep up the
appearance of stability and control. They do all of this in a variety of
ways.

[a] First of all, as a matter of course, the powerful and the influential will reinforce their impact by dint of accumulated *means;* people of class tend to be "people of means."

At a very elementary level, when we say "means" we mean *tools.*
Tools include, first of all, instruments of control over cosmic conditions: quality clothing, secure housing, not to mention fortifica-
tions and strongholds and walled cities; effective tools enhancing
the dexterity and the endurance required for fishing and hunting,
for clearing and cultivating the land, and for developing agricul-
ture and industry, as well as for the establishment of settlements
for the work force. In turn, these practices are a way of turning
territory itself into a merchantable commodity: land and edifices
can now be possessed and owned and claimed and proclaimed as
"private property" and "real estate"—no insignificant tool of power
and influence.

"Means" also includes instruments of locomotion and conveyance of both persons and chattel: beasts of burden, horses, chari-
ots, waggons, carriages, automobiles, ships, railway systems, executive jets. More importantly, "means" includes a whole range of implements to keep rivals and enemies both animal and human at
bay, to defeat them, or even to wipe them out: arms, armor, and
armaments, from the most elementary to the most sophisticated.
Far more importantly, "means" signifies instruments developed to

develop other instruments, from the rudimentary tools of the age-old smithy to the robotic devices functioning in the giant assembly plants of our own day; "means" thus comes to signify means of mass production.

Finally and most importantly, "means" signifies *wealth*. Today, wealth is no longer understood primarily in terms of ownership of real estate or the capacity to produce merchantable commodities and trade them, nor even in terms of the possession of cash and comparable monetary means of exchange and acquisition. For ever since the sixteenth century, which saw the rise of large-scale banking, money has become a productive (and hence, merchantable) commodity in its own right; *capital* is now the single most powerful means of production and hence, of wealth. One does not have to be a devotee of Karl Marx's *Das Kapital* to see that what now makes the powerful powerful and the influential influential is the power to *invest*: large capital resources put out at a profit now secures for its owners (nowadays usually large and even multinational companies with limited liability and many shareholders) not only a significant source of income, but also controlling access to the means of production and distribution.

Yet even this is not the end of the line in the accumulation of affluence and influence. Wealth and influence have become increasingly associated with those who have both the audacity, the dexterity, and the powerful information systems needed to understand, manipulate, and even control (ordinarily by means of their hugely powerful data processing capacity) the forces of the money market.

In sum, the twentieth century has seen the exponential growth of the human ability to develop *means*. Technological reason is enjoying a heyday; more than ever, humanity and its future are at the mercy of *homo faber*—man the instrument-maker. No wonder the ever more influential media, themselves one of the most notable products of technological reason, are basking in their own accomplishments and inviting (if that is the right word) everyone of us to stand in awe of technology and its marvels.

[c] This leads to a second set of observations. "Means" are not self-operating. They require a whole array of *workers* (the "work *force*"), not only to design and produce them, but also to operate them and to keep them in repair (not to mention, in the present context, the fact that they need a large and well-disposed throng of

loyal consumers to keep them in business and enable further development). In this way, control over "means" simply must be understood to comprise control over *human beings*. No upper class can survive without a working class: horsemen, footmen, craftsmen, perfumers, cooks, bakers, slaves (cf. 1 Sam 9, 11–13), bondsmen, serfs, vassals, indentured servants, stewards, assembly-line workers, office staff, typing pools, private secretaries, junior executives, corporate lawyers, and executive assistants, as well as domestics: maids, grooms, gophers, factotums, coachmen, butlers, valets, stewards, watchmen, chauffeurs, clerks, janitors, chaplains, agents, programmers, bodyguards, mistresses, private and not-so-private militias.

There is no doubt that in the past vast numbers of people owed their survival as well as a measure of real happiness to their dependence on the wealthy who employed them, often in a humane enough fashion. Squire Alworthy in Henry Fielding's novel *Tom Jones* (1749) is an icon of this benign use of power—a phenomenon still far from unknown in many places in the so-called Third World today. Still, the situation raises a disquieting, deeply moral question: in what sense and to what extent will "people of means" allow their "human resources" the freedom to have human lives *and goals* of their own?

[e] A third observation. "Means" includes symbolic paraphernalia *signifying power and influence* and reinforcing them. People of class will assert themselves and their influence by means of distinctive, often hereditary names and titles, along with distinctive clothing and emblems and seals and stationary and office furniture—all of them to convey superiority and authority. They will display ceremonial weaponry, coats of arms and other heraldic devices, charters, knighthoods, academic and professional diplomas, and solemn documents to proclaim their "acquired rights." Interestingly, even as today's influential and powerful maintain themselves and their status (and usually the *status quo* as well), these symbolic accoutrements of their class can be observed to spill over from them on to the "human resources" they employ: just think of clothing items like liveries, uniforms, company ties, and lapel pins proudly worn by devoted subordinates.

[f] Fourthly, the symbolic paraphernalia lay bare the fact that class creates a *culture of honor* without letting on that it is itself a creature of it. Emblems of honor are, of course, a distinctive part of any hu-

man civilization, and by no means the least admirable. But it is also true that they are at least partly designed to disguise the naked facts that the few do dominate the many, and that the dominant do tend to ennoble themselves by creating the impression that the pursuit of power and influence is far above the law of the jungle.

Idiomatic turns of phrase to convey this polite illusion are part of this culture of honor. People of class, clout, and rank will declare, with an earnestness all the more touching for being at least partly misleading, that they consider it an honor and a "distinct privilege" to be the "servants" of the people, whom they call, a little too diplomatically to sound true, "co-workers" and even "our real workers," and whom they assure ever so sincerely that they are really "equals." For their part, subordinates and people of low class generally, eager to have at least a touch of distinction in a life of civilized servitude, are apt to enjoy the honor derived from their association with the mighty. They will take pride in the importance lent to them and the protection given to them by their "betters" and by "the management," frequently with an earnestness that goes well beyond the naive.

In this way, cultures of honor encourage and maintain cultures of *loyalty*. Again, loyalty may be, and often is, a genuine virtue. But it is also two-faced. Cultures of loyalty capitalize not only on dependability but also on dependency, and in virtue of the latter they also have a proven capacity for means not only fair but also foul— for the sinister and the ruthless. All too often class and influence demands unconditional, undiscerning, and even criminal loyalty; all too often, too, the powerful allow themselves to be supported by loyalty of the same kind. And just as shows of nobility frequently mask ignoble designs, shows of loyalty often mask the latent discontent invariably associated with relationships of dependence and positions of inferiority—a discontent that will not stay quiescent forever, as mafia-style infighting and murder show. Thus, in typically cosmological fashion once again, power and influence and honor are, and will always remain, a matter of touch and go.

[g] Fifthly, in light of all this it is not surprising that class will protect, encourage, and enhance patterns of forcefulness by the cultivation, as a matter of principle, of *interdependence with their peers*— that is, interdependence based on power. Class simply *must* meet the basic dependency and security needs of its members and those dependent on them; at the same time it *must* furnish both of them

with an operating base for confrontation and contest with outsiders. Class, therefore, can be defined as human self-organization in support of forms of humanity's powerful yet precarious natural superiority—biophysical, psychophysical, and psycho-social. Put differently, *class is natural human influence and forcefulness supported and reinforced by social structures of dependence and interdependence aimed at self-preservation and self-advancement.*

[h] Sixthly and finally, all of this suggests that the forces that hold class together are highly and intricately developed forms of human self-maintenance and self-assertion supported by the two elementary passions: craving and temper (§127, 2–5). At bottom, therefore, power and influence are forms of instinctive self-protection and *ditto* intimidation. In this sense, class can be said to supply to human individuals and communities what the protective *Umwelt* (cf. §115, 8) leaves to be desired; no wonder territorial imperatives and property claims loom so large whenever and wherever one class meets another, or when class meets non-class. Thus, once again, human power and influence turn out to be, in the final analysis, a direct repercussion, at the sentient level, of humanity's struggle to survive in the play of forces we have called *cosmic process*; essentially, they operate at the biophysical and psychophysical, instinctive, sentient level (cf. §115, 5).

[4] It has been repeatedly observed that influence is the most elementary of human dynamics, and that this also makes it the least stable. A few observations to elaborate this are in order.

All things cosmic are affected by the dynamics of multiplicity and randomness (§117, 5). The less self-transcendent they are, the more they are exposed to the tug-of-war of cosmic process (cf. §116, 3–4). Accordingly, the continued existence of all cosmic configurations, even the most viable and stable, is and remains dependent on comparatively precarious balances.

Class and analogous structures of power and influence are no different; they exist at the mercy of comparatively precarious balances. To maintain themselves against the ever-present peril of defeat and death, the mighty are apt to feel driven to use *force majeure* as a first resort; self-maintenance (they instinctively figure) is best assured by facing rivals down, with a passion (cf. §127, 4). No wonder the influential sleep better when assured of their superior power, which they tend to view as the single best guarantee of peace, not only for themselves, but for everybody else as well. Not surprisingly, they tend to regard power and influence as very good things indeed— something right and essentially moral in most cases. Typically, therefore, they will be reluctant to criticize dictatorships, especially if they are of the benevolent kind. "Might is right" is liable to be the presumption (if not the unstated creed) of those who are unreflectively powerful and influential.

In spite of their forcefulness, however, the mighty will never find themselves completely at ease; their aplomb is regularly disturbed, especially in two ways.

[a] Firstly, in the dynamics of the cosmos, no control is ever complete; power is and remains relative. After all, forcefulness has a close affinity with the sheer multiplicity that is characteristic of cosmic phenomena (cf. §117, 5; §120, 3 and a). Accordingly, it is typical of power to occur in a welter of different forms: structures of influence, both actual and potential, are legion; rivals of uncertain origin and capacity are apt to crop up forever and everywhere. Thus, to have power means either to feel continuously apprehensive, or to suffer habitually from illusions of omnipotence, or at least of self-sufficiency (cf. Lk 12, 16–20).

[b] Secondly, more than even the most clever animals, human beings have the capacity to influence cosmic process by means immeasurably more refined than power and forcefulness. They enjoy, not only an amazing amount of animal shrewdness, but also, and above all else, intelligence and deliberation (§115, 10). This explains why animal fables, from Aesop to the present day, have reminded the powerful that they have not just the high and mighty to reckon with, but also the instinctively clever, the smart, and the deliberately purposeful—the "upstarts." Shrewdness and the superiority that goes with it is something the mighty instinctively recognize, distrust, and dread.

In sum, left to itself, the life of power and influence tends to become a incessant, wearying mixture of outmatching rivals and outwitting them. In practice this means that the powerful find themselves forced to settle for artificial (if often very artful) *balances of power.* But this, too, remains an uneasy compromise, for such balances are and remain impermanent, subject as they are to the happenstance inherent in cosmic process. Thus those among us who live by influence are compelled to live partly by fearful self-maintenance, partly by aggressive self-assertion in the face of many robust rivals and a fair number of sharp ones, not to mention the luck of the draw, inherent in a cosmos perpetually made chancy by large numbers and staggering odds.

In this way, the mighty must live on ground that keeps shifting, with little or no assurance of permanence. For them, life is a contest indeed—one not so much for *life* in any fuller sense as for *survival*. No wonder their efforts to survive have repeatedly come to nothing, as more than one Psalm explains (cf., *e.g.*, Pss 37 and 39).

[c] The accumulated wisdom of the Christian West has been well aware of this, too. One example comes to us from the high and late Middle Ages. When the spirit of enterprise took advantage of improved security on the highways and the high seas and of better means of conveying goods, it began to create a wealthy, influential merchant class with international connections. At about the same time, the unpredictable turns of the goddess Fortuna's wheel—an old pagan theme generally repugnant to the early Christian imagination[13]—became a favorite literary figure. It took the form of numerous moral tales told and numerous moral songs sung by comedians and troubadours. Giovanni Boccaccio captured its essence in the title of his collection *De casibus virorum illustrium* —"How Illustrious Men Have Fallen."[14]

Boccaccio was not the first medieval author to use the theme to advantage. Over half a century before Boccaccio, Dante had witnessed, in his native Florence, the rise of a merchant class not only prosperous but insolent as well, and of a clerical caste whose avarice was becoming proverbial. He had declared his moral disgust at both spendthrifts and misers by putting them together in the fourth circle of Hell, as mutual enemies. The sinful addiction to wealth that had depersonalized them in life was now perpetuated in a frantic scuffle for advantage, in which everyone's individuality had vanished and mutual taunts between faceless spenders and faceless graspers had become the sole form of communication.

Still, in that context he also had taken the theme of Fortuna's wheel a big step beyond the moral tale, striking a deeper, theological note. In reply to Dante's despondent laments about Dame Fortuna's short-lived favors, Virgil explains that there is elementary justice in cosmic happenstance. Created by God, whose knowledge of the universe is transcendent, angelic powers have the task of ensuring order and equity in the splendor of the heavens; as a result, on balance, every part of the earth gets its fair share of light. By a similar divine design, Virgil continues, a basic order of justice prevails on earth: in the pursuit of dominance, Fortuna ensures that all who are carried on her wheel get their moment at the top. In this way, at Dante's hands, Dame Fortuna becomes the elementary agent of God's Providence, tempering the crudeness of the human scramble for ascendancy in the midst of cosmic vicissitude.[15]

[5] In view of what has been explained, it is hardly surprising that the powerful and the influential should instinctively seek to maintain themselves—in fact, almost automatically. Nor is it strange that they will do so in typically cosmological fashion: they will try to maintain their own status, by endeavoring, at the very least, to maintain the *status quo,* that is, the conditions they know they can control. From a cosmological point of view, this is indeed the most natural thing in the world. In the cosmos, continuance in being is contingent on minimal maintenance of a prevailing balance of cosmic powers. However, this balance is a function of cosmic contest. Consequently, self-maintenance is always precarious and never assured. Cosmologically speaking, therefore, from the point of view of each participant or cluster of participants in cosmic process, balance of power is best assured by the capacity to wield power and use force to *at least some excess.* After all, the fittest to survive and even prosper in cosmic process are those participants that are the fittest to compete, compel, subdue, even destroy.

This is not to imply that power and violence and the upheaval generated in the cosmic process by the mighty will result in perpetual chaos. For, speaking cosmologically once again, more and more unintentional, mindless contest prevails in the cosmos as we look at it from the animal and vegetable kingdoms down; yet that very contest has shown, in evolutionary process, an amazing fertility and even purposefulness. This suggests the presence of a curious sort of pre-established fairness and justice. Seen from the vantage point of humanity, the potent dynamics of cosmic evolution, impersonal and purblind and undiscerning as they may appear, have obviously not been utterly haphazard; they have a proven record of constructiveness, culminating in that masterpiece of evolutionary process: humanity itself. Thus, if the dynamics of chance threaten every single participant in cosmic process with decombination and destruction (and they do), they also have a mysterious knack for successful configuration and development, and can be expected to continue to do so. No wonder that trial and error, heavy risk-taking, and a fair share of "dumb luck" have ordinarily been integral to the success of the powerful and the influential as they set up their systems of power and influence. Unsurprisingly, the history of science and technology has the same tale to tell.

There is a problem, though: everything and everyone forceful and influential wants to *stay* in power. The fortunate distrust the play of large numbers; they want to stop Fortuna's wheel, and they instinctively know that only force will do so. Not surprisingly, those *in possessione* will try to maintain themselves and their associates at least *somewhat* at the expense of competing forces, or in any case at the least expense to themselves; they will insist, often impatiently, that the best defense is a good offense. If contest and competition mean anything, they mean a visceral taste for rivalry, or in any case toughness, supported by a certain dexterity in cutting one's losses. Small wonder that the influential tend to assume instinctively (and sometimes with a *naïveté* that borders on the criminal) that *balance of power is best maintained by imbalance of power deliberately brought about*—that is, by the willful wielding (or at least flaunting) of superior power on the part of the stronger and the superior. "If you want peace, prepare for war," the ancient Romans said;.[16] The trade wars and the arms races of this past century suggest that the mighty have continued to concur.

[a] All this also explains why the influential are so strongly predisposed to experience and interpret human life mainly in terms of pushing power or *conatus essendi* (cf. §107, 5, c, [n]). The most "effective" way to get things and people to work right, they tend to feel, is the open exercise of power; in their view, forcefulness insures stability, law and order, and even morality.

The problem is, of course, that power and force tend to be inconsiderate; in and of themselves, they lack moral (*i.e.,* human) regard. To some extent, participation in cosmic process always involves the purblind give-and-take of cosmic mutuality (cf. §115, 8); cosmic participants are interdependent with no deliberate choice of their own; in the cosmic contest, rival forces are as much part of life as friendly ones. This creates both opportunities and risks. On the one hand, by virtue of natural mutuality and interdependence, cosmic beings do *de facto* often support one another; being cosmic involves having natural allies. Yet equally often, cosmic beings are natural threats to one another (§115, 8); being cosmic means having natural enemies. And just as, owing to the complexities of mu-

tuality and interdependence, natural good and natural evil are notoriously hard to tell apart (§115, 5; 10, b), so are natural allies
and natural enemies (as every ecologist now knows).

[6] By now it must be clear that humanity can (and thus should)
make a decisive difference in the cosmos, and how. The reason for
this is plain: while being cosmic agents, human persons and communities are more than cosmic. They can discover, right at the heart of
the precariousness of cosmic balance of power, the *moral* fact that no
cosmic participant, not even the most viable and the fittest, represents more than a *relative* value.

Let us rephrase this. Human beings are equipped to intuit (as Pascal did: cf. §96, 3), *in* the very vicissitudes of cosmic mutuality and
interdependence, the following higher-than-cosmological truth: *superior cosmic power or influence is not proof of superior ontological worth.* This
means that human beings must learn how to take their cues for action from *the fundamental relativity of all things cosmic.* The cosmos is
driven, to an overwhelming extent, by powers and forces and influences that are morally blind; in the cosmos humanity alone is capable of deliberately opting for what is more than merely cosmic, and
capable to do so by resorting to means higher than power and influence. To be fully human, human beings must, both individually and
communally, commit themselves to practices of intellectual and moral *discernment.*

This holds true, not only in regard to their human fellow-partici-
pants in cosmic process, but also vis-à-vis infra-human ones. Only by
the *considered, discerning* use of power and influence will humanity
succeed not only in managing itself, but also in utilizing and exploiting the infra-human cosmos in an integrally human—that is, morally
justifiable—fashion (cf. §120, 5). Put differently, humanity must use
its considerable ability to marshall cosmic energies and turn them to
its own advantage only in order to express and enhance its own integral, evolved self; that is, it must pursue the legitimate purposes of
present-day humanity along with the cosmic precedents that have
favored its emergence and continue to favor its survival and development (§115, 10, b). Thus, the willful wielding of power, force, and
influence with a view to controlling, subduing, and perhaps even destroying other cosmic beings, whether infra-human or human, is
morally justifiable only to the extent that the *direct* objects of such deliberate attacks constitute either a genuine *natural* evil (cf. §112) or
a *deliberate human* threat to legitimate human or natural goods.

All of this drives home the magnitude of the demands implied in the grandeur of hominization. It was in the teeth of overwhelming cosmic odds that humanity's evolutionary leap into the noosphere (§117, 5) occurred, but once human beings found themselves there (and thus, in an immediate affinity with God) acts and habits of immense moral courage were required of them. Humanity must move away from the purblind use of mere power, and move, in the very conditions of alienation, toward clear-sighted discernment and deliberation. That is, to become truly human, we must learn, before doing anything else, to discipline and direct the passionate instinct for power that we have inherited from the biosphere; both from our own humanity and to be properly human, we *must* learn that power is not the sole guide to life, let alone the principal one. If human behavior in the realm of passion, power, and influence is to be distinctly human, therefore, it will have to be guided by *right reason.*

[a] It is distinctively human to grasp that might does not establish right. This has a vital consequence. From the history of science and technology (not to mention of warfare of the military and the socio-economic kind), we know that human beings *can* accomplish feats of exceptional power. Still, physical ability does not by itself involve a moral *warrant,* let alone a moral *obligation,* to accomplish any *particular* feats of power. The "technological imperative" is something every scientist and engineer knows from personal experience; still, excitement at our potential for scientific and technological mastery does not constitute a *moral* imperative.[17] Every human exercise of power, and especially any exercise of highly effective, superior power, must show proper regard for both its object and its consequences. We must resist the bias in favor of the "arrow-straight will" (cf. §120, 3) that is so characteristic of our scientific technological culture; we must refrain from using crude, relatively a-moral, and often quite violent strategies to adjust the imbalances that beset the delicate systems that make up humanity and the cosmos. To be truly constructive and thus, morally acceptable, the use of force, power, and influence must be *considered* and thus patient—or, to use the traditional language of Catholic moral theology, *discerning* as well as *proportionate* [*l*].

[*l*] John C. Ford's famous article "The Morality of Obliteration Bombing," written as early as 1944, remains a powerful application of this proposition to the morality of warfare. Its publication antedated the deliberate reduction to ashes of the City of Dresden—an act of indiscriminate violence in which at least 35,000 defenseless noncombatants were killed. Needless to say, Ford's position was unpopular at the

[7] The themes raised and explored in this section are, of course, directly relevant to matters of a pedagogical and ascetical nature. It is part and parcel of humanity's participation in the cosmos that we should be vigorously driven by passion to exert influence. We naturally take advantage, to a large extent instinctively, of the powerful dynamics of cosmic process, including the ones that drive our own biophysical and psychophysical selves. Yet in so doing we equally naturally and instinctively threaten cosmic competitors with decombination and destruction. But then again, only human agents can (and should) *learn and discover* that instinctive feats of power and influence aimed at infra-human or human competitors are not self-justifying, let alone morally right; while the instinctive use of power may in and of itself be only a-moral, within the totality of human life it is at the very least pre-moral (cf. §115, 2, [a]). This implies that it is part of humanity's moral responsibility to discipline the passionate "lust for power" (*dominandi libido*; cf.§121, 3), whether this lust takes the form of craving or domination or both (cf. §128, 1–3; §137, 13, a– b), and bring it within the compass of human deliberation. How is this to be done and why? We must find answers to these questions, in a sequence of three sections of no little complexity.

TEMPERANCE AND FORTITUDE

[§130] TRAINING FOR TEMPERANCE: A MORAL ISSUE?

[1] Human beings have this in common with animals: they are naturally open to conditioning, training, and adaptation. All animals are constantly exposed to the dynamics of biophysical and psychophysical mutuality (§115, 8); this is, of course, more obvious to us in the case of those animals which, by virtue of our own elevated position in the biosphere, we are used to calling the "higher" animals.

---

time of its publication. Since 1944, many means of technological warfare, while enormously ingenious from a scientific and technological point of view, have become even more excessive in their consequences, and hence, wholly inconsiderate in practice. This, of course, raises the question whether such weaponry is capable of being used in any discriminating and proportionate manner. The Second Vatican Council suggested that this question must in all likelihood be answered in the negative (GS 79–82). This would seem to imply that even the manufacturing and stock-piling of such armaments would have to be called immoral, not to mention the threat to use them. In their pastoral letter *The Challenge of Peace*, the United States Catholic bishops have taught the same, in the strongest of terms and with far greater precision (cf. *Catholic Social Thought*, pp. 523–35 ([142–99]; David Hollenbach, *Justice, Peace, and Human Rights*, esp. pp. 145–49).

But in reality all animals are directly involved in vital, dynamic, relevant engagements with other cosmic beings, sometimes very actively, sometimes rather more receptively, sometimes as a matter of habit, sometimes on the spur of the moment. Some of these engagements are antagonistic; as many or more are supportive and even mutually supportive, as is shown by phenomena like parental care, support within the species or at least within the herd, and symbiotic relationships between different species. In all these situations, animals learn ("acquire") behavioral habits—many of them imitative ("mimetic"), many adaptive. These habits vary greatly, both in kind and in range; they depend on the level of refinement and differentiation proper to each species in regard both to biophysical and psychophysical properties and to their capacity for social habits; they also depend on the level of adjustment made available by particular environments and habitats, which in any case must be congruent with the particular psychophysical capacities and properties of each species (§115, 9). At any rate, within the specific range of the possibilities of each species (and in many cases within the range of experience of particular groups and even individuals within the species), animal dexterity is vigorously developed. It is *stimulated* by otherness and encouraged by it, and practiced to the point where it becomes spontaneous.

But animal spontaneity is also carefully *tempered* by otherness; in other words, it becomes *selective*. Animals engage otherness in recurrent situations; this prompts them to develop stock responses—some mainly reflexive, some highly perceptive, adaptive, and quite flexible. By and large, repetition will foster some behaviors and discourage others. Thus animals will learn, as a matter of fairly reliable instinct, the difference between allies and opponents; which environmental factors, which foods, which other animals, and which companions within the species are best sought out, which best avoided, disregarded, circumvented, or cowered to; which factors and actors can be taken advantage of, which can be faced down; which are best intimidated, which best ignored as irrelevant (invariably the vast majority, at least from the human point of view). In this way, animals develop not only a considerable dexterity in confronting the challenges that come to them from the outside, but also *an instinctive sense of their own limits*—the fruit of training and conditioning, whether environmental, symbiotic, parental, or social.

What further typifies acquired behavior in animals is this: while obviously useful and purposeful, animal habits remain substantially *self-serving and self-regarding*, at least in the sense that they serve the interests of the species or of groups and even individuals within the species, as the habits even of many domesticated animals show. In other words, while animal behavior does show altruistic features (cf. §122, 1, g), in the last analysis it is not moral. Animals deal, empathetically, with other members of the species; they deal, often very cleverly, with their *Umwelt*; but they do not deal with *the world as as a whole*; even less do they self-consciously and deliberately improve it. Much as we may observe reliable forms of acquired discipline, self-restraint, resourcefulness, skill, and loyalty in animals, both individually and socially, we know that animal behavior stays largely within the bounds of the animals' capacity for immediate and conditioned responses, and entirely within the park of instinctive experience. This is typical of the psychophysical life, driven by vital instinct and passion as it is (§116, 3).

Like all animals, and most conspicuously like the higher mammals, human beings acquire new behaviors at the sentient level. Like animals, too, they do so to a significant extent by dint of conditioning, mimicry, and adaptation. Likewise, not unlike many higher animals, human beings are open to *systematic training*: human beings will instinctively allow other animals—most notably other human beings acting deliberately—to teach them acts and habits of dexterity and enterprise as well as self-discipline and self-control *at the sentient level*. But besides, human beings possess a capacity found at best marginally in animals: *they can train themselves*. That is, human beings are capable of acquiring, in substantially deliberate ways, focused, disciplined *sentient* behaviors that will enable them to act more responsively, appropriately, and constructively *(again, at the sentient level)*, in regard to themselves and in regard to other persons and things.

Let us put this in frankly moral terms. Human beings are capable of allowing themselves to be trained for virtue and by seeking virtue even in the park of instinct, by *formative as well as self-formative acts and habits* of the cardinal virtue of *temperance*—acts initially performed by significant others and in due course also by themselves, both in regard to themselves and others. This proposition invites further reflection and development.

[a] Being a moral virtue, temperance is by definition distinctively human. Temperance is part of the deliberate life; as such, it is unknown in the animal world. Yet far more strikingly than the other cardinal virtues (cf. §134, 1, b), temperance operates in a domain which taken by itself is just *pre-moral*: "animal" instinct and passion

(cf. §115, 2, [a]). Where else in the moral life does the human spirit experience infra-human, cosmic process at closer quarters? Where else must human consciousness and freedom take on the powerful, always precarious dynamics of the sentient world more directly and immediately than at the point where human activity emerges from the biosphere and in the very act of emerging begins to transcend it (cf. §116, 2–3)?

Take on the dynamics of the sentient world—that is, acknowledge, accept, confront, temper, embrace, and focus these dynamics, and thus integrate them into properly moral acts and habits. Now at the *sentient* level, acts and habits consist largely of acquired behaviors of self-management and engagement with other human beings and the environment—behaviors of the instinctive, reflexive, and near-automatic kind. But acquired behavior typically occurs in *patterns*. Accordingly, we can say that human beings live—that is, live *morally*—to an appreciable extent on the strength of deeply ingrained, extremely complex, and often superbly purposeful as well as flexible behavior patterns at the sentient level.[18] No human life is possible apart from these patterns; hence, no theological or philosophical account of the responsible life can afford to overlook, let alone ignore, the deep-seated habits by which human beings are vitally in touch with cosmic otherness, drawing on it and contributing to it.

[b] As stated, the acquisition of sophisticated sentient behaviors in human beings bears an analogy to animal learning. Like animals, human beings acquire behaviors of both the individual and the social kind. Like animals, they do so to an significant extent by being unconsciously and involuntarily conditioned and trained as they engage otherness. They do so especially while young, but far from exclusively: old dogs do occasionally learn new tricks, and at least some of the leopard's spots can be changed.

This allusion to two common proverbs involving animals is an implicit acknowledgement that the ways in which human beings acquire behaviors at the sentient level is reminiscent of the ways animals do so. But there may be merit in reversing the analogy as well. For why do we, human beings, notice at all that animals learn automatc behaviors that are useful and purposeful? Obviously because we instinctively perceive an affinity. But why do we find this affinity *interesting*? Is it not because we find sentient learning processes in animals reminiscent of *human* behavior acquisition, and thus, humanly illuminating? Obviously, it takes human powers of intelligent, intentional observation to notice interactive habit formation in animals and to make it an object of systematic study. But is it not true that the valuable part of the payoff occurs when our observations and systematizations lead to a better understanding of *human* behavior at the sentient level? It is precisely this understanding that is in turn apt to make us more appreciative of the depth to which the many forms of genuine, responsible human living are indebted to the great array of human *sensibilities*.

[c] The point just made is part and parcel of the tradition of catholic thought. Thomas Aquinas was inspired by Albert the Great to draw the infra-human cosmos into the ambit of both philosophy and theology (cf. §80, 3). He found Aristotle's biological writings *anthropologically*—that is, philosophically and theologically—relevant and fruitful. In our own day, great, deeply humane lovers and students of Nature like Konrad Lorenz and Niko Tinbergen have been doing what Aristotle once did; their fascinating studies of animal behavior, now continued and expanded by an army of followers, have been opening our eyes to the intricacy, subtlety, and delicacy of human behavior at the sentient level, and thus, to *the relevance of sensibility to the responsible life* [m].

[d] This raises a question. What inspires *and* enables human beings to engage in the exploration and understanding of animal behavior? Answer: humanity is part of the biosphere, yet without being wholly immersed in it. We combine genuine participation in the biophysical and psychophysical order with a decisive transcendence over it (§115, 6). No wonder we instinctively intuit that animals acquire habits as we do; yet at the same time we realize that unlike animals, we enjoy the critical distance and the higher viewpoint required to appreciate and properly understand animal phenomena, and even more, to understand them as they are relevant to our own self-understanding.

---

[m] It is not out of place to venture a critical observation at this point. The period between the late Middle Ages and the early twentieth century saw the rise of many "modern" theories about what makes humanity unique in the cosmos. Most of these have a typically *modern* feature in common: they take a less integrated and more rationalist view of human nature; they tend to be blind to humanity's deep continuity with the cosmos as a whole (cf. §9, 1, [i]; §20, 2; §59, 6, [g]; §78, 3, [r]; §80, 3, [c]; §87, 2, a, [x], and d, [gg]; §94, 6, a; §99, 3; §102, 4, a, [l]; §103, 1; §115, 1; 6–8 and [g]). This raises questions. Were these rational anthropologies subliminally disdainful of human animality? Afraid of it, perhaps? In any case, in these "post-modern" days we are increasingly witnessing their fall, thank heavens.

[e] In the process of this study, we are likely to notice not only the numerous resemblances, but a big difference as well. Even as contemporary animal ethology is bringing to light the marvels of coordinated and disciplined behavior in animals, they are beginning to realize that behavior acquisition in animals, for all its intricacy, encompasses only a restricted number of specialized habits. Within each species, it is discovered, even the most resourceful animal behaviors are as restricted in scope as they are specialized; besides, useful and practical as such behaviors may be, animals pick them up only within the special conditions of their particular *Umwelt.*

By contrast, what distinguishes the human species *as a whole* is this: we have turned the wildest variety of environments into habitats, so much so that we think of ourselves as "conquerors" of *the world.* Human sensibility subsists in a multitude of exceedingly diverse sensibilities, each of them more distinctive and delicate than the next. And within the circle of each sensibility, human life literally once again teems with the most diverse and delicate forms of acquired behavior. Human beings, from the simplest to the most sophisticated, pick up and develop, and will continue to pick up and develop, both individually and socially, a wealth of extremely dexterous new behaviors to meet recurrent situations, both natural *and artificial.* The latter has been shown in a spectacular fashion not only by recent developments, say, in space technology and cardiac surgery, but also, and especially since the early eighteenth century, in the rise of technical virtuosity in playing string instruments. Human beings continue to devise and manufacture more refined or more powerful instruments; in doing so, they are also devising and constructing, at least partly deliberately, entirely new challenges for human beings to cope with. But whether the challenges we must cope with are natural or artificial, the ways in which we cope with them are analogous: in all of them, the instinctive and the intentional (*i.e.,* the psychophysical and the distinctively human, and ultimately, the pre-moral and the moral) are tied in with each other—so much so that their connections defy complete analysis or differentiation, and that separating the two is clearly impossible. Yet invariably as well as amazingly, human beings (or at least many of them) somehow succeed in training themselves and each other to meet these new self-made challenges, not only rationally, but at even the practical (or rather better, "sentient" and thus pre-moral) level. Some human beings end up performing highly sophisticated, coordinated, and disciplined as well as useful and purposeful behavioral skills in near-involuntary ways.

[f] Needless to say, these developments are awe-inspiring in their artfulness and virtuosity. Needless to say, too, they are apt to shape the sensibilities not only of those who achieve the feats but also of the countless who marvel at the achievements and stand in awe of them. But even more do these feats of rational ingenuity and sentient virtuosity shape the sensibilities of the many who take advantage of the technological developments that invariably come in the wake of the achievements. No wonder many of us tend to view the inventors, the designers, the manufacturers, and the operators of technological marvels in a near-heroic light. (Many of these dexterous, highly expert people are ready, of course, to offer disclaimers. They will point out that there is no heroism in ingenuity, that the skills in question are, or could be, practiced by countless other people, that being skillful is a matter of specialization and practice, and that *skill does not entail either wisdom or virtue.*)

[g] The disclaimers volunteered by virtuoso experts suggest that the awe in which expertise is generally held is elicited largely by the *powerful effects* of its performances, not by the moral caliber of the intelligence and deliberation behind them or by the nobility of the interests promoted by them. Once again, we must recall that whatever is powerful and influential is not in and of itself discerning, nor does it become discerning by being done either deliberately or skillfully. In fact, it *can* be undiscerning, and, in fact, it *can* be all the more short-sighted, purblind, and even downright immoral for being so advanced and so dexterous.

Let us put this differently, principally for emphasis. Thoughtless, animal virtuosity in human beings is splendid indeed—stirring in its very thoughtlessness, especially when undertaken by way of play or sheer delight. Yet no matter how well-coordinated, refined, and sophisticated it may be, physical virtuosity *can* be just mindless, and all the more mindless for being morally aimless— that is, when it is chiefly undertaken, in earnest and by design, by way of power, influence, self-assertion, and self-expansion, and indeed, of intimidation and domination.

[2] It was stated that temperance is the virtue on whose strength human beings attempting to live morally must deal directly and at close quarters with the powerful dynamics of the sentient life (§130, 1, a) —that is, human life and activity in so far as they are pre-moral and

in that sense mindless. This implies that temperance has everything to do with *human sensibilities.* This affirmation must not be taken in an exclusive sense. In its integrity, temperance is not a matter of sensibility alone; it is a true virtue—that is to say, it belongs in the sphere of deliberate, fully human activity. But it can be a virtue only to the extent that it acknowledges and integrates the powerful dynamics of human sensibility. No temperance and no mature moral living are possible without recognition of sense and sensibility—their delights and their demands. This requires clarification.

[a] First of all, sensibilities are complexes of mostly non-thematized, *per se* a-moral sentient awareness, shaped by habitual patterns of psychophysical activity, practiced as a matter of course, and experienced as fitting and quite often as enjoyable and gratifying as well. In the case of humanity, sensibilities are richly *varied,* and they exist across a broad continuum. Not only do human communities and individuals not feel in the same manner; they do not all feel the same things.

Secondly, while we may speak of individual sensibilities ("character and personality"), sensibilities are usually taken to be *shared.* This implies they create outsiders and insiders. To outsiders and from a distance, the sensibilities of others tend to look and feel *different* as well as *collective.* On the ground, people who are on the inside of a shared sensibility tend to be less conscious of this; sensibility is like the air they breathe and the water they drink. This does not imply that to insiders matters of sensibility are a closed book—quite the contrary. For sensibilities are never entirely of one piece in either space or time. Thus, within a larger region in which a fairly well identifiable sensibility prevails, those who feel at home in one particular village or town or province will still say that a neighboring village or town or province (or even the post-war generation in their own community) "has a different feel." Within a neighborhood (especially a cohesive one), people can still "feel the difference" between the recent arrivals and the residents of long standing, between the families where the grandparents and the parents have always been easygoing and the families where they have been demanding, or between the families where music is played, or bridge, and those where football is prevalent, or fly-fishing. Finally, within small towns, villages, and families, at least some truly individual sensibilities (usually called "characters") will stand out: she is nervous; he is shrewd; he is jovial but he also makes you feel like a subordinate; she is the power behind his throne; she is very funny but she just may have things to hide; the eldest of the So-and-so's is deep (or just taciturn?), and the middle child of the Joneses is somehow hard to get a handle on.

[b] These examples could, of course, be multiplied indefinitely; obviously, sensibilities are marked by cosmic multiplicity. But this does not mean that they are so miscellaneous as to be wholly un-amenable to classification or reason. What it does mean is this: sensibilities *function* at the sentient (and in that sense the non-rational) level; they are largely a matter of spontaneity; and they play very substantial roles in the formation of the morally responsible life. Put differently, although they are largely pre-moral, sensibilities are extremely relevant to the moral sense of individuals and communities, and to the changes and modifications to which any moral sense is subject (cf. §105, 3). This helps account for the considerable variety of life-styles that are, or have been, or are apt to be, considered morally responsible, not only "at home" but also "elsewhere."

[c] There is some else as well. Sensibilities at least partly result from formative processes operative at the purely sentient level: adaptation, conditioning, training. Sensibilities, therefore, *feel, look, and function* to a large extent as if they were simple biophysical and psychophysical givens—a matter of sentient habit and little else. Still, this is only apparently the case. For, as a matter of fact, sensibilities also include elements that are distinctively human. How?

Sensibilities, we have said, are patterns of "animal, thoughtless virtuosity" in human beings. These patterns develop first of all because human beings learn how to deal, as a matter of sentient routine, with characteristic natural (or almost-natural) situations. But there is more than sentient virtuosity even there: even the most primitive human communities deal with their natural environment *with at least some degree of deliberation.* This has resulted not only in sensibilities, but also in characteristic (if often very simple) "mind-sets" (as anybody knows who has met, say, forest dwellers, cowboys out on the range, or petty farmers in remote villages and their barbers). Not surprisingly, smarter sentient routines and more differentiated mind-sets typically occur in communities where both sensibilities and mind-sets have been shaped by *complex living situations deliberately and artificially created by human beings for their use* (as those who have met, say, crane operators, bartenders, surgeons, assem-

bly-line workers, graduate students preparing for examinations, executive secretaries, foremen at building sites, and—heaven knows
—academic deans, not to mention street-wise big-city dwellers, professional pickpockets, and other sharp operators).

Many of these things can also be said of sensibilities shaped by
other habits of artifice that have shaped us so deeply that we have
come to take them for granted. Any Western European or North
American who has ever spent time, say, in Central Java (and not in
hotels) knows how a wholly different housing culture can make
one feel not only clumsy but also a stranger. For the type of houses we are used to living in are artifacts that have become second
nature; they condition us in a thousand barely noticeable ways. So
do the liturgical and commmunity observances and customs that
shape our religious sensibities. Many Catholics feel they have not
really been to church if the service was not a proper eucharistic liturgy; Methodists may feel the same way if they have not sung at
least two rhyming hymns, and many Presbyterians (especially those
of German or Dutch provenance) feel out of sorts if the sermon
has not been long (or stern) enough, or if they have not sung a
rhyming psalm. Sensibilities are the lowly bottom layer of all cultures, and hence, of the moralities and the forms of religiosity they
commend.

Thus each and every form of human response to the world of
otherness, whether in regard to natural conditions or artifacts, involves a greater or lesser degree of deliberation—that is, of *mind*.
But all "mental" decisions, the fully deliberate as well as the merely
ingenious ones, will, along with their outcomes, affect us at the level of sensibility. They will often do so almost imperceptibly. That
is, they will often do so in ways that take us by surprise.

[d] How so? Due to *natural concupiscence* (cf. §113, 3, b), the human *mind* is seldom capable of appreciating, let alone anticipating,
each and every consequence that even its most deliberate decisions
and actions will have at the sentient level. Accordingly, the effects
of the mind's decisions and actions at the sentient level are only
very partly intentional. But the morally relevant fact is that at some
level there is mind involved in the formation of sensibility; and the
mere fact that sensibilities can be intentionally formed implies that
not only the formation of sensibilities but also the interpretation
and discernment of mind-sets and mentalities can become moral
issues (cf. §131, 5, b–c).

Let us put this differently. The fact that human beings act on the basis of sensibility raises a moral issue: the deliberate formation of character and mentality. This important conclusion requires exploration, clarification, and illustration, at some length.

[e] Given the complexity of these issues, our treatment will occur in two rounds. Neither will be brief. In the first (§131), we will concentrate on the issue of training for temperance as it occurs at close and fairly close *interpersonal* quarters—that is, in the setting of the family, of social units immediately associated with family life, and in smaller, largely face-to-face groups. The far-flung second round (§132) will also be far more ambitious. In it, we will inquire into temperance as a socio-political (*i.e., cultural*) moral issue.

Finally, this chapter will revert to its general theme (§133), and thus come to its conclusion.

[§131] TEMPERANCE, SENSIBILITY, SENSITIVITY

[1] Let us start the first round with a philosophical commonplace. As human beings, we are limited—that is, defined. We are "situated" (§125, 5; cf. §122, 3)—*i.e.*, positioned in the world of finitude as parts of it. We find ourselves both set off against otherness as well as involved in it (cf. §115, 5, c, [e]. One of the fundamental ways in which we *experience* finitude is that we find ourselves living to a significant extent by complexes of habitual sentient acts and habits or "sensibilities." Sensibility *defines* us, radically.

Having pertinent philosophical convictions is one thing; having a concrete, lived awareness of them is another. To be effective, philosophical commonplaces must come home to us with a certain sentient fierceness, in their particularity and tangibility. In the present context this means: we need a vivid, educated awareness of our sensibilities—of their extent and their defining power, but of their delicacy as well. Unless we become more aware of our sensibilities—our own and others'—we apt to forget just how, and just how deeply, we are indebted, for our experience of identity as persons and communities of persons, to the *particulars* of our situatedness. The problem is that in direct experience our awareness of the workings of our several sensibilities is largely spontaneous, and thus tacit. To develop a better awareness, therefore, we must reflect on direct experience.

Acquired habits and practices define us, it was stated, and definition implies *limitation*. This is where our exploration must begin. In the process of sentient behavior acquisition, human beings, like animals, develop *a felt sense of limits*—their own and those of everybody and everything around them. This sense of limits, as instinctive as it is subtle, is an elementary requisite for a successful sentient life. Animals must cope, survive, and flourish in a world rife with the powerful dynamics of combination and decombination. Instinctively, they must take their own measurements to do so successfully. They must discover, with sentient cleverness and sensitively, what suits them and what not, what they can use and what not, what they can handle and what not, what works for them and what doesn't, and which works for which or for what. Human beings are not exempted from these essential sentient discoveries.

In animals, this sense of limits is not just a prerequisite for the sentient life; it is also a positive enabler, and one of great subtlety; it is a source of *power*. Since we humans acquire behaviors on a range and with a scope unparalleled by any animal species (cf. §115, 9), our sentient self-definition is bound to be both incalculably more valuable and more subtle [*n*]. How could we be trusted to engage otherness with the distinctively human gifts of consciousness and freedom, without first developing, in the school of sentient experience, a keen and reliable sense of where we stop and otherness starts in the world we live in? At least two observations follow from this.

Firstly, it has been argued that human beings acquire valuable sentient habits, and thus achieve a useful sentient self-definition (*i.e.*, a sound instinctive sense of limits). Both the process of acquisition and the achievement of self-definition are very subtle and sophisticated. Thus, it makes sense to assume that the development and upkeep of human sensibilities is a delicate matter. But human sensibility is inseparable from the cardinal virtue of temperance. Our conclusion must be: human beings will be unable to acquire habits of temperance unless they acquire habits of *alertness, subtlety, sensitivity, and awareness of limits* that are as reliable as they are spontaneous.

This leads to the second observation. Unless unformed, untutored individuals and groups of individuals are *formed*, starting with the

---

[*n*] Even a cursory reading of F. J. J. Buytendijk's phenomenological masterpiece *Algemene theorie der menselijke houding en beweging* ("General Theory of Human Posture and Movement") will give the reader a sense of the sheer profusion of careful, self-adjusting attitudes and gestures typical of human beings at the psychophysical, sentient level, and of their dynamic variety, flexibility, subtlety, and meaningfulness. The search for balance between what Martin D'Arcy, in *The Mind and Heart of Love*, has discussed undere the rubric of the complementarity of *anima* and *animus* is operative even at the preconscious level.

sentient level, the truly moral, deliberate life (from temperance on up) is never going to become a genuine option for them. This suggests that it is a *moral* imperative for those who are already temperate to train and teach others not yet so fortunate a serviceable shared sensibility. In all human communities, therefore, it is morally incumbent on the sensibly and morally mature to help prepare other members of the community, especially the young and the marginal, for the more fully deliberate life. An fundamental way of doing so is to encourage them to discover their limits and thus to get to "know their place," especially by dint of active companionship with others like themselves, which frequently means: by fair play. But another part of this process of discovery is: actively to make them recognize the limits set by the community, and thus, to condition and train them for temperance them by dint of modeling and enforcing behaviors endorsed by the community.

To appreciate the importance of this claim, let us reflect in some detail on the subtlety of human sensibility and its vulnerability.

[a] Let us start our explorations by returning to a topic already touched upon at some length: *tools* (§129, 3, a). Human beings develop an extraordinarily broad range of tools, and they do so not only by dint of animal dexterity but also by clearly intelligent design. The tools may be primitive, such as almost wholly extempore cooking utensils,[19] stone-age axes, and simple machines entirely operated by hands and feet or both, such as wheel-barrows, potter's wheels, and weaving looms; they may also be means of locomotion and conveyance, both animal and mechanical, high-volume and high-speed; they may be refined instruments both musical and technological, such as violins and pipe organs, precision tools for micro-surgery, and computing-devices with a staggering capacity. What is more, human beings also learn how to *handle* these devices with an instinctive, often near-sensate dexterity.

In fact, many tools effectively function as *quasi-natural* extensions of our bodies, especially of our senses, our hands (cf. §115, 9, [i] and [j]), our feet, and our nervous systems, and ultimately, of our minds, of course. No wonder some of us will declare that they do not recognize their own faces without the glasses they have worn as long as they can remember; others will joke that while feet may well be made for walking, their true purpose is the management of the accelerator and the brake pedal of an automobile. The truth behind the jokes is that we all know from experience just how many really subtle tools and instruments have become second nature to us, and to what remarkable, even virtuoso, extent we have come to use them, and indeed, to identify ourselves with them.

[b] The points just made have a special relevance in our own day. On the strength of very powerful technologies and tools, wildly different human sensibilities around the globe are being increasingly forced into encounters with one another. Such encounters across sensibility boundaries have existed from time immemorial; their motor forces are the shifting alliances and antagonisms brought about by commerce and conflict ("coin and cannon" once again: §11, 6). In our day, however, these forces have been joined by a global expansion of literacy, and especially by massive technological growth and an unprecedented communications explosion. These potent developments are pushing some kind of global sensibility upon all of us.

We need not be alarmed at this realization, at least not immediately and without reflection. Père Teilhard de Chardin, hopeful as always, might conceivably have discerned in the developments just described another instance of creation's immense movement toward "unification by complexification" (§29, 5, c). But he also understood that creation's splendid advances come at a very high price; in fact, the saga of evolving humanity looked to him like "a way of the Cross" (§117, 5); his confidence in the future was not blind to painful facts whether past or present. For this reason, even our most optimistic interpreters of the new global technological culture are well advised to take note of the fact that the delicate human sensorium is under pressure everywhere, with consequences as yet unforeseeable, as Walter Ong has been explaining for almost half a century.

Today's enlightenment, in other words, is sorely testing many prevailing sensibilities. Untold people are living in societies that have been long and deeply formed by the Western capacity for distance and objectivity, and by the tools as well as the products of literacy, science, and technology. Many of them have for some time felt (often unthematically, of course) that their capacity for sentient self-definition is being stretched to the breaking point and beyond (cf. §120, 3, a). How much more, then, will the recent technological developments affect the many non-Western sensibilities of great antiquity—those that have for a very long time relied to a large extent on schooling and habit-formation at close quarters, on acceptance of limits as a source of strength and identity, and on the wisdom of oral/acoustical communication?

To make matters even more difficult, for all its technological sophistication, the new global sensibility and the methods it employ to commend ("sell") itself can hardly be called subtle. Despite the idyllic connotations of its designation, the "global village" is very much driven by the power-and-profit motive. No wonder that the professed ideals of this culture—openness without limits and global participation—are provoking some very authoritative traditional cultures: nervously, they will adopt stances of self-maintenance and of aggressive, often resentful self-definition.

[c] But let us return closer to home, to the sensibilities prevailing in the modern industrial powers. Having first defined "progress" in technological terms, they are now acting on the technological imperative (cf. §129, 6, a): under the banner of development, they are inundating the globe, and especially the "less advanced cultures" with the implements of technology.

How moral is this? Shall we say that the jury is still out on the long-range effects of these tools on *our own* sensibilities and thus, indirectly, on Western (and westernized) humanity's moral development? In the Western world itself, what is the future of the massive identification, *at the sentient level*, with the "knowledge" mainly understood as limitless power, mastery, and technological ingenuity? We are instrumentalizing, at the fiercest rate, our mastery both of the cosmos and of our own sentient (and even our deliberating) selves, often by default, impatiently, and undiscerningly; where is our insistence likely to lead us? Does it not make sense to say that our technological culture is *systemically* committing us to power, control, and influence as the dominant topics of our endeavor, our thought? And since it is doing so to a large extent at the level of mentality and sensibility (that is, tacitly), could it be that power, control, and influence are, imperceptibly but inexorably, becoming our real agenda—an agenda mostly hidden, and rather more hidden to ourselves than to others more perceptive than ourselves? And could it be that the lure of limitless power, control, and influence is surreptitiously eroding our basic instinctive sense of limits, and hence, too, depriving us of the psychophysical basis we need to attain a deeper, properly *human* sense of identity?

[d] These questions are not being raised here for the first time. When modern science and technology were still in their infancy,

Pascal was among the first to distrust the new confidence in the power of empirical knowledge of the cosmos, gained and conveyed with geometrical precision. He warned that the spirit of geometry did not guarantee *pensée*—the awareness of humanity's exquisite, distinctive privilege: the ability to understand both the cosmos *and ourselves*. He intuited that knowable and feasible *things* were potentially legion; he also sensed that the endless development of technological solutions to an indefinite multiplicity of fascinating problems could well run away with us, and lure the human spirit into the measureless reaches of space and time, where it might well get the knower lost (§96, 4 and [*a*]).

[2] Yet these realizations are only a first step. It is undeniable that humanity's uncommon talent for tools continues to enhance and improve the way we can function. But it is also true nowadays that our fascination with tools often eclipses the amazing capacity for instrumentality *inherent in the human body itself*. This raises questions. Are we overlooking the possibility that our technological tools, powerful and refined as they are, may well be far less refined than we think they are? Could it be that our dependence on tools is diminishing our ability to deal sentiently (and thus, in the long run, morally) with other human beings and the cosmos—the ability that lies at the basis of our deeper sense of identity? Let us inquire.

[a] By means of long training and conditioning, human beings develop behavioral complexes of an almost purely sentient kind which enable them to use parts of the human body as instruments far more delicate and sophisticated than even the most advanced of tools. These psychophysical instruments and the behaviors they enable are mainly automatic, yet very intricate and unimaginably complex and coordinated—marvels of self-control, efficiency, and freedom.

[b] First and foremost among them is *speech*. Years and years before human beings have anything (or anything much) to say, most of them find themselves conditioned and trained to *speak articulately*. At their best and most artful and artistic, speech (and *a fortiori* song) become acts of towering intellectual and affective self-expression and self-communication. But we tend to forget that even rustic speech and song are wonderfully expressive and communicative. Even the lowliest forms of vocal expression and communication vastly surpass even the most admirable and sophisticated vocal utterances of animals and infants (cf. once again §115, 9, [*i*]

and [j]); yet they are produced by means of organs very similar to those with which animals and infants produce their repetitive noises and strains.

What matters here is this. Speech and song, both of the elementary and the highly intelligent and expressive kind, are impossible without psychophysical organs managed by enormously complex sets of reflexes and routine behaviors. All these behaviors are rooted in almost purely imitative and naturally acquired skills. Firstly, there are the spontaneous, yet tremendously intricate, patterns of vocal, nasal, and oral *articulation* and *intonation* (cf. §115, 9). Added to that, there is our *lexical facility*, which builds on elementary "gestural" habits: hands-on dealing with of objects first, followed by hands-off pointing at them; for in due course we transcend these two types of "deictic" performance by first enhancing and then replacing them to a large extent by *words*; on the strength of the representative capacity of words, even the clumsiest speakers among us lift themselves and their hearers above the particularities of situations; in the end, we all use, amazingly, without much effort, abstractions ("universal ideas") to convey what we want or mean.[20]

On top of all this, human beings freely employ, almost wholly automatically, very complex *patterns of grammar and syntax*, which enable even uneducated speakers to convey subtle shades of both affect and meaning. By an even higher skill, we can deal with recurrent everyday situations because we can effortlessly resort to an arsenal of standard *idioms*, often wonderfully metaphorical, ranging all the way from highly efficient routine expressions to stirring and frequently profound vocal prayers—many, many of them first acquired by conditioning, training, and imitation, and only on that basis enhanced, perhaps, by deliberate study and practice.

The thing to be noted in all this is that the distinctively and irreducibly human ability (not just to speak but) to *say something* is supported and enabled by substantial systems of coordinated skills at the psychophysical, reflexive, near-instinctive level. To appreciate the delicacy of these skills as well as their fragility, let us recall what happens, say, in moments of sudden illness or acute embarrassment, or in outbursts of barely rational or uncontrolled passion, both in individuals and in groups. Ordinary speech collapses and turns linguistically deviant: we find ourselves or others "being stuck for words" or "becoming incoherent." But these crises occur to a large extent *at the purely sentient level*: what breaks down at such moments is the *psychophysical* ability to be articulate, to put to *spontane-*

ous use the rules of grammar and syntax, to tap into our *unconscious* lexical wealth, and so, to perform *with ease* generally accepted forms of speech. In other words, in such situations people do not "lose their *minds*"—their *spiritual* ability to rise above the situation by dint of thinking, judging, and acting. What defeats them far more immediately, at least momentarily, is overwhelming, unmanageable anxiety and malfunction at the level of *sensibility;* control and self-control break down; the pressure of the here-and-now situation bars access to their habitual facility of sentient performance.

[c] Analogous things can be pointed out in the area of that other basic domain of the sentient life: *manners*—the whole array of routine gestural forms of expression and social communication that we pick up partly by conditioning, partly by mimicry, partly by conscious effort. Standard manners are a matter of tempered sensibility; they occur on a wide range, from little knacks to formal protocol, from the relatively coarse to the very refined; they are acquired not only in close units like families, but also by association with wider zones of social communication, as well as more vaguely, from the culture at large. What is relevant here is that knacks and manners occur and have their impact at the emotive, sentient level. They may well have been intentionally acquired and even deliberately rehearsed, but in the performance they are operate instinctively rather than by design; they are behavioral statements that have more in common with the *signals* that herds instinctively use to stay together or to disperse than with the *signs* used by societies for the purpose of deliberate communication (cf. §122, 1, e, [g]). Thus, groups and individuals driven by strong needs for a high profile will deliberately put together from the large arsenal of publicly available manners a blend of idiosyncratic behavioral routines, some less refined than others. In this way, fairly small groups can become the nuclei of highly expressive (if often idiosyncratic or even ominous) sub-cultures characterized by shared displays of offbeat manners. Analogously, individuals can become "characters," whose eccentricities, whether of the irritating or the amusing kind, have their chief impact at the sentient level. But what all manners and mannerisms accomplish is this: *they create limits,* largely at the sentient level. In this way, they create a base for more conscious forms of identity.

Taken in their totality, the manners of individuals or communities, like their speech, are very much part of the *deliberate* life; think of some of the more ostentatious mannerisms willfully rehearsed and practiced, or some of the more far-fetched forms of etiquette. Yet it is also true that many forms of civility (or incivility) become automatic, because they occur at the reflexive level—imitative behaviors acquired largely involuntarily and practiced out of a fundamental need for contact, under the pressure of social conditioning and training.

Like articulate speech, manners are a source of stability at an elementary, instinctive level. When for some reason our routines and mannerisms fail us or become unusable, all access to otherness appears to be taken away from us; we feel cut off and estranged. This, too, is worth pursuing for a moment.

To the extent that manners are acquired behaviors, they are habitual and hence, largely involuntary. In that sense and to that extent, they are thoughtless and non-deliberate. Yet most of us know that being prevented from effectively using them is a paralyzing, alienating experience—unsettling not just intellectually and morally, but emotionally as well. Yet on reflection, this is only to be expected. Rising above sensibility is far more easily thought about than achieved. It is inherent in alienation that otherness *can* be at odds with our sense of identity; it can even push us into downright estrangement (§122, 1, a). And at times, that otherness is our very own. Our own body and its instincts (as well as its extensions, both the instrumental and the self-expressive) *can* weigh heavy on our souls; in fact, they often do, without any fault on our part, when they surprise us by malfunctioning in an otherwise familiar context. Which among us polite, literate, reasonable people, has not been out of sorts or infuriated and unable to act properly, say, after dropping a potato on the floor at a dinner party, or after breaking a leg, or after a ridiculous sneezing-fit, or, for that matter, when we were unable to find our glasses, or when the family car or the computer broke down at the worst possible moment? Equally often, though, we are confounded by otherness not our own—that is, when we find ourselves stymied for lack of support or sympathetic context. Those of us who have been (or are) confined by incarceration, or crippled by illness, or caught in situations of sheer terror can bear witness to this: when manners fail us, we not only become tongue-tied; we are also at a loss as to "what to make of ourselves." (Clearly, *maners makyth man.*)[21] And who has not felt "turned off," immobilized, viscerally intimidated, or driven to irrational fury in environments dominated by the coarse language and the uncouth manners of individuals or groups that seem to insist on being non-conformist, deviant, or even downright offensive?   Or perhaps more frequently, how many of us have felt vaguely hurt by the mass media, and especially by the televised displays of sex and violence, whose impact on our sensibilities has been looming larger and larger, despite the networks' contention that there is no scientific evidence of this claim?

[d] To ponder the issue of human sensibility and its delicacy a bit more deeply, let us briefly ponder two concrete instances.

The first is taken from the world of mass-entertainment. For years now, crass talk-show hosts have been invading the privacy of their victims—unsuspecting lambs publicly led to the slaughter—and inciting their studio audiences to join in and do the same. Some of the victims are little people; some are stars of sorts; many of them are loud and curiously self-important, if often in silly ways; some are artless, many embittered and spiteful; almost all are anxious; all of them are pathetic, hungry for attention, and only too ready to debase their sad or kinky selves by airing their tacky victories and *ditto* agonies. Some fall apart. What is it that enables us to watch these scenes of human regressiveness and listen to them, except the circumstance that we are "only watching"? How would we feel, and how would we want to respond, if the event were taking place without cameras and microphones and audiences, in the privacy of our back yards, with only the family and perhaps the neighbors present and participating? What makes us think that as long as we are "only watching" we will not be suffering what amounts to psychophysical violence? That we are not exposing our impressionable sensibilities far too wide to the mindless opinions and mannerisms broadcast by *à la mode* but shameless media experts operating under the banner of sincerity and caring? That we are not letting callous media clowns with big incomes and cheap tastes coarsen the common culture?[22]

To reinforce the claim that sensibilities, however virtuoso they may be, remain very vulnerable, our second example takes its cue from a common enough experience taken from the realm of intercultural communication: failure of sensibility.

Once in a while, we come upon other human beings who do not pick up even our most ordinary, conventional vocal and gestural signals, or who appear to be amazed at the clothes we wear and the devices we use. Sometimes such people show that they find our behavior impolite or (worse) farcical. Sometimes they seem to misinterpret our manners (as well as ourselves) as outright threats to themselves. In front of such strangers most of us (except, perhaps, the very adventurous and the very obtuse) are apt to lose both our bearings and our nerve. In such situations, we will feel stymied, dissociated, and estranged, or at least insecure. So, with the immediacy of raw passion, we feel at a loss, or offended, or even threatened.

As we find ourselves thus viscerally startled by the abrupt actuality of unfamiliar otherness, our conscious selves are turned off, so to speak. Sentient affect takes over, but to little avail: our sensibility, normally so dexterous in meeting contingencies, is not prepared for this disconcerting encounter with unanticipated otherness. Thus, with the same instinctive immediacy as (presumably) the aliens we are encountering, we find ourselves not only speechless but also unfocused; so we quail or bristle or dissemble or feign total obliviousness; in any case, we will feel very self-conscious and quite nervous. For the fact is that in standoffs like this, we are alarmed and unstable at the level of instinct. We smell embarrassment or conflict, or at the very least contest. And as if feeling powerless and frustrated and irritable were not enough, the rush of emotion we experience becomes all the more disconcerting in proportion as we try harder to rise above it or control it. In fact, judging from the embarrassing results our efforts to regain control, our conscious efforts to *respond humanly* (that is, deliberately and morally), and not just to *react viscerally* (that is, animally) is making our visceral reaction worse, not better.

[3] In the interest of further reflection, let us go back to an issue already touched on. Why is it so hard on such bewildering occasions to speak or to act in a studied manner—that is, humanly and consciously? What keeps us from deliberately rising, at least to some degree, above this close involvement in purblind, instinctive psychophysical process? What keeps us from taking a disciplined, focused, reasonable interest in otherness as it surprises us without warning?

The answer is that in quandaries like those described above we experience ourselves as captive and defeated, without ado, by some of the banal realities of cosmic interdependence and mutuality (cf. §115, 8). We are finding out, by unambiguous, direct experience, that we have taken for granted a host of practically unconscious but highly ingenious behavioral routines which empower (!) us to deal constructively with the world of otherness and which, by "force (!) of habit," have become "second nature" to us. Put differently, precisely when our reflexes and habitual behaviors fail us do we discover the extent to which we unconsciously rely on them as the psychophysical preconditions for every human (that is, moral) move we make—*i.e.,* for every temperate, controlled, *deliberate* form of engagement with otherness. We discover just how intensely, as cosmic participants, we are "creatures of habit"; we find out just how deeply *sentient* we are. We also discover just how delicate are the control mechanisms— the psychophysical skills and routines on whose stability we must habitually count if we are to have our higher, human, "spiritual" faculties and our sense of identity at our disposal.

At the root of our every *deliberate, moral* act of cultural self-expression and engagement with otherness, therefore, we are deeply dependent on ingrained, disciplined, focused, but largely instinctive, *reflexive* behavioral routines. They are acquired habits—the outcome of mimicry encouraged and reinforced by conditioning and training of long standing, and kept up by regular practice. These routines include, as natural and quasi-natural parts of our sentient selves, a knack for refined linguistic and gestural behaviors and for the management of technical tools. These routines set us free. Deep-seated as they are, they are powerful supports of human self-maintenance and self-assertion. Indirectly, they act as elementary, immediately available tools of social control as well; they enable us to define ourselves and negotiate the part we play in the world of otherness.

These realizations open new prospects. For this is exactly where the genuinely *moral* issue begins to surface—right at the point where we emerge, as human beings acting humanly, from the dynamics of the infra-human, sentient cosmos. Let us elaborate this proposition, in two ways—the first fairly succinctly, the second at greater length.

[4] It has been explained that our properly human, deliberate (*i.e.* moral) acts, while indeed transcendent over our largely instinctive, routine acquired behaviors, are never independent of them. This entails the conclusion that in the virtue of temperance two integral elements meet: sensibility and deliberation. Firstly, temperance requires that we accept the passionate, instinctive life both in ourselves and each other and befriend it as truly our own; passion and sensibility must be *integrated,* not denied or stifled, let alone repressed. Secondly, temperance requires that we discover that the passionate, instinctive life calls for *management;* sensibility must (to use a Thomis-

tic idiom) be *ordered*—*i.e.,* brought under the rule of reason and will. Thus, "rightly ordered passions are good, and wrongly ordered passions are vicious."²³ Thus, once again, but now in a fully *moral* sense, *maners makyth man.*

[5] A second point to be made about the interface between the sentient and the deliberate is this. Recall that the *virtue* of temperance (*i.e.* temperance as a *moral* habit) can be acquired and developed only by *intentional acts* of temperance. Thus, genuine humane self-discipline and self-control consists in the *deliberate* use of our ability to use power, exert influence, and assert control over the natural passions of the moment (in the park of both craving and temper), in order to bring them under the rule of reason and will. Morally, this *deliberate* practice of temperance is only fitting, on two grounds.

[a] For one thing, it is part of mature, civilized human self-regard to wish to transcend the realm of untutored passion. We generally do so by mustering up the civilized manners that humanize us, not just on occasion, but habitually: *Maners makyth man.* Yet we feel that genuine humaneness has a rather more altruistic side as well. Even if other human beings or indeed things should in some fashion turn out to be our cosmic competitors, we feel that moral maturity requires that we resist the elementary, passionate impulse to ward them off, and even more the urge to attack them. We instinctively feel that it is part of temperance to be *considerate* in regard to other human beings and things, even if they should pose a threat to our composure, our tastes, our well-being, perhaps even to our lives. Temperance, in other words, turns out to have a natural affinity with another cardinal virtue, in which deliberation plays a far more obvious part: *fortitude.* Those who aim at living temperate lives, therefore, will discover that the forces of intemperance, both within themselves and around them, threaten the life of right reason and deliberation—a realization that calls for firmness, endurance, and even assertiveness and readiness to act vigorously.²⁴

[b] In this way, temperance and fortitude together lead the way to the cardinal virtue that will take pride of place in the next chapter: *justice*—the virtue most characteristic of the fully deliberate life. For if it is by temperance that we control the sensuality that is *ours,* and by fortitude that we sustain the persistent demands of sensibility—*our own and others'*—it is by justice that we deliberately give to each and every *other* the respect that is due to *them* quite apart from our own feelings and spontaneous preferences, but simply because

in and of themselves *they* command respect; accordingly, *they* have rights: *suum cuique.*[25] The sentient life is indeed an integral part of the deliberate, moral life, but it is so only to the extent that it lets itself be disciplined, and thus induced (and occasionally forced) to yield to the just claims of otherness in every form (and not just of those instances of otherness that are naturally congenial to us at the level of sensibility).

[c] This has significant consequences for the moral interpretation of the *pre-moral,* automatic speech and behavior patterns which are the preconditions of the acts and habits of temperance that are require if we are to practice justice. We can acquire these patterns in two ways: either mainly actively, by deliberate (and hence, *moral*) effort, or mainly passively, by being exposed to conditioning and training. Let us put this a little more descriptively.

Human beings *can* acquire new, almost-automatic behaviors actively and intentionally—that is, morally. When, for instance, we decide to live abroad, we will make *efforts* to master the foreign culture's language and to assimilate its manners; we will do so slowly, by dint of observation, practice, and study. In the process we are, of course, aided at some half-conscious or unconscious level by our daily immersion in and exposure to the foreigners and their ways. But we differ from these foreigners in this: the majority of them have acquired (and, like ourselves, continue to acquire) most of their distinctive speech and behavior patterns not by design but by immersion—that is, largely un-self-consciously, simply by dint of conditioning and training. This is how "natives" acquire their distinctive manners, and "native speakers" their characteristic, automatic language habits.

This latter observation has a moral corollary. *Communities* that cherish and cultivate *moral* maturity (of which habits of temperance, fortitude, and justice are integral parts) will insist on the acquisition of certain disciplined, "conditioned," *pre-moral* behaviors on the part of all. In other words, they will be convinced that *modeling and reinforcing accepted manners and accepted speech is a moral duty.* They will recall, of course, that not all individuals and communities are equally open to modeling efforts. Accordingly, they will regard as excusable (at least for the time being and in particular situations) certain shortcomings in the practice of generally received manners and speech; they will excuse certain kinds of deficient discipline and self-control, especially in children and in the mentally and socially disadvantaged. But they will not resign themselves to these weaknesses, let alone romanticize them as "only natural" or as forms of "sincerity." For they know that without discipline and control the abundant energies stored up in the life of passion will never become a humane asset. Thus, they will regard the training and restraining of the instincts and passions of the young and the unformed as the most natural and obvious thing in the world. Thus, too, they will regard modeling behavior and reinforcing it, but also *the temperate, proportionate use of psychophysical and even physical force* as a genuinely moral duty, and consequently, as a *shared* responsibility. For the same reasons, such communities will regard the modeling of undisciplined manners and speech as *morally* unacceptable (cf. §123, 7, [*p*]). And for comparable reasons, they will view the restraining of the morally incompetent and the delinquent (and, at least as much as possible, their healing and rehabilitation) as shared *moral* obligations, not to be sidestepped by sentimental appeals to the liberty of each human individual.

[d] Shared values, in other words, occur even at the sentient, psychophysical level; consequently, the pursuit of some kind of "premoral common good" at this level is a moral duty incumbent on all those in the community who are culturally and morally mature. They, therefore, are the ones who must practice both temperance and fortitude. That is to say, they must patiently shoulder the moral responsibility for the *pre-moral formation* of the immature, the stunted, and the downright intractable. They must do so to prevent the latter from coming to grief—hapless victims of their own and each other's instincts, and further down the line, the likely target of judicial rigor, which will find itself compelled to force on them the limits they are incapable of establishing for themselves (cf. §128, 2, a).

[e] Let us end on a lighter note (or at any rate a more practical one). In light of what has been stated, it would appear that it is at the very least ill-advised to argue, *as a matter of moral principle*, that *any* form of *deliberate* corporal punishment and *any* form of other less physical but equally coercive forms of discipline are in every instance inhumane, and hence, unethical or immoral [*o*].

[*o*] On September 20, 1951, in a letter to Sally and Robert Fitzgerald, expecting their fifth child, Flannery O'Connor banters: "I hope this one will be a girl & have a fierce Old Testament name and cut off a lot of heads. You had better stay down and take care of yourself. Your children sound big enough to do all the work. By beating them moderately & moderately often you should be able to get them in

[6] Temperance, it has been explained, involves the management of psychophysical (that is, sentient and in that sense cosmic) process and habit in us. It follows that temperance is never assured. In the life of deliberation, even such higher (that is, in context, properly moral) activities as articulate speech and civilized manners are prone to falling victim to the pressure of passion. In other words, the possibility of intemperance never quite ceases to jeopardize the exercise of even our most distinctively human functions.

This disconcerting conclusion implies a disconcerting fact. Behaviors that *look* human, deliberate, and other-regarding may in cases be largely a matter of sentient affect. It is part of the human condition that under the semblance of distinctively human demeanor we may in fact be engaging in behavioral routines that are essentially instinctive and self-regarding. This will embarrass the self-aware among us. Still, since such routines are to a significant extent involuntary and automatic, we may turn unaware of them, and accustomed to them even to the point of addiction; we may even unconsciously use them for purposes of manipulation—to gratify our craving for the favors of others or to relish our temper as we put others in their places.

[a] Quite often, these forms of intemperance take the shape of *speech.* Language, whether spoken or written, is ambivalent. It can be used constructively—to create room for truthful self-expression and transparent communication; it can also be used to build walls to hide behind and fortresses to attack others from. In and of itself, in other words, not even the most articulate speech guarantees that something is being said, let alone that something is being said to someone. It is by no means rare for people to talk and converse almost purely involuntarily and instinctively—a far cry from distinctively human communication, whether intellectual or affective or both. Thus we may find others (as well as ourselves) speaking elegantly and eloquently in public without really saying anything—that is, speaking simply in the interest of self-maintenance or self-assertion. Or we mumble and mutter and swear under our breath to soothe or encourage ourselves; we babble and prate to avoid having to focus on our tasks; we gossip compulsively out of a

---

the habit of doing domestic chores." She must have enjoyed the phrase, for less than a month later, on October 18, congratulating her friend Betty Boyd Love on the birth of her first child, she turns it into a maxim of general validity while adding a characteristic touch of common-sense polemics: "My advice to all parents is beat your children moderately and moderately often; and anything that Wm. Heard Kilpatrick & Jhn. Dewey say do, don't do" (*The Habit of Being,* pp. 26, 29).

hidden fear of having our own conduct assessed; we find ourselves prattling aimlessly as, under cover of speech, we try to outtalk others, or to silence, bait, flatter, or intimidate them, or to get them sexually interested; we find ourselves unable to stop chattering at a business meeting in order to evade the embarrassment of having our unfamiliarity with the agenda unmasked; we carry on with such instinctive intensity that all we are doing is forcing others to become partners in our confusion or frenzy. Or we repeat slogans and camp phrases; with the cleverness of instinct, we mindlessly mimic the pronunciation and intonation patterns of movie stars and television starlets because it makes us "sound good" and appear "tuned in." Or, carefully avoiding saying anything that might rock the boat, and borne on the tired wings of pious platitude and hallowed cliché, we put ourselves through the motions of yet another homily. And in a sudden emergency, at our wits' end, we find ourselves reciting prayer upon childhood prayer instinctively, mechanically, and as hard and forcefully as we can, our eyes tightly shut, figuring that this must be religion at its most real.

These examples are, of course, largely taken from the microcosm of individual experience and fairly close-up human relationships. Needless to say, similar patterns unfortunately occur in macrocosmic shape as well, especially (or so it would seem) in the world of advertizing and other forms of double-talk and hidden manipulation. It occurs even more frequently in socio-political and religious movements that engage in the sort of overt or covert propaganda in which reason and self-discipline play very little part.

[b] Analogously, intemperance catches up with us when we revel in *mannerisms* that are as empty as they are automatic. In many cases they are merely a matter of innocuous habit, but they can be dangerously compulsive and even downright manipulative as well. In any case, they can be tools of instinctive self-maintenance and self-assertion. At a party, we unwittingly wrap ourselves in an air of high-minded correctness or cold elegance, either out of fear, or to avoid facing an uncomfortable acquaintance. Or we act briskly and energetically, though subliminally all we are doing is throwing our weight around, to affect unspecified others. Or we utter compliment upon standard compliment in a desperate effort to avoid having to face, or discover, or tell, the truth. Or, to take an example from the larger world, it is possible, by overt or covert manipulation aimed not at reason but at prejudice, to get entire popula-

tions to practice political conformity and correctness, to develop subhuman tastes in forms of entertainment posturing as art, to adopt mindless habits of consumption, or to march in goose-step and shout rallying-cries in the service of vicious causes.

Summing up: the fact that there is no morality that is not rooted in an underlying sensibility makes it possible that in the very act of *ostensibly* engaging in distinctively human, deliberate behavior, human beings act (or rather, "act out") in purely instinctive, intemperate ways, on the basis of questionable sensibilities fostered either deliberately or by benign neglect.

[c] From a moral point of view, acquired sentient behaviors and developed sensibilities, as well as the inappropriate forms of manners and speech connected with both of them, may well be regarded as pre-moral, and hence, as excusable, especially in the young, the thoughtless, the humanly incompetent, and the acutely embarrassed or distressed. Occasionally, and from a developmental or clinical psychological point of view, it may even be the better part of wisdom to practice fortitude and to treat intemperate speech and uncouth manners as "permissible," at least provisionally. Finally, in certain circumstances (say, in some forms of treatment of the mentally and emotionally troubled), it may even be therapeutic to allow patients to act out, or perhaps even to occasion them to do so.

Still, persons and communities who live by refined sensibilities and moral maturity are apt to stop to think at this point. They typically appreciate the fact that sensibility and instinct are part of human culture; nevertheless, they will not put their trust in so frail a set of ingrained habits. They are inclined to realize, both experientially and intellectually, that basic craving for self-defense and deep thirst for influence are always apt to resort to passion and instinct, even under the appearance of distinctively human pursuits and behaviors, especially in people who are under pressure. The truly temperate, in other words, are aware of humanity's latent capacity for almost purely sentient, regressive, intemperate behavior, in the interest of self-maintenance and self-assertion, even in situations where fully human behavior is both called for and possible.

[d] Because the temperate respect distinctively human integrity and dignity, their own as well as others', they will appreciate sensibilities and even encourage them, but they will also make efforts to be consciously and deliberately considerate, both in private life

and in public life. They realize that every form of genuinely humane life is precarious. Accordingly, while acknowledging and positively enjoying the vitality of passion and the excitement inherent in it, they have a healthy distrust of untutored sensibility and uncontrolled passion. They understand that sentient activity can disgrace not only others, but also ourselves, especially the morning after; they also know that blithe displays of emotion can be utterly ludicrous. They are especially wary when passion is commended, or paraded, as "spontaneity," "honesty," or "candor." They understand that vital instinct and spontaneity, short-sighted as they tend to be, are transitory and capricious. Sensibility will be genuinely human, in a sustained manner, only to the extent that it is formed, controlled, disciplined, tempered, seasoned.

Accordingly, the emotionally and morally mature are apt both to develop personal habits of self-examination and to commend them to others, especially in the form of "examination of consciousness."[26] Typically, they are not authoritarian: they are accessible to feedback about their own behavior, and to friendly advice and correction. Typically, too, they will seek to draw profit from adversity, often with the aid of others; they will even try to learn from hostility. The reason is that their engagement with otherness is habitually prompted, not just by the largely sentient dynamics of action and reaction, but also, and predominantly, by sensibility informed by right reason. In this way, they almost involuntarily (and thus, habitually) transcend the play of cosmic power. That is to say, on the sound foundation of a refined sensibility and acquired habits of discipline and self-control, they practice the virtues of temperance and fortitude.

[e] If the deliberate formation of sensibility is an integral part of temperance and fortitude, then informed, knowledgeable asceticism must be an integral part of the practice of these two virtues. It is precisely in this area that, in recent times, the human sciences, and social psychology in particular, have made important contributions, as Aimé Solignac, in a commanding monograph, had hoped they would (cf. §139, 1, [v] and d). In particular, from the nineteen-fifties and -sixties on, a number of important studies in the dynamics of group processes have appeared, especially in the United States, where research began to take its cue from Kurt Lewin's "field theory."[27] Only a little later did Max Pagès, in France, develop his theory on the human relation as an affective event.[28] In

North America, the corporate world tuned in surprisingly quickly, inspired chiefly by Douglas McGregor's ground-breaking *The Human Side of Enterprise*. Predictably, teachers at all levels, intent on learning about the influence of affect on the life of the mind, became a notable part of what was rapidly becoming a nation-wide movement in "sensitivity training."

Early on, too, religious groups seeking personal and spiritual renewal in the wake of Vatican II picked up the subject, expecting to arrive at a badly-needed understanding of how feelings both tough and tender have a way of influencing the quality of religious and community life, and often discovering that it was a good thing to learn how to acknowledge feelings and deal with them in practice.[29]

Before long, the practice of sensitivity training was giving rise to a fair amount of reliable literature, especially in North America.[30] Of singular ascetical and therapeutic fruitfulness were models and instruments designed not only to animate experiential learning by group interaction in controlled settings, but also to provide enlightening conceptual frameworks enabling participants to give themselves an account of these (often surprising) learning experiences. One such model is the well-known "Johari Window," developed by Joseph Luft and Harry Ingram.[31] Simply by way of illustration, let us describe it and show its relevance to ascetical practice.

[f] The Johari Window is based on two assumptions. The first is that *common goals* can be achieved only to the extent that *individual needs* are taken into account. The second is that human communication will be more effective according as there is more *openness*. Luft and Ingram argue that the more open the field of communication, the more intellectually *and affectively* relevant data are likely to be brought into the open and shared by all those involved; as a result, communication is apt to be both successful and personally satisfying. The first problem is, of course, that in no group are the rational and emotional data ever entirely shared. In and of itself, this is not inappropriate: the level of openness in any group must be proportionate to the group's aims and purposes. There is a more fundamental problem, though: communication between persons (and groups of persons) will be hampered, understandably but in principle unnecessarily, by relevant but unknown factors obstructing openness. Put differently, it is often insufficiently clear which persons (or which sub-groups) in the group are aware of

which *relevant* data, not just at the level of thought and opinion, but also, and especially, at the level of sensibility.

This requires elaboration. Let us begin with a figure of the Johari window.

SELF

	Known to Self	Unknown to Self
Known to Others	I *Area of Free Activity*	II *Blind Area*
Unknown to Others	III *Avoided (Hidden) Area*	IV *Dark Area*

OTHERS

Among the data relevant to all those in the group and at every level are the following. Firstly, there are items which I (we) notice /know about myself (ourselves), but which remain unnoticed by/ unknown to other parties; such data are called "avoided" or "hidden." Secondly, there are items, in various degress relevant to all, which I (we) do not notice/know about myself (ourselves); still, they *are* noticed by/known to other parties; such data are called "blind." Now if communication is to improve, all the group members must cooperate in *expanding the area of needed openness.* They can do so by reducing the domains both of the hidden data and of the blind. To reduce the domain of the hidden, all must venture to share the data they keep *hidden,* mostly by avoiding them. This is achieved by the intentional practice of mutual "self-disclosure." To help reduce the domain of *blindness,* participants must agree to get the relevant data to which they themselves are blind shared openly, by practicing the mutual giving and receiving of "feedback." In all this, it is important to deal appropriately with *affective data.* Expressions of feeling, whether intentional or unpremeditated, are part and parcel of our sense of identity and the quality of our relationships, yet they are always hard to convey. Quite often they are confused as well as confusing, especially when they are

spontaneous and involuntary. Spontaneous feeling, after all, occurs largely at the level of our sensibility, and matters of sensibility
are delicate and hard to pin down. Besides, feelings of this sort are
for the most part out of our control; no wonder we find them painfully hard to acknowledge. To communicate well, therefore, we
must learn how to deal appropriately with feelings, carefully as well
as sensitively. In practice this means we need training, not only in
order to learn about sensibilities (our own and others') but also to
acquire the sensitivity we need in the practice of communication.
Part of this sensitivity consists in developing habits of verification:
every item of both self-disclosure and feedback must be "checked
out," to make sure they have been accurately perceived and understood (and thus shared) by as many group members as possible.

An important negative element in sensitivity training consists in
learning how to be careful with *reasonings* and *judgments*, and when
to refrain altogether from stating or otherwise conveying them.
One reason for this is that they may obstruct the exploration of
feelings and emotional situations in the group. Now affect is often
highly relevant to the quality of communication in groups. Yet,
since it is mostly a matter of *present,* spontaneous experience, and
since, unlike thoughts and judgments, it is only seldom fully retrievable, it is often best expressed while it occurs and dealt with as
soon as possible. Another reason to be wary of intellectualization
is that spontaneous feelings are to a significant extent pre-moral;
for that reason they frequently are inappropriate matter for (moral) judgment—whether approval or censure. Finally, since spontaneity is hardly ever reducible to thought or explanation, or manageable by instruction, judgments (especially general ones) are often not immediately relevant to the present situation; that is, they
tend to reduce the group's ability to focus on what is actually going
on here and know.

How, then, are we to learn how to deal with matters of sensibility? The answer is once again: by seeking training in the venturing
of non-judgmental self-disclosure and feedback. Of these two, *self-
disclosure* is more effective to the extent that persons voluntarily
overcome their habits of anxious self-protection, and proceed, in
front of others in the group, to own up to present feelings; self-disclosure helps reduce the domain of the hidden data; and those
who practice it implicitly convey that they are willing to invest in
the quality of communication in the group. *Feedback*, on the other
hand, is more effective to the extent that persons voluntarily "sit

on" their immediate, *feeling* responses to events in the group, and offer (not enjoin!) perceptive observations to others on their present or at least very recent behaviors, preferably in *descriptive* (*i.e.,* non-judgmental) language; feedback helps reduce the domain of blindness in the group. (Obviously, feedback and self-disclosure can be expressed together, as in "I notice that you pound the table with your right fist at the end of almost every sentence; frankly, I find that hard to take, and it makes it very hard for me to follow you.")

One issue remains. Besides the open, hidden, and blind areas, there is a fourth area of data in every group: the domain of darkness—the data that are obscure to *all* members of the group. Dark data are conceivably rational but far more often they are entirely affective; and the members of the group are aware of them only in the dimmest of ways. Dark data may very well be relevant to the communication that is being attempted; but then again, they may not be. The only thing we can say about them is that they are neither in the open, nor hidden, nor blind. That is to say, it is impossible for anyone to deal with them; it is impossible even to determine if they are real. It is practically impossible, therefore, to get a handle on them and to judge their relevance, though they may be felt to be powerfully present, as an uncomfortable, even ominous presence. In every group, such "central shadows" exist.[32] Like all shadows, they will create anxiety; they will also appeal to anxieties that are already present in and among participants. That is, central shadows will invite unsubstantiated and unverifiable interpretations of what is "really going on" in the group. Most often such interpretations are little more than *projections:* "the whole problem is" that the chairman wants to cover up he is getting angry, that Julie hates André, right next to her, because he is French and probably has an eye on her, that Fred has terminal cancer but won't resign from the board because he wants to get his son a nice job first, that Ursula is flattering the people who count in order to get a raise, and so forth. If group communication is sound, participants will acknowledge that domains of darkness exist; they will also resolutely resist the temptation to be drawn into guessing games. After all, nothing is to be gained from speculating about the unknown; offering judgments based on "data" that are neither shared *nor shareable* is one of the most effective ways to hamper communication. Groups that do not realize this will feel frustrated; they often will vent their thwarted energies in erratic, even hurtful ways; equally

often the energies ready in the group will turn the group against itself, make it impossible to deal with data that *are* shareable, and so
cause depression. Floating anxiety is part of human life; it always
calls for fortitude, and for analysis only in appropriate settings.

[g] Anybody familiar with the practice and theory of faith-sharing
and spiritual direction will have recognized, in this description of
some of the principal dynamics of interpersonal communication in
groups, ideas and practices that have long been known (often under different names) in the tradition of ascetical practice and theology. Let us mention a few, in no particular order.

Typically, religious communities (both the more institutional
and the more loosely organized) have shared religious goals—always in the form of concrete practices of dedication to the love of
God and the love of others. Like any group, communities can accomplish freely undertaken, shared goals; but they can do so only
on condition that the human and religious needs of individual
persons and of smaller, more closely personalized units *within* the
group are met. However, in order to meet them, or in order to get
them met, such needs must be appropriately brought out in the
open. For this reason, people seeking to live lives of dedication to
God in some form of community setting can ill afford to keep each
other (and thus, indirectly, themselves as well) second-guessing
what is going on (and thus, indirectly, what is going on with themselves as well); habits of guessing can only result in a climate of oppressive non-communicativeness. Yet this is exactly what will come
about (and has come about) when religious people develop habits
of concealing their lives from fellow religious, spiritual directors,
or superiors. Thus, communities of religious should learn how to
share—discretely, of course—not only their observable activities,
but also their more private struggles, their practices of devotion or
penitence, and even more the special graces, favors, and encouragements they have experienced, as well as the opposites of the latter: afflictions, temptations, falls from grace. However, because all
these things are to a large extent a matter of sensibility and affect,
it is impossible to feel poised and temperate about them; they are
awkward to share in an appropriate manner. Thus, religious persons often tend to keep them wholly private. This is a temptation.
Men and women seeking to lead interior lives usually have deeply-
felt and deeply-held affections, ideas, and desires; the dark side of
this is that they are susceptible to illusions and disillusions. On the

one hand, therefore, sensibility and affect (and deeply-rooted and deeply-felt affect in particular) are vital to any religious vocation; on the other hand they are hard to negotiate, communicate, and interpret. To grow in the Spirit, therefore, religious people must learn how not to be taken aback by what is going on in and with and around themselves. In practice, this means finding guidance and supervision, in setting where they can safely practice appropriate self-disclosure. In this way, they are apt to gain an experience-based understanding of the benefits of self-disclosure, which in turn will encourage them to seek deeper guidance by more generous self-disclosure leading to deeper self-awareness. In connection with this, the ascetical tradition has stressed that spiritual people must acquire an understanding of rules of "discernment of spirits" of one kind or another; this will not only clarify their own sense of identity and purpose, but also enable them both to find growth in the spirit for themselves and to foster union of minds and hearts in the community.

It is, of course, foolish to expect that all of this can come about in a harsh, insensitive, authoritarian, judgmental, impersonal environment. No wonder the ascetical tradition has appealed to the Gospel injunction to refrain from judgment (cf. esp. Mt 7, 1–2 par. Lk 6, 37–38; Mk 4, 24). But habits of suspending judgment are difficult; they amount to more than mere temperance. For the temperate must endure the "crudities, doubts, and confusions"[33] that will forever beset the struggle for temperance, and they must endure them not only in themselves, but also in those whom they endeavor to train for temperance. The temperate, in other words, need *fortitude*—the cardinal virtue by which we learn not to suppress by dint of force either their own temptations to intemperance or the intemperance of others, but to quench them by kindness, patience, as well as gentle firmness, especially in the face of anxiety, uncommunicativeness, miscommunication, and misunderstanding. In particular, the ascetical tradition has urged those in positions of leadership to do so.[34] For wherever persons attempt to communicate openly (that is, deliberately *and* affectively) with God and each other, nothing is so badly needed as *habits of patiently noticing* both inner experience and outward behavior. No amount of approval, criticism, diagnosis, or other forms of judgment (even informed judgment) can match the quiet, enduring, contemplative perceptiveness of the truly observant. An essential part of offering spiritual direction to others, therefore, consists in helping those who seek direction to take note of what is going on with and inside themselves and increasingly also with those around them. This will create an atmosphere of consideration and acceptance, in which, in due course, people will become interested in feedback about themselves. This in turn will also help them gradually discover habits of resistance and and overcome them; thus, too, they are apt to develop an enlightened, tough-minded, carefree openness and spontaneity both at the level of sensibility and of thought and decision. Less and less anxious and defensive, they will grow in the direction of a genuine (and thus attractive) humility rooted in self-knowledge, self-acceptance, and self-discipline—all of them vital preconditions for growth in habits of mature self-disclosure and of sensitive and respectful openness to others, combined with the the kind of frankness that betrays genuine affection. Needless to say, all these dispositions are essential for mature habits of all kinds of prayer, and especially of meditative and contemplative prayer.[35]

The above is no recipe for Utopia, of course. Even communities in which the wisdom of the tradition is habitually practiced will struggle with elements of real darkness; in fact, a heightened sense of crisis and frailty is quite often the price paid for the heightened awareness prevailing in communities where clear-sightedness and openness overcome defensiveness and pretext as a matter of habit. But then again, total freedom from anxiety is not a sign of sound living at all; quiet fearlessness and acceptance of awkward differences are; maturity is not the removal of either sensibility or anxiety, but their transformation, by dint of both temperance and fortitude.

[§132] TEMPERANCE IN A CULTURE CAPTIVATED BY MEANS AND TOOLS

[1] It is time to move on to the promised second round of our treatment of temperance and training for temperance. As promised, the first round (§131) has focused on temperance and its rather more deliberate companion, fortitude, as cardinal virtues to be practiced predominantly by individuals and by people in familial and fairly close interpersonal settings. For a long time, Catholic moral theology, and Christian ethics generally were content to limit their treatment of temperance and fortitude to the domestic sphere. It is true, references to temperate, steadfast conduct as a duty incumbent on people in positions of public power and authority were not lacking

in the tradition; still, they were brought in almost as an afterthought. However, in the world we live in, shot through as it is with large-scale social communication processes making use of every conceivable means and affecting the sensibilities of entire communities and even cultures, the wisdom of continuing to treat temperance and fortitude in such a narrowly domestic way is doubtful.

In this second round, therefore, the focus will be on large-scale settings: society and culture. In today's world, it will be argued, there are very good reasons to think that temperance has become a *social* virtue of the most pressing significance, thanks to the exponential growth of humanity's ability to manipulate not only its own psychophysical makeup but also its cosmic environment. Needless to say, the treatment offered here owes a large (if mostly implicit) debt to the ecological movement, and through it, to the various movements that opposed the nuclear arms race—that immoral menace to the survival of human culture for so many decades.

Let us introduce the issue of temperance as a social virtue under the rubric of what we will term the "literate-technological mentality."

[2] Let us begin by recalling a theme touched on a few times already in *God Encountered*, namely, that the foundational developments of what we now call Western civilization have occurred *systemically*, by processes of increasing *objectification*. A centuries-long process of development in literacy ended up giving rise to the assumption (frequently kept implicit) that objective, "literal" truth and geometrical precision are the outstanding instances of real and reliable knowledge (cf. §7, 1, a; §28, 2, a; 6, b; §32, a, [*f*], §56, 12, a). Eventually, the motor forces of this process led to the acceptance of scientific and technological reason as the civilizing power *par excellence;* not surprisingly, technological accomplishments came to be viewed as the crowning glory of Western civilization. These affirmations require elaboration, at some length.

[a] The journey's point of departure is the development of *alphabetic literacy*. Decimal ("digital") and alphabetic notation systems enabled the West to record spoken words and numbers with near-complete accuracy and objectivity. Here it is exceedingly important to note that Arabic numerals (unlike, *e.g.,* the Roman ones) and alphabetic lettering (unlike, *e.g.,* the Chinese ideograms) have two notable features in common: (a) both consist of *purely formal* elements, namely, letter and number signs, and (b) these signs are presented in *one-directional sequences*—whether from left to right or

from right to left, whether from top to bottom or from bottom to top. This invites further explanation.

In principle, each single *letter* sign invariably represents roughly the same sound *and nothing else*—no intonations, no accents, no nuances, nothing of the vocal kind, to say nothing of gestures. Even more significantly, the sound ("phoneme") corresponding to each letter sign is in and of itself *meaningless;* the *sounds* signified by letters like "a" or "p" are totally abstract and formal. Not until letter-signs are "sounded out" in the correct sequence (*i.e.,* not until *visual letter signs arranged in space* are correctly turned into *vocal sequences occurring in time*) do *words and sentences with meaning* begin to result. Interestingly, the etymologies of the words for "reading" in, respectively, Latin, Greek, and the West-Germanic languages convey this fact. Reading is *"picking things up by scanning them and putting them together,"* and when we read we *"turn silent letter-signs back into resonant knowledge";* reading is decoding: we *"make sense of something obscure."*[36] Learning how to read, therefore, means: to learn how to discover and recognize words known thus far only orally/ acoustically by interpreting visual letter-sequences. Once this initial step is taken, practice and interiorization can be trusted to do the rest.

Exactly what does practice achieve? Firstly, we learn how to *synthesize* elements we perceive visually. Rather than reading just letters and putting them together, we recognize, initially words and short sentences, then longer sentences; eventually, far more subtly, we take in entire *contexts.* Interestingly, as we progress, *we no longer notice every detail of the written or printed text.* We learn how to read in *word-Gestalts.* But secondly, and very importantly, practice makes us *overlook and forget* a fact of vital consequence. It is this: a large number of important meaning elements are scarcely conveyed by written language, or even not at all: intonation, emphasis, innuendo—that is to say, most of the *vocal and rhetorical elements.* These elements, so prominent in live speech, are not just a decorative feature of human language; they are vital to *meaning.* When we are reading, we are bviously not just picking up written or printed series of words; we are also supplying elements that are not on the page at all. That is, *we are interpreting.* In this regard, texts are like printed musical scores; we *perform* them, even when we are alone.

We keep doing this even when we no longer sound out the letters we read. Having interiorized the tools of literacy, we somehow succeed in reading both sufficiently nimbly and imaginatively to "hear" internally and half-consciously interpret in oral/acoustical ways the text we read visually. Very much later, many of us will use that inner voice and ear less and less; thanks to the printing press, quite a few of us become extremely dexterous, purely visual readers and writers, taking in or putting out the "data" or the "info."

But differences remain, especially *affective* ones. Unlike print, *handwriting* is always somewhat idiosyncratic; besides, handwritten texts allow us to touch physically the paper the writer has touched; no wonder we find ourselves reading hand-written texts more slowly, deliberately; we "read between the lines"; we interpret with feeling; we supply intense meaning; we understand what we read by participation. By comparison, printed text is flat, even, and thus "cool." No longer slowed down by affect, we read almost entirely with our eyes; we skim; we speed-read, *dispassionately;* we "assimilate the data," or just the main points, on the fly.

Quite apart from mental understanding, such advanced reading and writing (and, in cases, *type*-writing) behaviors involve, at the *sentient* level, extremely sophisticated acquired skills of neuro-visual (and neuro-manual) coordination, and of near-instinctive grammatical, syntactic, and lexical alertness. These skills are comparable to, but far more sophisticated and astonishing than, the spontaneous dexterity that allows violin *virtuosi*, micro-surgeons, and astronauts to do their work with such astonishing facility.

Still, impressive as these *sentient* reading and writing skills may be, we tend to forget that reading of any kind also involves considerable *mental* abilities. *We interpret.* Interpretative skills may very well be less spectacular than reading skills, but it is a big mistake to take them for granted. They are far more relevant to *knowledge and understanding* than the dexterous manipulation of objective data conveyed by letters on a page.

Analogous things can be said of *numbers,* with this exception that the individual number signs represent not isolated, meaningless sounds, but *words with a purely formal meaning.* That is to say, when we hear "three," we immediately know what is said, but we also wonder, "Three *what?*" There is another difference. In arithmetic, the *visual,* sequential arrangement of the numbers on the page only approximately conveys the order of the numbers in *oral* performance. In English, for instance, the written number 476 is altogether logically sounded out as "four hundred and seventy-six," but Germans say "vierhundert sechs und siebzig" and the French go even further and say "quatre cent soixante-seize." But when it comes to objectivity of reference, the sequential arrangement of numbers is very sophisticated as well as utterly accurate. The value of each digit is determined by its position in the sequence: by itself, the figure 4 represents "four", but in 476, it represents "four hundred". Finally, just as in reading texts we supply elements not seen on the page, in reading numbers (except when we are first learning or practicing arithmetic) we implicitly think of the *things* we are counting, adding, subtracting, multiplying, dividing, and so on. This implies that we somehow understand that the *full meaning* of numbers (that is, their *significance)* changes according as the things represented by the numbers vary. For instance, counting the inhabitants of a city differs (or at least should differ) from counting cars or stars or stripes. Put differently, numbers have tacit hermeneutical implications; when we are counting, we are *supplying meaning elements not conveyed by the numbers.*

It is a good thing to be aware of this, for the formal objectivity of numbers can mislead us. Clearly, just as we can lose sight of unstated meanings when reading a written *text,* so we can lose sight of the unstated meaning of *numbers.* It is quite naive to think that the meaning we draw from numbers is as objective as the numbers themselves; that is letting the medium curtail the fuller message.

An important conclusion follows from these reflections: not only the notation systems but also the written *documents* that they make possible are *instrumental* in nature; they are *tools to convey facts or truths* rather than truths or facts themselves. To get to the latter, we must be so familiar with the capacity of the tools as *to be able to go beyond them.* That is, we must learn how to *supply* the meanings which the tools can only *suggest.* And so, once again, *we must learn how to interpret.* In other words, if we are to be fully literate readers and writers, our *humanity* must match our *dexterity;* that is to say, we must learn not only how to read interpretatively but also to write interpretably.

[b]   So far, our reflections have emphasized the *limitations* of the tools of literacy. Now we must observe that for all their limitations, these tools are towering achievements of the human spirit. When they were first developed, they enabled human beings to encode and thus *make habitually accessible* four things that had always been by nature transient and thus, impermanent. Yet (we now know) all four of them are vital to the development and growth of civilized, reliable ways of human life together.

The four are the following. (1) *Celestial and climatic occurrences*— the regular as well as the fairly irregular. (2) *Trade agreements* of the *oral* (*i.e.*, wholly fiduciary) kind. (3) *Political, poetic, sapiential, and religious oral performance*, both of the contemporary, memorable kind, and of the immemorial, formulaic kind—the latter tradition-ally only known by heart and flexibly rehearsed from memory; the Hebrew Scriptures and those of the Christian New Testament are in this category. (4) *Musical performance*, both of the traditional and the *extempore* kind. But let us be a bit more specific.

(1) Once encoded in *calendars*, celestial and climatic occurrences became understood and thus, predictable—an indispensable con-dition for survival and well-being in any human community. (2) Once trade agreements took the shape of written instruments— *contracts, bills of lading, invoices*, and the like—trade became more reliable than it had ever been, especially since written instruments were often attested by identifiable witnesses. (3) Once oral perfor-mance was encoded in *written texts*, it got stabilized and became, in a sense, timeless; memorable linguistic matter ceased to be at the mercy of linguistic shifts, particular occasion, and social and cul-tural circumstance; this in turn made it possible, at least in princi-ple, for "authors" (as distinct not only from *viva voce* reciters and narrators but also from single readers) to *write* prose texts and po-etry before they were ever *heard;* it also enabled the development of what we have come to call "literary classics"—that key ingredient of literacy as we know it. (4) Finally, once musical scores were de-veloped (of the four, it is the most recent), *musical performance* (like oral performance) became repeatable (again, at least in principle); this in turn made it possible for composers (as distinct from per-forming singers and instrumentalists) to *write* music before it was ever *heard.*

Of these four developments, the first three may very well have had one-time beginnings. Specifically, alphabetic literacy and Ara-bic "numeracy" as we know them appear to have arisen only once in human history and only in one place: in the Near East, about six centuries before the Common Era. However, both of them spread rapidly and indeed globally, and their effective history has been phenomenal. All of this invites reflection.

[c] Before the arrival of writing, immemorial traditions, immemo-rial myths and narratives, and the face-to-face trade agreements of every day had this in common: they depended on living memory

and living witnesses for retrieval, survival, and attestation. But oral tradition and communal memory, no matter how reliable, and living witnesses, no matter how authoritative, have clay feet: they die. Sound and voice are transient, fugitive, and precarious; they can even be deceptive and downright fraudulent; in any case, time and death will (as we have come to put it) consign them to oblivion. In the very process of being remembered and handed on, the treasures of living oral/acoustical traditions are always threatened by contamination and oblivion; in any case, they will get modified, if ever so slightly, to suit new situations; over time, they are transformed, *imperceptibly* and (more importantly in the long run) *unverifiably*.

When numerical and alphabetic scripts were invented and developed, and even more when they came to be used in combination with each other, they enabled our remote ancestors to *stabilize and fix spatially* (that is, *visually*) what thus far had been known only by oral tradition, live memory, and live witness. Changes in the oral tradition could now become perceptible. Transactions and performances hitherto carried out only orally/acoustically (that is, in passing), borne on the ever-changing winds of time (and often carried off by them), could now be turned into durable, reliable, documents—*objects of examination and analysis.* That is to say, sayings and events could now be lifted out of the particular circumstances in which they had first occurred, and be *made* memorable —retrievable, objective, verifiable, replicable, durable, virtually permanent, and hence, very authoritative. Eventually, this made possible not only public recitals of authoritative texts to attentive audiences (read Neh 8, 1–12) and oral commentary on such texts exchanged among devoted readers, but also of individual study, in silence and solitude. What better way to demonstrate that *the documents themselves* (and not just what they really "meant" or "had to say") had become *objects of study?*

So what does it mean to be literate? It means: having privileged access to (and, in pertinent cases, to have personally examined and evaluated) information ("data") available in encoded, stored, retrievable, and verifiable form. The consequences are staggering.

[d] To begin with, writings could henceforth be hailed as more secure than the impermanent word of tradition and oral rehearsal. Rough-and-ready types with some weight to throw around have, of course, always dismissed "book learning" as irrelevant; they are still

doing it today, typically with the rough-and-ready *voice* of power and authority; it is not for nothing that we call the insolent "big-mouthed." To mention a New Testament example, the Roman procurator Porcius Festus was neither the first nor the only one to dismiss as insanity Paul's proclamation of the resurrection of the Messiah; what is interesting about his particular dismissal is that it involves a diagnosis: "Paul, you are raving mad; *your great book-learning* is turning you crazy" (Acts 26, 24). By contrast, it takes a self-conscious *author* like Geoffrey Chaucer, talented and ae of his ability and influence, to belittle orality and to call it ephemeral and unsubstantial: "Soun ys noght but eyr ybroken, / And every speche that ys spoken, / Lowd or pryvee, foul or fair, / In his substaunce ys but air."[37]

Thus literacy began to forward *claims to solidity, argument, and accountability,* and with these, *history.* In non-literate cultures, oral tradition and oral commitments are the present's sole link with the past. In literate cultures, the maxim *verba volant, scripta manent* will gain territory. Certifying truth by oracular and proverbial wisdom, oaths, and the word of honor uttered by the honorable will no longer do if it can (and thus, should) be certified by "hard data." The Western process of "cognitive stabilization" took off. "Writing is a technology that transforms thought," as Walter Ong has put it.

Not surprisingly, the advent of encoded knowledge soon made it possible to raise questions about the difference between volatile opinion and stable truth. That is, *philosophical reflection became possible.* In the long run, this had consequences. For instance, the Middle Ages could still consider the "literal sense" of the Scriptures the foundation of the higher, and in that sense "truer" meaning of the biblical text (cf. §54, 1). But eventually, and especially since the sixteenth century, "real" truths came to be called "literally" true. A privileged form of truth had arisen: the proposition that was true because it was verifiable by means of documentation, experimentation, logical analysis. It was only a matter of time before the New Learning came up with an even more certain form of truth: statements about invariable natural occurrences and formulations of natural laws formulated *quantitatively.* The authority of rhetoric had begun to wane; the triumph of logic and geometry had begun.

[e] These clearly were enormous triumphs of human reason and resourcefulness. Equally clearly, they were not without risks. Let us explain.

The first and most notable risk of literacy is clearly this: documents have this in common with lifeless matter that they cannot explain themselves. They are at least once removed from the actuality of live speech-events; while they *convey* information, they can only *suggest* connotation, tonality, affect, interest, human relationships, and the voice of tradition. Aquinas is a good example of a mediaeval theologian aware of the problem inherent in textually fixed formulas. Even in the *Summa theologiæ*—a wholly new venture in theological education—his method of treating theological issues still reflects the old oral question-and-answer practices of the scholastic classroom; but it is the man who read everything he could get his hands on and succeeded in composing this *magnum opus* who can write, in the context of a treatment of the articles of the faith: "When people believe, their focus is not on the proposition, but on reality. For in matters of faith as in matters of knowledge, our only purpose in devising propositions is: *to have knowledge of realities by means of them.*"[38] Aquinas, in other words, knows that texts are liable to make us overlook the fact that they are not free-standing entities, but *instruments with a purpose.* That is, taken by themselves, texts *can* not only mislead and deceive but also be misread and misinterpreted (for instance, by being taken at face value, or by being read or taken out of context). This is the chief weakness of literacy, and it is systemic.

Plato, a *homo politicus* who also cherished intellectual integrity, had become painfully aware of this. His involvement in the Sicilian power politics of his day gave him an opportunity to explain himself on this topic. The pursuit of virtue and wisdom, he writes, is subtle and demanding, so it is foolish to address oneself in writing to the general public on these matters and expect to be understood [*p*].[39]

Whence this reluctance to trust written texts? Literacy (so it was widely and for centuries realized) is a powerful and demanding skill, and one that is safe only in the hands of the truly educated— *i.e.*, of *discerning readers.* The ill-educated may well be able to read, but they will invariably misread and misinterpret; they either lack

---

[*p*] More than fifteen hundred years later, Plato's sentiment was to be echoed by the author of *The Cloud of Unknowing.* Right on the first page of his treatise he pleads with the reader not to let this text fall into the hands of others; only followers of Christ in search of perfection will understand it. Cf. *The Cloud of Unknowing and the Book of Privy Counselling,* Ed. Hodgson, pp. 1–2.

the criteria to interpret properly, or if they don't, they will misuse them to suit their own purposes. They will forget (or expect others to forget) that written documents do not produce, let alone guarantee thought, understanding, sound judgment, virtue, and wisdom; they create only the *presumption* of them. Without discernment, the only thing literacy will accomplish is deliver half-literate, obtuse, foolish readers to their own ignorance and folly. This implies that the ability to read and write will tempt the unwise to act as if they understood. Even worse, pretensions to literacy and understanding will tempt those who are not only ignorant but also powerful to resort to the kind of writing that not only lacks understanding, but is also apt to foster violence (cf. §137, 10, a–c); they may even consider such violence excusable, as Albert Camus was to realize with such great clarity more than two thousand years later (cf. §140, 6).

The second risk inherent in literacy is the fact that written documents are the work of *authors*. Now documents (unlike their authors) are enduring; they *look* reliable and authoritative (especially when printed, as every modern teacher knows); that is, they are likely to mask the errors and the ignorance of their authors. This is apt to grow worse according as readers have more confidence in literacy's inherent powers of objectivity, which encourages them to insist that, simply because they "can read," they can "get it right." Thus, to his friends in Syracuse, Plato had to explain that the murderous Dionysios had actually *heard* him teach only once, and that he had obviously gotten nothing out of the experience. This, however, had not deterred him from writing down what he claimed to have learned; and the fact that the people of Syracuse had trusted his writings as well as himself had been a big error of judgment.

There is a double moral here for all lovers of literacy. Ever since the advent of literacy, all empty, flat surfaces, whether paper or walls or fences or billboards or polished granite and tiled surfaces, have invited lettering of every kind. They have also been long-suffering and silent. They will not quarrel with anyone who writes on them; even less will they warn incompetent or gullible readers that what they are reading is not true; least of all will they warn them that they are misreading what they are reading or that they are missing the point altogether. For only to the truly educated is neither the writing nor the reading of texts a perfectly straightforward (and in that sense completely neutral) proposition; rather, reading things written are demanding *exercises* in both trust and suspicion.

Accordingly, a hermeneutics of both trust and suspicion is an integral part of being reliably literate.

[f] Acts and attitudes of trust and suspicion are humane only if they are acts not of naiveté or anxiety but of *discernment*. But discernment is a matter of freedom, and freedom is never assured; specifically, freedom of expression is always threatened by ulterior motives, especially the pursuit of *power*. For this reason, there is another point to be made. Many genuinely learned and literate people will get more than a little embarrassed when it is pointed out to them that literacy is inseparable from vigorous elements of *competition*. How can accomplishments so distinctively humane as reading and writing have affinities with power—that is to say, with *cosmic process?*

The answer is that literacy is dependent on *tools* and the ability to use them (§132, 2, a). This suggests that literacy has closer relationships with power than the humane and the literate tend to appreciate—an insight that will prove quite pertinent further down. For now, let us briefly illustrate the claim just made.

First of all, literacy is apt to foster curious forms of *conspiracy*. Whatever is written and read can be used for purposes of concealment in ways oral performance can never be. The more elevated the level of literacy, therefore, the more probable it is that both the idioms of the literate and their errors will enjoy the protection of silence. Professional literates and "numerates" tend to love the privileged privacy of technical terminology, of the faculty common room, and of the professional organization, with their penchant for the cultivation of labyrinthine specialties and sub-specialties. Texts, even texts that are in the public domain, share in that privilege: printed texts of any kind create their own reading publics, members of which are liable to form communities of insiders impressed by the privileged and quasi-privileged understanding that they have in common. We all know how every form of cultivated literacy will create alliances of initiates—from astrophysicists and canon lawyers to C. S. Lewis fans and Catholic Traditionalists. Literacy also spawns *clubs:* science fiction reading circles, Dickens Societies, philosophical and theological "schools of thought," coffee houses and *Stammtische* for literary critics (especially for those among them who read little and should write less), not to mention academic conspiracies and other dubious covens of self-protective literates.

In the very act of enabling communication, therefore, texts and numbers also create divisions. The literate and numerate world is full of factions and institutionalized disagreements, some overt and vehement, many more tacit. The latter are apt to be fiercer and more stubborn for being unacknowledged or unexpressed, as numerous academics know from bitter experience. Literacy, initially developed to secure cherished truth and to communicate knowledge and understanding across the vicissitudes of time and space, thus turns out to have unexpected powers of misrepresentation, deceit, division, and fragmentation, as Plato's story illustrates all too well. In this regard, literacy and numeracy are often less candid and straightforward than oral/acoustical performance of the traditional kind.

To mention a typical example of such candor, oral/acoustical cultures typically make no secret of their penchant for contest and confrontation. In such cultures, people will typically exercise themselves as well as others by challenges, taunts, dares, displays of defiance, and oral invective. In fact, orality positively revels in such "agonistic" (but seldom lethal) forms of human communication-by-confrontation, as all readers of Homer (and all who have witnessed the immediate aftermath of traffic incidents in Rome, or have tried to buy something in the East both Near and Far) knows. By contrast, those who live by the tools of literacy tend to be (or profess to be) less savvy about power and influence. They are apt to ignore (or deny), whether in good faith or bad, that words written and printed, like so many other tools, can kill. Off-stage, in the wings, without blinking an eye, always ready to cast a stone and plead not guilty, writers and publishers can look on as their words produce the intended effect. They are protected by the freedoms of speech and opinion; even more, they rely on that powerful tool of influence: the *printing press*—a subject to which we will return.

[3] Something very important is implicit in all this. Literacy is and remains, of course, a stunning accomplishment of humanity's ability to free itself from the domination of place and time, and in that sense, to transcend the powerful dynamics inherent in cosmic process. Still, it never accomplishes *complete* transcendence any more than humanity itself does. That is, *even literate humanity remains radically cosmic* (cf. §9, 1, [i]; §115, 1; 7, [g]; §116, 3). Consequently, much as literacy is a superb instrument of humane civilization, it *can* become a tool of human communication that is merely apparent,

and hence, a means to bring about thoughtlessness, misunderstanding, and estrangement.

For a long time, this was obvious. Literacy was a privilege. Accordingly, its practitioners emphasized the hardships inherent in it. They did so by proclaiming that reading required *interpretation,* and hence, familiarity with *a tradition of understanding.* Maximus the Confessor (cf. §53, 2, c) provides us with a good example of this. In one of his commentaries on debated scripture passages, he explains that the Church is the lampstand needed to make the light of Scripture effective and illuminating (cf. Lk 11, 33 par. Mt 5, 15). To support his argument, he appeals to a truth that was manifest not only to his Christian contemporaries, but to all cultured people of his day:

Those, therefore, who stop at the mere letter of Scripture, will get only the *perception,* which captures what is natural; accordingly, all this [perception] will disclose is what results from the relationship between the soul and the flesh. Clearly, if a text is not *spiritually* understood, it will not go beyond the perception contained in the *words pronounced out loud,* and this perception does not allow the *gist* of the written text to get through to the *mind.*[40]

But what was plain for a long time may not be as plain in our own day, with its massive emphasis on the *advanced tools* of literacy. Still, on reflection, is it not obvious even today that in and of itself the skills of information management *can* (and often do) degenerate into exercises in mere self-maintenance, self-assertion, contest, competition, and outright domination? Even worse, is it not true that in our literate and numerate culture the tag "knowledge is power" is often "literally" true? The Master of an unnamed Oxbridge college is reported to have a message over his office door announcing: "I am the Master of this College, and what I don't know isn't knowledge." The story may be apocryphal; it was not created out of nothing.

[4] This allusion to an academic institution reminds us of a late fifteenth literary and technological development whose impact on the world of learning is hard to overstate: *the printing press.* Within decades of its invention and development, it started to have an impact on the formation of public opinion comparable to the solid-state radio in the nineteen-fifties. Most importantly, it caused a landslide in the schools (as Walter Ong has shown in *Ramus, Method and the Decay of Dialogue*)—one comparable to the effects of computer technology in the nineteen-eighties and -nineties. We must briefly reflect on this.

[a] The printing press represents a quantum leap in the history of literacy. It is also one of the most typical products of the literate

mind's pursuit of precision in expression, geometrical objectivity, and technological ingenuity. Printed matter of every kind started to appear on the scene just before the turn of the sixteenth century. In less than half a century, it produced a torrent of tracts, pamphlets, handbills, and holy cards, as well as books of every size, weight, and quality, from the monumental to the diminutive—the latter often devotional. It was the books, many of them handsomely, dramatically, even lavishly illustrated, that became most influential in the long run. Expensive though they were, books came into their own at a phenomenal rate. They made their mark especially in libraries both public and personal, and of course in the schools. Not being ephemeral, they held their ground as the most impressive instruments for the storage and retrieval of thought and information in the history of human knowledge. And being portable, they enabled and encouraged individual reading; they became tools—instruments packed with learning for the *savant* to ingest or at least consult; scholarship became a virtuoso accomplishment of gifted individuals who had the luxury of being able to accumulate knowledge undisturbed by the interference of others. Knowledge became a form of banking,[41] and like money, "genius" became more and more concentrated. Besides, just as the world of banking gradually discovered that money was also a tool to acquire more money, so the world of book learning, too, became self-referential: books began to contain their own tools, first in marginal references and soon after (far more efficiently) in alphabetic registers in the back. Only one small step now separated the world of learning from the reference work *pur et simple*. In *encyclopedias,* all things worth knowing (or so it was claimed) came to be stored: a wealth of neutral, true information, waiting for retrieval in the most unprejudiced fashion imaginable—under the banner of that symbol of enlightened impartiality: the alphabetic register. The New Learning became unthinkable without encyclopedias.

This also accounts for the New Learning's clamor for individual freedom of thought, of scholarly investigation, and of political expression. Rulers and parliaments of every stripe immediately recognized and feared the power of print since they saw through its claims to impartiality. Accordingly, they saw to it at once that all printed matter was censored, and that no books were printed and sold without licence, lest they go out into the world to cause trouble. Despite these obstacles, however, books never ceased to increase and multiply, ever since the mid-sixteenth century. Even in our day we are witnessing an unprecedented deluge of printed matter and books of every kind. Curiously, the deluge is produced thanks to the very electronic technology of which many experts have predicted that it was going to make print obsolete for good.

Illiteracy continues in many parts of the world, yet alphabetic literacy and print technology have become global phenomena; people everywhere read and write these days of literacy campaigns, or are being taught to read and write. In the teeth of C. P. Snow's manifesto declaring the estrangement between the West's "two cultures,"[42] humane literacy and scientific technology have been mutually supportive far more than they have been mutually obstructive. Is it not largely due to evermore efficient means of transportation that the global trade in books and other printed materials has been with us so long, and that it is still expanding? Is the dissemination of literacy not unthinkable without the technologies that use electrical power that now run high-capacity printing-presses even in developing countries? Everywhere, literacy has been made possible by, and in turn has enabled, ever more effective rapid and instantaneous long-distance communication technologies by both cable and wireless: telegraph, radio and telephone. Even though the latter two of these means of communication are oral/ acoustical in nature, they are still inconceivable and inoperative apart from alphabetic and numerical notation systems. Obviously, the world as we know it is still being pulled together by an alliance of literacy and technology.

Since the late nineteen-fifties, however, even this short list of successful communication technologies has been turned into a wild understatement. Literacy has been both intensified and revolutionized by solid-state circuitry and switching technology: an inundation of ever more powerful, sophisticated, and flexible electrical and electronic means of communication and data storage-and-retrieval devices has come on the scene. Never before, nor ever on such a scale and at such a rate of speed have literacy, technology, and mathematical logic been operationalized and put to the service of the dissemination and management of information. The information explosion is becoming more daunting by the day, at exponentially mounting levels of both volume of storage and speed and sophistication of retrieval. Clearly, know-how and knowledge are conquering space and time.

[b] But not only space and time. Tools, it has been argued, have a way of profoundly shaping *its users* at the sentient level. The in-

struments we use are extensions of our bodies; they enable us to do very ingenious things we would not be able to do without them, and to feel and even think in ways that would be inaccessible to us without them. Still, our bodies themselves are instruments of far greater sophistication, capable of far more subtle skills than the instruments we devise. But if our sensibilities are marvelously flexible, they are also very delicate. If, in the name of intensified literacy, more and more (and more and more powerful) tools enabling knowledge and dexterity are put in the hands of more and more people, human sensibilities around the world are bound to be reshaped to an unprecedented degree. Are they bound to be overpowered as well, by tools of humanity's own devising?

These issues must be raised because power and capacity are inadequate standards by which to measure *humanity*. Being cosmic, humanity is indeed a participant in the cosmic contest; but cosmic goods, including the tools we develop to engage the cosmos, are *relative goods* (cf. §128, 3, c; §129, 5, a). This implies: even the most effective use of tools, taken by itself, leaves the distinctively human (*i.e., moral*) questions unanswered. As stated before: no advanced literacy without nimbleness; but besides dexterity, literacy requires imagination (cf. §132, 2, a)—a subject to which we will have to come back at length in the next chapter (§138). Intelligent capacity for *interpretation of texts viewed as humane documents* is as crucial an asset in the life of literacy as sentient proficiency in *operating the texts viewed as tools of data storage and retrieval*. Over the centuries we have become ever more dexterous readers; the tools of literacy have increased and multiplied both in quantity and sophistication: records full of hand- and typewritten letter signs and numbers; newspapers, journals, and volumes chock-full of printed texts and figures; and lately, marvels of solid-state technology replete with "info" visually conveyed in letter and number signs.

So the moral question is, Are we also becoming better *interpreters* of what we read and retrieve? Put differently, Are *we* keeping up with the *tools* that put the data at our disposal? And if so, to what degree? Or should we ask the question, Which of the two of us is running which, and to what extent?

[c] These questions are not posed here by way of rhetorical ones, to suggest, in a spirit of cultural pessimism *à la* Oswald Spengler or (more recently) Allan Bloom,[43] that the answers are clearly negative. Earlier in this systematic theology it was stated that these neu-

ralgic developments and estrangement are part and parcel of the
dynamics of human culture, but that they also have their liberating
aspects: they can "marvelously stretch the range of available human experience" and "demonstrate the depth and the breadth of
humanity's capacity for fulfillment" (§28, 6, d). But for that very
reason they require philosophical and theological reflection as well
as the kind of hermeneutical delicacy that is being urged here.

[5] In a series of far-sighted books, Marshall McLuhan and Walter
Ong, the most original North American interpreters of the anthropological and cultural aftermath of the developments just surveyed,
have shown how profoundly literacy has rearranged the human sensorium.[44] Large sections of humanity are now born right into a sensibility profoundly affected by literacy. In increasing partnership
with "numeracy," technological literacy now shapes our first learning
practices, our teaching methods, and thus, our first attempts at self-
definition. For more than twenty-five centuries now, alphabetic and
numerical notation systems have helped store large amounts of textual materials and make them retrievable and communicable. They
have also more and more been dictating, tacitly but successfully, the
normative shape of "real" (that is useful, objective, reliable) knowledge. Whatever learning used to mean in the past (and probably
continues to mean in many predominantly oral/acoustical cultures
—the outposts of a vanishing world), in today's world to *learn* means,
more than anything else, to become *literate*. The problem is that the
preponderance of tools increasingly conveys the impression that literacy is primarily an *instrumental* skill—one that is best developed by
means of ever more powerful, refined tools. It is not. Texts, as well
as the documents and the books, the printing presses and the computers that preserve the texts and make them retrievable, are indeed
tools; reading and writing are indeed skills, and enormously intricate
ones to boot, and hence, far from superficial. Like all tools and acquired skills, they do shape our sensibilities; as a result, they deeply
(if indirectly) shape our human (*i.e., moral*) lives. Yet tools and skills
are humane only in the hands of those who can supply what is wanting in the tools—from the words and figures on the page of printed
books to the data produced by computers. What, then, is wanting?

In one word: *goals*. To be genuinely literate and humane means:
to be able to use tools and skills, especially the more powerful and
fascinating, in the service of human understanding, choice, and deliberation.

It is time to bring to a close our exploration into the nature, the promise, and the precariousness of literacy viewed as an elementary step from humanity's sentient life into the responsible, properly human and humane life. However, before we can do so, we must reflect on two dynamic connections: the affinity between literacy and power, and the correlation between mentality and sensibility.

[6] It must be obvious by now that his entire chapter serves to explore the implications of one fundamental proposition: it is part of humanity's moral responsibility to discipline the passionate "lust for power" in its various forms, so as to bring it within the compass of human deliberation (§129, 7; cf. §130, 2, b–c). Let us pursue this subject as it relates to literacy.

In the West, the educated have typically been the upward bound as well. It is true that for centuries literacy was a craft rather than a cultural requirement; writing materials were often primitive and even more often scarce, so penmanship was a difficult skill; orthography was non-existent. No surprisingly, the highest leadership could quite often afford to remain illiterate. But neither they nor the upper echelons in society were ever without their retinue of scribes, clerks, secretaries, and chroniclers. Thus, one way or another, literacy shaped, and has continued to shape, the social stratification of Western and Westernized societies. Specifically, in the sixteenth century, reading, writing and the printing press became the tools, not only of education and humane culture, but also of far-flung influence and power, as the massive amounts of government correspondence bequeathed to us by the sixteenth- and seventeenth-century monarchies testify. Since that time, no establishment of power or influence has been stable without chanceries full of clerks and without access to the printing press. It has already been noted that rulers and parliaments long clamped down on these influential means of social communication. To maintain the prevailing order, they deemed censorship and forms of covert diplomacy by means of classified correspondence a political necessity, and thus, a moral duty. Once again, who in the modern West has not heard it said that "knowledge is power"?

Once again, this question is not rhetorical; it invites needed stock-taking and reflection. Our literacy and numeracy have taken close to three millennia to develop. Enabled by a long series of more and more reliable, sophisticated, and far-reaching tools and methods, humanity has succeeded in surmounting the barriers which the ever-changing circumstances of time and space will put in the way of significant, memorable, and (especially) *durable* human self-expression, self-management, communication, social organization—in short, *reliable humane civilization.*

Obviously, only intelligent and resolute human beings could have set out on this very long and for a long time extremely slow journey of self-transcendence and kept marching. In this sense, there is absolutely no doubt that, at bottom, the progress of literacy has been, and still is, an anthropological undertaking of the highest distinction. Yet it is also true that the development of the *tools* of literacy has gathered speed as it has advanced, especially since the sixteenth and seventeenth centuries. As a matter of fact, in recent decades the pace has become so fierce as to be exponential. This especially calls for critical reflection.

Has human self-transcendence by literacy and numeracy kept up with the progress and the capacity of its tools? Exponentiality is an arithmetical, numerical phenomenon; this suggests an affinity with the powerful dynamics of cosmic multiplicity. Does the exponentially gathering speed of humanity's scientific and technological journey indicate that its true motor forces have become cosmological rather than anthropological? Surveying literacy's more recent stages—say, the past three or four (not millennia but) centuries, and even more the past three or four decades—do we not have reason to wonder if cosmology has increasingly been taking anthropology by the nose, dictating the speed, leading the way? Is it conceivable that the literacy campaign has been losing the sense of *proportion* that is such a distinctive requirement of genuinely human—that is, *moral*—enterprises? Could it be that ends have been lost sight of for the means? Is it conceivable that we have become so fascinated with our increasing understanding of cosmic process that we have allowed it to run away with us, at the expense of what is most human about us—consciousness and freedom?

[a] These sobering questions also come to mind when we recall that the tools of today's literacy—devices capable of massive data storage and retrieval—are so powerful *and* so manifestly associated with power systems. The human capacity for virtuosity at the sentient level, we have already observed, is awesome indeed, but brilliance makes neither persons nor actions discerning or even moral. In fact, brilliance may be a symptom of an underlying illness, as every psychiatrist knows. In the same way, virtuosity may mask that something very undiscerning is going on—splendid but pointless

facility at best and sheer flexing of muscle designed to intimidate at worst. So much for the affinity between literacy and power.

[7] We must now raise the issue of the correlation between mentality and sensibility. Let us start with a distinction and a proposal for a definition. Human sensibilities, it has been argued, are shaped by patterns of "sentient virtuosity." These patterns develop because human beings learn how to respond, as a matter of sentient habit, to characteristic, "formative" situations in their environment.

Some formative situations are natural. To some of them, human individuals and communities will react instinctively, and in that sense "naturally." To most of them, however, they have learned how to respond rather more humanly—*i.e.*, ingeniously, with *at least some deliberation*. Characteristically, they do so by developing tools; even the most primitive human communities deliberately develop various *habits of dexterity* to respond to each other and to their *Umwelt* by means of implements.

But human beings are naturally loath to settle for mere habit, however ingenious. Further deliberation and design will induce us to create new, different type of situations: almost wholly artificial ones. The tools we already have will forever continue to enable us to develop tools that are even more advanced and even more difficult to use; in order to use them, even more deliberate training is going to be required. This intelligent, distinctively human type of incrementally instrumental engagement with otherness fosters, of course, the formation of characteristic *sensibilities;* communities with state-of-the-art equipment "feel" different from pioneering ones. Still, since *all tools* are products of *conscious* ingenuity, *all* tools will help shape "mindsets" or *mentalities* (as those of us know who have encountered, say, cowboys out on the range, forest dwellers, or petty farmers, carpenters, bee-keepers, blacksmiths, and cobblers in remote villages).

Mentalities are a prime instance of knowledge and understanding *of the participative kind* (§63); they are fairly stable, often shrewd, always flexible, largely implicit habits of familiarity, perception, and appraisal of feasibility; mentalities enable people to deal wittily and tastefully with the practicalities of their cosmic and human environment. Very importantly, since they are truly mental, they can be intellectualized and verbalized. In other words, human communities and their leading representatives, especially when under pressure to change, can appeal to prevailing mentalities to account for and justify "why we think this way and do things this way around here."

[a]   In this sense, *mentalities are conservative;* it is not for nothing that Jacques Le Goff, long before he wrote his distinguished and controversial *The Birth of Purgatory,* suggested, in a commanding article on *l'histoire des mentalités,* that mentalities are the element of *inertia* in history; accordingly, the historical study of mentalities is "the history of slowness within history."[45] Formulas like this are, of course, vague and very imprecise; this makes the history of mentalities suspect in the eyes of the purely "professional" academics. But then again, this very imprecision makes the study of mentalities attractive from the experiential ("human") point of view. Purely "analytic" history (to say nothing of "quantitative" history, so *en vogue* today)—they all somehow lack that curious quality, that *je ne sais quoi* which makes history such a source of insight and wisdom.

And indeed, Le Goff explains, appreciation of mentalities goes a long way to endow the more objective, data-based forms of history with the kind of living soul that makes it meaningful. What, after all, is a medieval crusade apart from a "religious mentality"? What sense does the early-medieval economy make without that "feudal mentality" whose core is a wide-spread willingness to be at the service of someone higher up and proud of it? How can we account for early capitalism without also noting the new mentality in regard to labor and money, associated with what Max Weber saw as the Protestant work-ethic? What sense are we to make of Gregory the Great who, while still an abbot, on hearing that a dying monk had admitted to the possession of three gold pieces, forbade his monks to attend to the man in his agony, and instead of giving the body a proper burial, ordered it pitched on the garbage heap? What else could this be but a case of the Rule of Benedict being overruled by a "barbarian mentality"? (Imported to the West long ago by the Goths? Some kind of throwback to elementary psychic impulses?)

"So [Le Goff writes] things seemingly rootless, born extempore or out of reflexes, mechanical behaviors, undeliberate words, come to us from a very great distance, witnesses to the fact that systems of thought and consciousness have long-lasting echoes."[46] The largely negative connotations of the word "mentality" would seem to lend support to this observation; after all, mentalities are frequently regarded as relapses into sensibilities that psychologists feel they have to call archaic, atavistic, or infantile.

[b] Le Goff also offers advice to *practitioners* of the history of mentalities—some of it important to our discussion. Negatively, he cau-

tions that it is an intellectualist misconception to reduce mentalities to the history of *ideas,* just as it is a behaviorist mistake to reduce them to the fortunes of mindless, strictly *automatic reactions and responses.* Similarly, he warns that reviving spiritualist notions about the collective soul is as unsatisfactory as hanging on to the Marxist, materialist postulate that non-material superstructures are simply functions of hard socio-economic infrastructures. The truth about mentalities lies somewhere in the middle. The treatment of sensibility offered in this chapter has suggested that this "middle" is: *the places where deliberation and sensibility meet and blend.*

Positively, Le Goff proposes two areas of history where the processes of this meeting and blending can be found and examined; hence, they are singularly valuable sources for the study of mentalities. The first is *"mental equipment":* vocabulary, syntax, idioms, commonplaces, notions about place and time, frameworks of logic. The second is *"models":* the monastic patterns of asceticism and solitude, or the aristocratic, courtly ideals of generosity, beauty, fairness, loyalty, prowess—in short, the sort of civilized demeanor that has come down to us as *courtesy.* It is not difficult to see that the two areas of human behavior suggested by Le Goff correspond nicely to the two elements of *sensibility* already explored in this section: *articulate speech* and *civilized manners.* Interestingly, both are largely habitual as well as substantially deliberate—*i.e.,* they are matters of both sensibility and mentality.

[c] Another question of some moral interest. Where are mentalities born, and how do they spread? Le Goff suggests that we must look to places where *creativity* and *capacity for dissemination* occur. Thus there are the medieval palaces, monasteries, castles, schools, courts, and increasingly also the towns and cities. For the era of the industrial revolution, we should visit the mills, the steel factories, the taverns. Places like these are "the nebulas out of which mentalities crystallize"[47]—the environments concentrated and intense enough to give birth to new galaxies. And, Le Goff adds, for a long time the mentalities of the Christian West were shaped, of course, by sermons and images both painted and sculptured—to limit ourselves to developments "on the far side of the Gutenberg Galaxy."[48]

A revealing remark. The medievalist Le Goff is alluding to a seminal book on contemporary, literate, instrumental mentality, entitled *The Gutenberg Galaxy: The Making of Typographic Man.* The author: Marshall McLuhan. Quietly but unmistakably, Le Goff is endorsing an intimation conveyed by the subtitle of that book, *viz.*, that in the closing decades of the Late Middle Ages print literacy was the beginning of a landslide in the history of mentalities. And once again, the treatment offered in the present chapter agrees.

[8] But far more than that. We must recall that this chapter is an inquiry into *the dynamics of power, influence, and forcefulness as a moral issue.* Obviously, "the making of typographical man" is a great and powerful achievement indeed. But it has turned literacy into a landslide: having gathered speed without much of a sense of direction, it is now capable of destroying humanity. This drastic instrumentalization of literate human activity has succeeded in shaping the sensibility of the most influential segments of humanity in one particular direction: toward sentient virtuosity, proficiency in overcoming problems, and technological ability to compete for power. As a result, we are dealing with a perception, as unspoken as it is wide-spread, that these three—sentient virtuosity, problem-solving ability, and capacity to compete—are the norms by which human accomplishment is to be evaluated. In turn, this perception has helped foster the "literate-scientific-technological mentality"; its unspoken assumption is that human civilization is simply a matter of ingenuity, know-how, and power.

[9] Needless to say, there are dark and ominous sides to these developments. It has already been pointed out that *at the sentient level* it is hard, if not downright impossible, to tell means apart from ends (§129, 2, g). But ever since Descartes equated ideal knowledge with geometrical knowledge, and ever since geometry came to determine the progress of technology, means have become far more fascinating (as well as manageable) than ends. Dietrich Bonhoeffer, who had no illusions about the French revolution because he had no illusions about national socialism, was working on the manuscript of what we know as his *Ethics* when he was arrested in April, 1943. It contains one of the most somber moments in all of his writings. It may well have been one of his most prophetic, too. He wrote:

The French revolution has created the new spiritual unity of the Occident. It consists in the liberation of humanity as *ratio*, as mass, as nation. In the struggle for liberation the three go together; once liberty is achieved they become deadly enemies. Thus, the new unity already bears in itself the germ of decadence. It also shows—and here a fundamental law of history becomes apparent—that the desire for absolute freedom will lead humanity to the most abject slavery. The master of the machine becomes its slave;

the machine becomes humanity's enemy. The creature turns itself against its creator—a remarkable re-enactment of the Fall! The liberation of the masses ends up as the reign of terror of the guillotine. Nationalism inevitably leads to war. The liberation of humanity [pursued] as an absolute ideal leads to humanity's self-destruction. What meets us at the end of the road taken by the French revolution is nihilism.[49]

The pursuit of freedom with a vengeance, with every weapon and tool wielded on every front, has had terrible consequences in the realm of power and influence. "People of means" have always been relatively few in number, but at least their persons, the size of their means, and many of their goals, were for centuries a matter of common knowledge; in that sense, they were shared. Glaring as they may have been, the injustices were at least above board: the eighteenth-century squire encouraged hard work so his tenants would improve the yield of his estate; the local factory owner habitually underpaid his labor force, rationalizing his unjust practices by appealing to the need for investment and expansion in order to create more work places, which would enable an expanding labor force to share in the benefits of employment. But in our day, the very influence enjoyed by the "people of means" also enables them to make themselves *as well as their goals* (if, indeed, they have any acknowledged goals at all) difficult to identify, and even more difficult to endorse or share; no wonder they are extremely hard to police and discipline. Yet at the same time the influential enjoy the most fantastic ability to force and reinforce their impact on the lives of the vast majority of the less powerful and the less influential depending on them, *regardless of any goals*. This distinctively human (*i.e.,* moral) problem demands careful exploration and evaluation, not only in the present context, but also at a later point in our reflections (cf. esp. §163, 3–8).

[a] A very disquieting symptom of the problem is the fact that employment has long been becoming more and more problematic and unpredictable. What used to be life-long trades and professions are more and more being replaced by impermanent "jobs"; ability and desire to work—both of them specifically human, *moral* factors—are becoming irrelevant; the labor market is turning into a lottery; increasingly, the privileged class consists of those *lucky* enough to have jobs. No wonder there prevails a justified sense of both impotence and exclusion in many quarters.

Such fierce and *unjust* socio-economical imbalances caused by self-serving (and hence, purblind) power give rise to apathy. This in turn is bound to foster violence, both of the unfocused and of the purposeful kind, in the form of desperate, entirely irrational and disproportionate acts of insurrection and even terrorism—often the only way the marginal and the wholly excluded have the ability to attract notice (cf. §128, 1, a; §133, 5). After all, when the dynamics of power and influence replace deliberation and moral decision, and are left to run the course of human affairs, all they can be expected to "obey" is the fundamental law of cosmic process, which is: thoughtless action invites mindless reaction. And only rarely does this process allow any but the fittest to survive.

The social encyclicals of a whole series of late nineteenth-century and twentieth-century Popes have insisted that human beings must never be employed in such a way as to become, to all intents and purposes, mere means of production, exploited almost exclusively with a view to company profit, without a just wage to enable them to care *and* stand up for themselves and their dependents in a socially and economically responsible fashion. More recent papal writings, especially Pope John XXIII's *Pacem in terris,* have broadened the horizons of the call for justice, by introducing the issue of global injustice into the discussion. Even more recently, new social encyclicals, including Pope John Paul II's *Laborem exercens,* have raised an even more fundamental moral question, namely, work as a requirement of human dignity. The social systems managed and even owned by the rich and influential are nowadays often so complex that the work force that keeps them operating is becoming irrelevant to any goals and ends; workers can be allowed to operate only at the level of means; in this way, human persons become a function of tools. This not only makes work humanly (and thus, morally) unrewarding. It also raises a fundamental *moral* question —the one which so profoundly troubled Karl Marx, and which has had Pope John Paul II equally exercized, as Gregory Baum has shown in *The Priority of Labor,* a commentary on the encyclical *Laborem exercens.* The question is: To what extent does this form of employment amount to a demand heartlessly imposed on the work force to lead depersonalized, inauthentic lives, victims of an oppressive mentality packed with fascistoid implications?

[b] This theme has come up more than once in recent literature. Thus the British-Japanese novelist Kazuo Ishiguro has raised it in *The Remains of the Day,* a comic novel that tells the story of an aging butler with the most elevated conception of his office—hardly a factory hand. The butler's life takes an unexpected turn when a

wealthy, jovial American acquires the country estate which has been his universe for years. Alarmingly, the new, egalitarian master practically forces this consummate "gentleman's gentleman," who is only residually aware of himself as a person with an individuality of his own, to take the car and go on a holiday. All the poor butler can think of for a vacation is a visit to a retired maid, whom he might possibly have loved long ago, if only his position had permitted him to give evidence of romantic attachments to members of his staff. In the event, neither the trip nor the meeting amount to much, but during this first holiday of his life the butler does manage, with the little that is left of him, to put the scattered pieces of his life together and come to the conclusion that his former gentleman-employer, whom he had idolized with blind devotion, had been criminally involved in high treason.

[c] In exploring the same theme, the German novelist Martin Walser has mostly dispensed with comedy. The title of his novel *Seelenarbeit* ("Travail of the Soul," 1983) alludes to Isaiah's Servant who agrees to suffer, burdened by the offenses of others (cf. Is 53, 11). The book tells the story of Xaver, the private chauffeur of a modern captain of industry. He is a quiet, helpless man inwardly oppressed by the sheer status of his boss—a taciturn man forever wrapped in self-important anonymity. At Walser's hands, the driver's life becomes a painful parable of the lives of the countless who have no choice but to let themselves be reduced to mere instruments, and thus to live bleak, permanently anesthetized lives. They do not even have the satisfaction of realizing that their service to "the system" and the powerful, faceless agents who operate it (and who, as often as not, are operated by it as well) is a form of martyrdom—one no less real for being wholly secular and implicit.

More recently, Walser has taken another, far more drastic step in the same direction. Turning tactlessness and the naming of names into an art form, he has insisted that oppression by power and control has now reached the point where depersonalization affects not just individuals, families, or even classes, but society as a whole. His novel *Fink's Krieg,* finished in 1995 and published the year after, is an object lesson in what happens when systems of power and influence command more respect than persons and personalness.

The protagonist of the story, Stefan Fink, is a highly placed civil servant close to retirement. Without even the semblance of due process, and for reasons of pure political expediency, he finds himself moved over to a different department of government. He decides to seek redress. The government minister who removed him —a career politician of course—justifies his action by alleging unspecified complaints about Fink from people in high places. The old-fashioned civil servant surprises the political establishment by going on a mad crusade. Energized by sheer rage, he builds up a circle of supporters and correspondents exceeded in size only by his own ever-growing collection of documents and dossiers. As he fights for his life, in a rehabilitation battle made interminable by his own unreflective obstinacy, the copying-machine and the computer—once considered the despised symbols of mindless modernity—become his secret weapons. The campaign soon becomes meaningless, first to his family, and eventually even to those whom he regards as his true friends and supporters. In due course, the inconceivable happens: mortally offended, the once-polite Fink is transformed into a lone warrior, dour, bitter, desperate, pathetic. He breaks apart; a mechanical, run-away bureaucratic *persona* in him reduces his human, accomplished, responsible self to the impotent observer of his own disintegration. With each stubborn headshake, Fink's unspoken *No* to the world becomes more deafening. Unheard by anybody, his muttered invectives reach levels of anal vulgarity which he would once have considered ill-mannered, but which (so he furiously concludes in the end) are in fact wholly appropriate to "the system" and to those who run it or let themselves be run by it—even those among them who mean well.

The cause of Fink's regression is apparent. In the world of today, something the honorable civil servant could never have imagined has come about: the ways and means of power have ceased to regard persons not just in the world of factory labor, but everywhere. The sense of personal and professional honor, by which Fink has always lived and worked has become unaffordable—a fact all too easily understood by the sun-tanned, unscrupulous, ambitious political operators now occupying positions of power and enjoying them.

At last, just before his retirement, Fink prevails. By a supreme, unaided effort he gets a parliamentary committee to force the responsible goverment minister to order his reinstatement. But by then Fink has already buckled under the pressure and run for cover in the Swiss Alps. Only there does he finally "gain altitude": his awakening occurs, if only barely.

At this point, Fink's story gets a literary precedent. Walser specifically alludes to Thomas Mann's famous novel *Der Zauberberg* ("The Magic Mountain"), which also turns the Alps into the setting of an inner awakening. Mann's hero, young, naive Hans Castorp, finds himself forced by tuberculosis to turn a two-week stay with a sick friend recovering in Switzerland into a prolonged period of recovery for himself. There, in the bourgois, deeply conflicted atmosphere of a sanatorium for the affluent and the idle, Castorp finds himself stripped of his immaturity and discovering, slowly, the meaning of life and the significance of love.

By contrast, Walser's disillusioned civil servant finds a "second *naiveté*" in a setting that could not have been more different. First, there is the refreshing, healing climate Fink discovers in the monastery where, disgusted with himself and desperate for relief, he has begged for asylum. The gracious abbess, a young-looking woman of the same age as Fink's wife Thea, encourages Fink simply to live and be at ease. In this, she is backed up by the community—a group of quiet nuns, whose very distance is reassuring. In this unassuming place, not a single novice has entered in the past twenty-seven years (so Walser explains, with a pointed reference to 1968 and its aftermath), yet no one seems to have grown a day older. What is the source of this curiously constant youthfulness? Fink intuits it is a deep serenity, mysteriously connected with the comeliness of worship chanted in common, day in day out, in a community of self-effacing tranquillity no longer known down below, in the so-called real world, where only those count who busy themselves attracting attention. Accordingly, when his wife Thea brings him the happy news of his victory in parliament, she is surprised to find him as uninterested in his rehabilitation as she had found him obstinate in pursuing his rights. Thea, loyal but conventional as she is, can no more follow her husband upward in his inner illumination than she had been able to follow him downward in his harsh crusade. A most important aspect of Fink's awakening is that he regains imagination; he even has dreams of entering the monastery or joining the priesthood, wearing the clerical garb of the monastery's dead chaplain, whose ill-fitting wardrobe mother prioress has invited him to use.

Secondly, to enhance the life-giving climate of the monastery, there is the beauty of the thousands and thousands of crocuses and gentians on the mountain slopes. Here Fink's long-lost better self (whose still inner voice often curiously sounds like a voice of

God) finally manages to coax the desperate warrior into listening. He begins to realize that the amends he has won have been as callously bestowed and are as void of human meaning as the injustice he had so senselessly fought. Accordingly, he is also forced to conclude that his craving for victory had been nothing but a bid to join the powerful by trying to beat them at their game—an attempt doomed to failure, since only those who pursue power for its own sake are in the know and know how to win. Clearly, then, the name of the game played in "the system" is throwing one's weight around and nothing else, and it is a sign of health that Fink is not up to that. In fact, he concludes, the only constructive way to do justice to the mighty is to praise them to the skies; the mindless cynicism that has infected those who pursue power can be healed only by the studied cynicism of the enlightened. The more the powerful are encouraged to indulge their illusions of significance, the less prepared they will be for their fall from power—which, it seems, is the only road to inner awakening nowadays.

So, in the end, Fink the crusader is relieved to admit defeat. For the first time in years, he nods again, almost invisibly, high up on a mountain slope. How beautiful—he says *Yes* once again, if ever so feebly! But at least this weak *Yes* is genuine: in a world dominated by power, Walser subtly suggests, only *elected weakness* can restore access to the sources of humanity's transcendence (cf. §110, 4–5).

Walser's proximate focus in this novel is, of course, the mood of modern Germany, but his disgust with the mentality of the power-driven Western world at whose sufferance the new Germany came into being in 1945 is never far to seek. Victors, not victims, write history, and Germany's recent history is no different: it was written by the victors because dictated by them. No wonder modern Germany's principal theme is power. This hideous fact was well demonstrated by the power-struggle of 1968; it was demonstrated even better just over two decades later, when the end of Germany's long division was hailed not with public rejoycing, but by public qualms about the demands of the reconstruction of the East and by a wave of revulsion at the prospect of a recurrence of the Third Reich. And the shocking part was that this occurred not just in the Western world at large but also—in a show of frightening self-degradation—in Germany itself. But then again, Walser insinuates, what can we expect from a society that has become insensitive to the human agonies great and small generated by "the system"? And in a Western world that allows itself to be the captive of *both* the lust for power *and* the fear of it, what can we expect, except the virtual death of humanity's sensitivity to the *symbolic* facts of life—benevolence and beauty both humane and cosmic, and, within them and beyond them, the immemorial intimations of Transcendence?

[d] The symptoms of modern humanity's powerlessness in the face of its own enslavement to power are not just visible in the political sphere. More and more, power and technology and successful engineering—including human engineering—are being taken, in the West, for the authoritative yardsticks of human growth and development *tout court.* But, ironically, that same West is now also finding itself in the position of the Sorcerer's Apprentice: the very tools of power that have carried it to its present position of dominance are now reducing it to moral impotence.

In a classic passage, Max Weber explains the permanent character of what may be called the "dynamics of instrumentalization" and their impact on the social order, especially through the power of bureaucracy.[50] In recent years the pressure produced by ongoing instrumentalization have been having paralyzing effects, not merely on individuals, small social units, or particular classes, but across the board. In many developed social economies, sophisticated (but frequently, at least in the long run, humanly unreliable) instruments are now (not assisting or empowering but) replacing and excluding human beings *at every level;* poverty without any prospect of improvement *("grande pauvreté"),* socio-economic precariousness, and random exclusion from the labor force *at every level* are becoming *systemic.*[51]

In this way, a socio-economic scandal of long standing in the industrial West is changing for the worse. For a long time, our characteristic social sin was the disproportionate contrast between the wealth and the power of the few, and the suffering of the untold poor who were being deprived of their fair share. After World War II, in the wake of the fall of political imperialism, this injustice became global: the developed countries kept increasing their affluence even as they were assisting the developing ones. Now yet another phase of injustice is taking shape: even as the experts continue to predict a brave new world of global sharing and communication by the most sophisticated means, those very means are eclipsing our grasp of the ends; we are allowing ourselves to be captivated by the aimless dynamics of instrumentalization. In the public domain, it is very poorly realized that *rapid technological development* (like everything else in the park of power) *is no less cosmological for being sophisticated.* And all things cosmological have a built-in dynamic of their own: in and of themselves, they operate erratically. In and of itself, the universe as we understand it is and remains a Pandora's box. That is, Nature will see to it that our every ingenious solution will bring new problems to the surface; cosmic randomness will forever be around, appealing to our need for control and testing our ingenuity; the conquest of the cosmos is never finished, as Pascal intuited more than three hundred years ago (§96, 3–4). But what is liable to happen if we should really agree that the pinnacle of civilization is the success of humanity's efforts to stay abreast of more and more cosmic challenges? Might we not lose sight of the fact that *in and of itself technological progress does not respect persons any more than the purblind blind cosmos itself?* Put differently: allowing ourselves to be governed by the appeal of the technological imperative is tantamount to agreeing to live by honing human instinct and sensibility, not by forming human reason and morality. If left uncontrolled and undisciplined, technological sophistication can only result in a concentration of means of production and earning power in the hands of the *lucky* few.

This is now even a matter of established fact. Increasingly, the "people of means" are nowadays not just the rich and influential, but those who are still "capable of insuring access to the labor market." *The working class is becoming part of the privileged class.* Yet at the same time, those lucky enough to have employment are becoming less and less assured of being able to keep it. In this way, a new and extremely alarming form of poverty is now spreading, visibly: more and more people, willing to do "productive" work and capable of it, are falling victim to the technological rationalization of the production process as it is still functioning and even developing. Being made not only superfluous but irrelevant by the growth of technological devices, they are finding themselves, first progressively marginalized on the labor market, and in the end, erratically excluded from it, often definitively.

[e] The now traditional welfare state has no answer to these dynamics. Often, it is true, the unemployed receive unemployment benefits of some kind. Still, in the long run, being on the public payroll in return for remaining passive cannot possibly be a source of meaning in human life. Besides, there are signs that the capacity of the welfare state to care for its "unproductive" citizens has its limits. In this context, too, employment itself ceases to be a source

of human satisfaction; being "productive" in the traditional sense is becoming a source of embarrassment. How could reasonably compassionate persons possibly enjoy being employed in a society that blindly, and as a matter of sheer socio-economic fact, *systemically* forces their children, relatives, friends, neighbors, and peers to be unemployed—a society, that is, where employment becomes inseparable from the painful unemployment of relevant others?

Morally speaking, labor with at least some degree of satisfaction is the most ordinary way in which human beings actively and constructively engage otherness *and thus grow in the human identity that is their common birthright*. No wonder that in many places systemic unemployment, aided by stultifying entertainment offered by the media, has already led to both massive demoralization *and practical illiteracy*—a phenomenon especially noticeable among the countless young people who have given up even trying to gain access to the labor market and are threatening to use their muscle rather than their minds. We have every reason to wonder if the fundamental tools of human transcendence over place and time are losing their significance.

The present situation, therefore, calls not so much for forcefulness and more sophisticated scientific and technological endeavor as for *interpretation and discernment*. It has been explained that our ingenious electronic media are jeopardizing more deeply humane (*i.e.,* interpretative) reading habits. That is to say, now that humanity's God-given ingenuity has enabled it to conceive and manufacture extremely powerful instruments of social communication, it is turning these same instruments against its better, higher self. It takes only a little thought to realize that this is a case of social sin. After all, Augustine granted that the good things that are the object of sinners' appetites (let us say, positions of influence and sophisticated instruments) are in no way evil (cf. §121, 1). He went on to state that free will (*i.e.,* our freedom to use our God-given ingenuity) is not evil either, but simply an indifferent good. But he clinched his explanation by stating that evil consists in free will being used to turn away from the unchanging good (say, the human capacity for genuine understanding and virtue and for the true knowledge and love of God) and to voluntarily *turn toward changing goods* (say, instruments of power that systematically keep human beings from actualizing their deeper, more spiritual potential). The moral question must be: Is this what is happening today?

Alasdair MacIntyre has proposed in no uncertain words that the answer to this question can only be Yes. At least, this is how he concludes his penetrating study *After Virtue:* "What matters at this stage is *the construction of local forms of community within which civility and the intellectual and moral life can be sustained* through the new dark ages which are already upon us. And if the tradition of the virtues was able to survive the horrors of the last dark ages, we are not entirely without grounds for hope. This time however the barbarians are not waiting beyond the frontiers; they have already been governing us for quite some time. And it is our lack of consciousness of this that constitutes part of our predicament. We are waiting not for a Godot, but for another—doubtless very different —St Benedict."[52]

Is it not time, then, to make it plain that technology—without any doubt a distinctively human achievement—is now widely jeopardizing values that are even more distinctively human? Is it not time to argue that *human dignity* is incomplete if it does not include the freedom to work? And by the same token, is it not time to argue that *human rights* are incomplete if they do not include the freedom to work? In Western Europe, the latter question is regularly asked nowadays by people who have barely survived communist régimes. Those régimes were inhumane, of course, and no less bent on power and influence and technology than the democracies in the free West; but at least they long guaranteed employment for all as well as a minimal standard of living. Now that their survivors (who were systematically and for a long time discouraged to take initiatives) are exposed to the random (*i.e.,* clearly infrahumane) mechanics of the free market, just exactly where is the human—*i.e.,* moral— gain?

[f] In this ominous landscape, thank heavens, points of light are appearing. Thus we have the writings, not only of the very versatile, very intelligent utopian Wendell Berry, but also those of a respected social scientist like E. F. Schumacher, whose deceptively simple *Small is Beautiful: A Study of Economics as if People Mattered* calls for the *deliberate* development of "Intermediate Technology." Interestingly but not surprisingly, Schumacher's book ends with (of all things) a little treatise on the *cardinal virtues*—a clear indication that the author is aware that it will take *human, moral* decisions to take on the mentality of the technology race in which people matter little or not at all, and perhaps even less than they did

in the period of the arms race, now a quarter century ago. Recently, F. Byron Nahser, the chief operating officer of a sizable big-city advertising business, obtained a doctorate in philosophy with his book *Learning to Read the Signs: Reclaiming Pragmatism in Business*. Citing a profusion of expert witnesses, he shows that commercially, intellectually, and morally honest business practices involve a lot more than the mechanical approaches encouraged by "number crunching." On a different front, but inspired by the similar concerns, Alwine de Vos van Steenwijk, in a splendid report discussed at the World Summit for Social Development held in Copenhagen in the Spring of 1995, has explained why the current concept of labor and productivity as well as the practice of both of them must be entirely reconceived and reorganized creatively—*i.e.*, not by recourse to technology and market forces alone, but in properly *human and cultural* terms.[53] In this situation, could it be that the respect for the delicacies of sensibility and narrative, felt and cultivated in many places in Latin America, Asia, and Africa, and the consequent reluctance to adopt the rational-technological Western life style may in the long run turn out to be an important resource for a new humanity? And last but not least, is it not possible to observe in the ecological movement the formation of basic communities, in which commitment to a healthy environment and, in that environment, to a healthy humanity is viewed as an authentically moral responsibility [*q*]? Could these be some of "the nebulas out of which mentalities crystallize" (§132, 7, c)—the environments concentrated and intense enough to disarm the scientific-techno-

---

[*q*] In this context, it is pertinent to point to applied behavioral science and the various forms of experience-based education developed by it, sometimes lumped together under the rubric of "sensitivity training." There are good reasons to interpret this type of formation as an attempt at introducing leaders and leadership teams to *an alternative mentality*—one decisively more humane than the prevalent, coldly literate-scientific-technological one. Still, there are two aspects to any effort to promote such a mentality. Firstly, since mentalities have at least remote connections with deliberate decisions, deliberate efforts to change mentalities are within the park of morality, and hence, a matter of moral commitment. Secondly, since mentalities are inseparable from sensibility, efforts to change them simply *must* broach issues of sensitivity. Together, these two go a long way to explain a well-known phenomenon, *viz.*, the deeply moral (and sometimes even religious) experiences that regularly occur during exercises like small-group sensitivity training, organization and community development, and training programs aimed at the discovery and development of the participants' human potential. How so? Both the decision to offer training programs of this kind and the decision to participate in them are deliberate (*i. e.*, moral) acts; why, then, should it surprising that participants discovering and developing sensibilities different from their prevalent ones, should end up feeling morally and religiously changed and even "healed"?

logical mentality and thus, capable of giving birth to a new human-ism—one more in accord with the great traditions of Jewish and Christian humanism?

[g] The main contention of the present exploratioms should be clear by now: *temperance must become a socio-political virtue.* So must fortitude. In the West, the milieus that have the capacity to engen-der a post-scientific-technological humanity are likely to be those where temperance and fortitude are treated as *social* virtues. Tem-perance demands that we learn how to deliberately discipline our immature, largely instinctive fascination with runaway technology and powerful means. As a community, we must learn, systematical-ly, how to look past ways and means, in order to discern and em-brace distinctively human *ends.* Only then we will be choosing ways and means to pursue systemically what we can responsibly want, with whatever technologies will prove to be both affordable and helpful. The world community must begin to put at least some brakes on its breathless quest for greater material wealth and pro-ductivity, and its most powerful members must set the example. Power must be tempered by reason and a moral vision; fortitude must replace the breathless quest for success. Otherwise humanity may well end up, under the banner of freedom, doing a disastrous injustice to its true, more-than-cosmic self, by chasing after domi-nation and influence instead of attaining to a mature pursuit of justice and prudence.

[10] Our analyses have led us back to a theme touched on before. Class, it was suggested, has a "quasi-cosmological" quality (§129, 2, a); establishments of power and influence have the ability to impress and enthrall us *tout bêtement,* by dint of sheer *facticity* (cf. §129, 2, g, [k]). We must now add that the modern mentality, by letting itself be captivated by the literate-scientific-technological passion for *means* rather than *ends,* has implicitly accepted power and can-do as the yardstick of all development, including *human* development. But there is more to humanity than the mindless fact that all things, in-cluding human beings, are naturally exposed to the dynamics of cos-mic happenstance. While it is true (as well as fundamentally moral) that we must take things in hand in order to exist, it is inhumane to act as if we owe it to ourselves to use each and any conceivable means to contend with otherness in all its forms and to assert our in-dependence and mastery as much as we possibly can. To act consis-tently in such a manner dangerously favors the notion that power,

influence, and class are humanity's chief moral issues and that the acceptance of weakness of any kind is a moral defeat. It also amounts to an implicit refusal to accept the natural *as well as moral* fact that humanity, no matter how developed, is and remains a participant in the cosmos, and that even its most ingenious devices will leave both the cosmos and itself unfinished. This is a troubling realization, of course, but it is entirely frustrating only for those who live by the tacit conviction that lies at the heart of the technological mentality, namely, that the essence of humanity's transcendence over the cosmos lies in its superior power over it. On this assumption, the best that human beings can do is: exploiting everything cosmic that is available and turning it into tools for human success. That is to say, *pushing power* will become the dominating theme of human growth and development (cf. §107, 5, c, [n]), and in its wake, *mastery over matter*—including undiscerning mastery over the human body and all its functions.

Should this theme ever succeed in becoming the prevailing mentality, the ever-pressing demands of cosmicity are likely to become all-consuming. That is to say, humanity's distinctive privilege—its transcendence over cosmic process, which is rooted in its native self-transcendence—will become a lower priority than forcefulness, and humanity will become (in Emmanuel Lévinas' idiom) unscrupulous. Along with this loss of moral sensitivity, humanity's distinctive (that is, *moral*) undertakings—namely, the deliberate pursuit of the genuinely common good and the practice of the love of God "with all your heart and with all your soul and with all your mind and with all your strength" and of the love of the neighbor "as yourself" (Mk 12, 30–31)—will become, at best, optional (or worse, "interesting") extras.

[a] These observations and analyses also serve to reinforce and detail an earlier contention: power, influence, and class are, at bottom, cosmological forces (§129, 3). They also help settle the claim that, of the three dynamics operative in the life in alienation—influence, inclusion, and intimacy—the first is the most primitive and unsophisticated from the integrally human point of view.

We can now add that the characteristic mentality of the powerful and the influential serves to corroborate these claims. The mighty appreciate morality and religiosity and proclaim their ability to propel humanity to the top of its potential for ingenuity, but typically they do not count on them, and even less on God. They love to operate (or feel they "have to" operate), not by consideration or discernment, but by *fait accompli* and *faktisch Vorgehen*. Accordingly, they tend to think simply, and will declare themselves proud of it. They enjoy applauding straightforwardness and directness. Disinclined to differentiate, they typically commend "trial and error" and "the school of hard knocks." They are apt to show little respect for the wider humanity around them (which they typically think of as confused, ineffective, and in need of coordination); they show even less regard for the "academics" and the "wets" who advocate means rather more subtle than power and willfulness, and ends rather less tangible than immediate effectiveness; in the eyes of the mighty, such means are likely to betray "lack of leadership capacity" and such ends are apt to be "pie in the sky." In their view, only "the tough" can successfully engage both the world and humanity, and deal with them in a "productive" fashion. Not surprisingly, the influential will point out with some regularity that those who will not be "taught" will simply "have to suffer." In their characteristically cosmological view of the world, forcefulness and power are the most dependable road to almost everything; they are also the only "language" that "everybody" can be made to "understand," especially when combined with implied or explicit threats of ridicule, punishment, dismissal, or the outright use of force (cf. §135, 2, b).

So much for the dynamics of the powerful and the forceful and their ilk. The question explored in this section is not only, How moral can human societies be if they are mostly driven by fascination with power and forcefulness? It is also, Is it possible to help create a mentality that is open to something higher?

[11] It is time to conclude this long section. The questions raised in it are too broad for quick answers. Any conclusions, therefore, must remain provisional. Let an interesting essay by the historian Karlfried Froehlich entitled *Cultivating a Symbolic Mentality* and (alas) never published, serve to convey our main thesis; a few sketchy further observations will have to suffice to round out the picture.

Medieval literacy, Froehlich explains, invariably took its cues from biblical literacy. Besides, it had this in common with the literacy *and* the liturgical art of the Christian East that it was consistently "iconic"; it appealed to the *imagination* of its readers and implicitly expected them to *discern further meaning*. That is to say, reading was far more than a sentient skill; it was invariably formative, civilizing, humanizing. Leaving aside ledgers and bills of lading and records and pure chronicles, all writings, whether sacred or profane, were reminiscent of Scripture, and thus were felt to possess (or rather "to be possessed of") a curious form of *normativity* [r]. They were neither written down nor read to others for the sake of information alone, just as no medieval pictorial representations ever aimed at mere photographic realism; even numbers were rarely without intimations of higher meaning [s]. All things artistic or even merely artful or elegant suggested layers of further significance (cf. §54, 1, a)—accessible to people with developed imaginations, to whom it would never even occur that a text was just a text and an artifact just an artifact, and that there was nothing significant to be found behind either. This "symbolic mentality" firmly supported (and was in turn firmly supported by) the Church, with its understanding of divine revelation conveyed in a whole world of signs and symbols inviting both discovery and interpretation.[54]

In his book *Models of Revelation,* Avery Dulles has carefully retrieved and reaffirmed the thesis that divine Revelation is a matter of *symbolic mediation.* Even more importantly, he has argued that in our own day this understanding can reconcile a number of needlessly conflicting conceptions of revelation (cf. §95, esp. 11, c; cf. also §78).[55] It would seem, then, that it is vitally important for the Christian community to recognize the need for a symbolic mentality in the culture at large, and to support and encourage any and all efforts to foster it, especially in milieus where people learn how to live by more than tools alone. A few modest remarks to add detail to this proposition.

---

[r] The teller of *The Nun's Priest's Tale* in Chaucer's *Canterbury Tales* quotes the Letter to the Romans ("Whatever is written is written for our training": Rom 15, 6) for the secular (but intensely human and thus, moral) purpose of telling his listeners not to stop at the mere *story*—the *sensus historicus*—of the fable of Chauntecleer and Pertelote he has just told, but to draw the moral lesson from it (VII 3441–42). As a matter of fact, Chaucer himself, speaking in his own behalf this time, can turn the end of *The Parson's Tale* into a little homily to urge his readers, *on the authority of the same Pauline text,* to believe in his good intentions and put a favorable construction on his own writings, even where they find them morally hard to take (X [I] 1080–85)! Cf. *The Works of Geoffrey Chaucer* [ed. Robinson], pp. 205, 265.

[s] Froehlich mentions a German research project. It "began by investigating the 'new literacy' in the trivial literature of the time such as handbooks and book-keeping records, [but] soon realized that the mass productions of a biblical culture— multiple copies of Bibles, commentaries, sermon books and devotional tools— were of interest not only for the statistics of book production but deserved attention as a literature which was meant to powerfully affect, and actually did so affect, everyday life at its deepest level for the people of those centuries." In this context Froehlich also cites Hagen Keller's interesting article "Vom 'heiligen Buch' zur 'Buchführung'."

[a] Mentalities are the element of *inertia* in history (§132, 7, a). A first conclusion must be the following. It is both good history and good theology to emphasize, contrary to what is often alleged nowadays by the media and other sources uninterested in history, that the symbolic mentality did *not* by any means die out with the start of the New Learning and the rise of science. It is obviously alive and well in Andreas Vesalius' anatomical atlas of 1543, with its meticulous drawings of the human skeleton in poses that convey meditations on death and mortality.[56] About the same time, Albrecht Dürer was using the iron laws of optical perspective to evoke dramatic perspectives of a moral and spiritual nature (cf. §56, 12, a, [*i*])—a manner of "visualizing" which was to be carried to brilliant extremes a good century later by the Jesuit Brother Andrea Pozzo, in the visionary splendor of the ceiling of the church of Sant'Ignazio in Rome. By then, the Metaphysical Poets in England (like other *concettisti* elsewhere in Europe) had for some time drawn new and surprising intuitions and perspectives not only from what the New Learning and the voyages of discovery were bringing home to them, but also from books proposing matter for mental prayer, of the kind encouraged in the *Spiritual Exercises* by Ignatius of Loyola, as Louis Martz has so well explained in *The Poetry of Meditation.*

The sixteenth century also witnessed the birth of the emblem books;[57] from Andrea Alciati's highly polished and much reprinted and plagiarized collection of 1535 till the late eighteenth century these immensely popular little volumes, replete with texts that were as puzzling as they were pointed and with pictures that were as cryptic as they were memorable, were to invite their users to find moral reflection and even religious contemplation in and beyond what they were seeing and reading on the printed page.

Not until the late seventeenth and early eighteenth centuries (and then only in the leading circles) did "dissociation of sensibility" (cf. §99, 5) begin to be part of the normative cultural climate; feeling and objectivity parted company—a move that in the long run turned the former into mere sentiment and the latter into merely rational knowledge.[58] This gradual move away from a culture attentive to deeper significance was completed by the *Encyclopédistes,* who left affect for what it was, and insisted (though not always with a clear conscience) that only descriptive, factual knowledge was *certain,* effective, unprejudiced, and thus "true"; in their eyes, knowledge and awareness on tradition and interpretation were "dogmatic," probably obscurantist and hence, always suspect (cf. §28, 6, b– d). In the eyes of the Enlightened, the crassest form of such knowledge was, of course, the revealed knowledge claimed by Christianity, foisted by self-interest and priestcraft upon the simple-minded and the uneducated in the interest of preserving the *ancien régime.*

Yet even under the pressure of the Enlightenment and the dissociation of sensibility it promoted, the symbolic mentality died hard. Not until the conduct of ordinary human life was significantly affected *at the level of environment and hence, of sensibility* did the scientific-technological mentality take hold. Powerful mechanical engineering achievements such as large bridges, large seaworthy vessels, ingenious technologies capable of controlling water levels, and faster, motorized means of conveyance gave travelers, merchants, farmers, and entrepreneurs significant ascendancy over natural barriers; consistent division of labor in small shops that grew larger and larger increased to an unheard-of degree the production of common artifacts; increasingly mechanized labor practices in large factories changed the cities, the dynamics of commerce, and the daily living conditions of countless people; new medical knowledge and surgical techniques stimulated population growth and general well-being. It was as if the implements of progress were becoming so powerful and so authoritative that it began to look humanly irresponsible not to work as hard and efficiently as possible with every tool available. One of these instruments was "religion," hailed by John D. Rockefeller as the supreme means to thrust the human mind forward and upward to the highest accomplishments. Only as the scientific-technological mentality (along with its favorite offspring, philosophical utilitarianism and positivism) continued to ride the crest of such waves of "progress," could it gradually begin to claim moral authority and cast doubts on the symbolic (or at least the allegorical) mentality and eventually displace it in many quarters [*t*]. In other words, the symbolic mental-

---

[*t*] It is fashionable nowadays to glorify symbol and decry allegory. That there are differences between the two is clear: symbols (as well as their effects on us) are more "holistic," while allegory appeals, in a fairly one-sided manner, to our rationality. Nevertheless, it is often overlooked that *both* symbol *and* allegory are part of the same inclusive mentality. Its chief element is the generally received habit of *actively interpreting* written truths and facts (including those written in the Book of Nature, as Alain de Lille had taught in the twelfth century). In other words, both symbol and allegory invite being taken not just at face value, but also in reference to morality and mystery. Cf. M.-D. Chenu, "La mentalité symbolique," in *La théolo-*

ity is far from dead, even in the West. In fact, the "post-modern" mood is embracing it again (at least for the time being). And who knows, the countries of the so-called Third World, where the symbolic mentality is very much alive, could turn out to be among those "nebulas out of which mentalities crystallize" (§132, 7, c).

[b] But this argument has another side to it. Once again, mentalities are the element of *inertia* in human history (§132, 7, a). It is wise not to suppose that the scientific-technological mentality will prove an exception to this rule. Mentalities are carried by patterns of "sentient virtuosity"—shared habits of doing things that have made sense so long that they have become part of a cultural community's developed sensibility. Over the past century and a half, and especially in North America and Western Europe, our sensibilities have become so deep shaped by modern technology and its successes that we can hardly imagine living differently. The problem is, of course, that technology has served not only to round out our sensibilities and to enhance certain sentient skills that are now part of our sensibilities; it has also left some of our sentient skills underdeveloped and dulled others outright. In all likelihood (but who is to tell?), it has even perverted some of them. By way of example, let us recall that instant painkillers, contraceptives, walkmen, and other forms of portable sound equipment (including cellular telephones) are now broadly advertized and readily available almost everywhere. Small wonder that their use is both widespread and casual. Yet there is little doubt that these developments have helped alter our sensitivities in regard to pain (cf. §120, 3, a–c), sexual intimacy, and the whole world of sound, silence, and oral/acoustical communication. Without doubt they have *stretched* and *expanded* our sensibilities; besides, it is not inconceivable that they will grow on us, so that we may end up living with them in a truly humane manner (cf. §28, 6, d). But is it obvious, at least for the time being, that they have *improved* them? *Refined* them? *Civilized* them? What has been the dynamic underlying these developments? Is it not true that we tend to be so interested in, and awed by, the *immediate power and effectiveness* of these tools that we have lost our awareness of their effect on our delicate sensorium, and thus on our sensibilities? This awe in regard to the power and ef-

gie au douzième siècle, pp. 159–90 (ET "The Symbolist [*sic*] Mentality," in *Nature, Man, and Society in the Twelfth Century* [pp. 99–145] and "La théologie symbolique," [*ibid.,* pp. 190–209).

fectiveness of our tools has also tended to blind us to a significant extent to the enormous subtlety of the accumulated sentient skills in us that are *not* assisted or enhanced by any tools— the example of articulate speech comes to mind. And who is to tell any longer what subtle sentient skills we may have lost altogether, by allowing them to be wholly *supplanted* by tools? *Humanly* (*i.e.*, morally) speaking, could it be that some of these "improvements" have not been entirely beneficial?

Let us resort to another example. Judging from the media, the capacity of the human nervous system is best measured by comparing it (often unfavorably) with the ability of advanced computers; the latter can process data at speeds and in quantities far beyond the capacity of the unaided human brain and the organs directed by it. But leaving aside the fact that even the most advanced computers would not do anything without human ingenuity, does fairness not demand that the capacity of such computers should also be measured against the immeasurably greater subtlety and capacity for discrimination of the human brain and the organs directed by it (cf. §130, 1, e–f; §131, 1, a; 2, b–c)? What is it that makes us take the latter for granted and stand in awe of the former? Is it not because the pursuit of *power and effectiveness* rather than subtlety and sensitivity lies at the heart of the scientific-technological mentality—the mentality we now almost instinctively live and judge by (*i.e.*, fail to properly *judge* by)?

[c] Let us now make an attempt to appraise, simply by way of suggestion, the enormous difficulties inherent in overcoming the scientific-technological mentality, in two ways.

First of all, visionary social scientists like Harry Stack Sullivan, David Riesman, and J.H. van den Berg have pointed out in different ways that *we live in a situation of culturally induced stress:* the sheer *multiplicity of roles and tasks,* and the profusion of means at our disposal to help us play our roles and perform our tasks, make it difficult to sustain the sense of coherence, the focus, the concentration, and especially the sense of identity we need to see our way toward *ends,* especially shared ends (§120, 3, a; cf. §112, 4–5). Besides, the mouthpieces of the scientific-technological mentality keep on assuring us loudly (but more often tacitly) that the attainment of great goals and the alleviation of stress and even its complete elimination are ours if only we avail ourselves of the many means and "resources" placed at our disposal by science and technology. The problem is, of course, that the very glut of means and resources is one of the primary factors that *produce* the stress and the sense of aimlessness. It takes more than a profusion of means to develop a focused understanding of our world and a vigorous inner sense of communal and personal integration and identity. Put differently, in the end, ingenuity and mastery, even in large doses, are inadequate to the task of building a distinctively *human* culture. Only capacity for interpretation and discernment and judgment can do that, as the next chapter will argue, and they are not available apart from a symbolic mentality, carefully and persistently cultivated by institutions, communities, and individuals prepared to take on the prevailing culture, not by force, but with discernment.

Secondly, one of the most obvious features of the scientific-technological mentality is a deep respect for the Expert and the State of the Art. Clearly, it would be foolish as well as mean-spirited to disparage expertise and cutting-edge research. Yet it remains true, as Hans-Georg Gadamer has so compellingly argued,[59] that expertise by itself guarantees neither judgment nor wisdom, and that nothing is less definitive than the state of the art. Not surprisingly, therefore, to mention only two notable examples, many modern technological and medical developments have a record of considerable lack of ecological and socio-economic and humane discernment and prudence. By itself, doing everything we possibly can is no sure sign of either humanity or morality, yet the signals we keep on picking up from the prevailing mentality is precisely that our future will be assured as long as we do everything we possibly can, with the best (*i.e.,* latest) means at our disposal and relying on "the best people in the field." But surely the answer to the question as to what are the best means and who are the best people is a matter not of scientific-technological prowess, but of good judgment and wisdom.

[d] A final, more theological observation. It would be curious if the scientific-technological mentality, so characteristic of Enlightenment and post-Enlightenment rationalism, had had no impact at all on the Christian world. In fact, over the last few centuries many Christians and Christian mileus have unconsciously traded the symbolic mentality so essential to the Christian profession of faith for something more in tune with the prevalent culture, antisymbolic and rationalist as it is. Thus the Catholic traditionalists

and fideists of the nineteenth and early twentieth centuries could assert that the "supernatural" truths and facts of the Catholic faith were just that: objectively true and entirely factual. These truths and facts, after all, were immediately revealed and caused by God and truly *known* to be thus revealed and caused; accordingly, they could be adequately told apart from "merely natural" truths and facts; in fact, the former could even fly in the face of the latter (cf. §12, 1, a; §68, 2, b). The same anti-symbolic, rationalist mentality goes a long way to account for the fact that many pre-Vatican II neo-Thomists argued that it was possible to demonstrate the truth of the Catholic faith by recourse to incontrovertible proofs based on certainties establishable by natural reason (cf. §86, 2–6).

Some of this continues even after the Second Vatican Council, which set so much store by discernment ("being attentive to the signs of the times") and symbolism (the primacy of the liturgy: cf. §34, 7, a). The scientific-technological mentality of our own day is so overwhelming that it would be nothing short of miraculous if contemporary Christians, including Catholics, had remained unaffected by it. Catholic integralists and Christian fundamentalists of every stripe are once again only too willing to insist that the formulas of revealed faith are the adequate expression of revealed faith, and hence its only test; they will likewise insist that every fact of faith is as "historical" and indisputable as any other proven facts. In making these claims, they are overlooking the positivist bias that underlies their notion of divine revelation. Interested in clarity and certainty rather than mystery (cf. §19), they mistrust symbolism and especially hermeneutics as forms of modernism and liberalism. The problem is that, when they profess the faith they love and cling to, they invariably end up protesting too much. In the Roman Catholic Church, some of these groups and persons seem to be forever imploring the Church's teaching authorities to give them as many truths to believe in as possible, and to speak infallibly as a matter of course.

[12] We must move on. This section has argued that most forms of human engagement with natural and artificial situations involve *mind*. This proposition also holds true for engagements that make use of means and tools—mechanical, electrical, and electronic tools, as well as the tools of literacy and of its latest shape, electronic literacy.

Now the life of the conscious mind is always to some extent influenced by passion, instinct, and sensibility—something the mind of-

ten finds hard to acknowledge (cf. §131, 6). There is something else
the human mind finds hard to appreciate, let alone anticipate: the
impact which its own decisions and actions are apt to have at the
sentient level (cf. §130, 2, c). Thus the habitual use of advanced
tools such as books, mechanical appliances, and computers, and the
habitual study of specialized subjects may develop some skills, both
sentient *and mental,* to a high degree, while allowing others to deteriorate. Many car drivers make poor pedestrians, just as many data
processing experts and many specialists make poor, or at least bor-
ing, conversation partners. The blessings of the printing press are
numerous indeed, but one of its curses is hack journalism. Under
the banner of freedom of expression it is now considered humane to
find and write up any "data" (especially of the contentious kind)—
i.e., any random opinion or "state-of-the-art" knowledge or any piece
of information that people at large are moved to enjoy seeing in
print for any reason whatsoever, including for no reason. Are our
instinctive news consumption habits and the fancy of the moment
really a human blessing? Is is really such a sound idea to teach very
small children that they are "advanced" once they know how to look
for the *truth* ("the facts") in newspapers, dictionaries and encyclopedias?

[a] Needless to say, many providers and handlers of texts in which
only such "data" are relevant are themselves primitive readers—
skillful and dexterous, but unreflective, undiscerning, and thus often prejudiced. To make matters worse, they tend to assume that
all there is to reading is what *they* make of *it—i.e.,* an assemblage of
data and dexterity. No wonder they think that all readers are like
themselves; unsurprisingly, they fail to acknowledge deeper, wider,
more temperate, more patient forms of intelligence. Still, being
human, even second-rate writers and readers have choices; for example, they can learn that reading is not the same as speed-read-
ing. *Reading* is not so much an exercise in storage as in interpretation. The road to humane literacy remains open to those willing
to convert.

[b] Something analogous can be said about the relationship between mentalities and sensibilities, except that the forces of habit
and inertia bulk much larger here. Mentalities are always to a significant extent predicated on sensibilities, and one reason for the
thesis that mentalities function as forces of inertia in the history of
human ingenuity and initiative (cf. §132, 7, a) is the fact that sensi-

bilities are deeply ingrained and largely unconscious. Yet it is also true that mentalities often prevent us from appreciating, let alone anticipating, the real or potential impact of decisions and actions on our sensibilities. Mentalities are shared mental habits rather than deliberately held convictions; accordingly, they are hard to defend, harder to challenge, and even harder to change. Besides, mentalities are typically kept in place or (as the case may be) modified by prevalent sensibilities. But sensibilities are largely involuntary, so it is hard even to identify them; no wonder they are even harder to change, challenge, or defend.

Earlier on, it was argued that the formation of sensibility can be a moral issue, especially with regard to the young, the thoughtless, and the humanly incompetent (§131, 5, c–d). We can now add to this that mentalities are, at least in principle, *matters of mind;* no wonder they *can* be intellectualized and verbalized, accounted for and justified (cf. §132, 7). But this implies that they are also proper objects of *moral* exploration, discernment, judgment, decision-making, and action. In other words, appeals to mentalities are not an acceptable excuse for immoral behavior.

[§133] PASSION, POWER, TEMPERANCE, AND THE LURE OF VIOLENCE

[1] It is time to bring this lengthy chapter firmly to a properly theological and anthropological close. It is not by accident that Paul, writing to the Christian community at Corinth, demanded that the better-off and the influential among them be temperate and considerate enough to refrain from eating and drinking until the less fortunate members of the community had joined them, and that he told them to "examine themselves" before partaking of the bread and wine of the Eucharist—both out of "consideration for the Body," and to make it possible for "all things to be done courteously and in proper order" (1 Cor 11, 21. 28–29. 33; 14, 40). For the fact is that the forceful and the influential are tempted to be insensitive (sometimes to the point of total unawareness) of the seductions of instinctive self-maintenance and self-assertion. This does not make them simply immoral. Rather, being so closely identified with power and influence, they tend to interpret the moral life almost exclusively in terms of effort, forcefulness, and short-term victories. They tend to stress, with a vengeance, that what really matters is that everybody do their duty and work hard at it. In practice this means, unfortunately, that they frequently (and sometimes with a fascistoid sincerity that

will amaze the discerning) think that it is part of moral responsibility to be inconsiderate and heavy-handed, lest the world and human society be overwhelmed by what they take to be moral chaos and instability.

[a] Small wonder the powerful and the influential are inclined to adopt positions that indirectly commit them to a simplified world view. That is, they will interpret the world they live in almost entirely *in the way they experience their own lives* in the world: *i.e.*, in predominantly cosmological (that is, less than fully human) terms. They *require* such a world view; it helps them justify their habit of meeting the challenges offered by new situations with their favorite approach, which is: availing themselves of the tensions and uncertainties inherent in the dynamics of power and turning them to their own advantage. They will typically try to *create* situations of imbalance of power, in which they can gain the advantage at the expense of others, whom they will usually regard as competitors and even as enemies. They will habitually opt for contest and competition, sometimes without even entertaining the possibility of collaboration.[60] They are apt to be so captivated by the persistent, never quite predictable play of power that they do not realize that even the natural dynamics of cosmic power and influence involve not just contest and competition, but also combination and concurrence ("synergy"). Unable to take a discerning view of either their own worth or the worth of other agents, they will divide the world into enemies and (some) allies and blindly and instinctively act on that perception. In this way, they will end up creating for themselves a universe of meaning in which *relativity and relatedness give way to polarization and division*—a dangerous dynamic to which we will have an opportunity to return (cf. §137, 10, a, [*i*]; 13).

[2] This is, therefore, where the distinctively human (that is, *moral*) responsibility, both for humanity viewed as a cosmic agent and for the cosmos itself finds itself at a critical juncture. The *human* institutions of class and its variants, it has been argued, support themselves chiefly by relying on the largely *cosmic* dynamics of influence and power. This is far from surprising. Humanity is radically involved in cosmic process, and participating in the cosmic dynamics of power and influence is the most radical way in which creatureliness and finitude are etched into the human condition.

But humanity is *also* natively transcendent. This clearly and urgently demands that we habitually transcend mere cosmic involvement; we must see to it that the natural forces of human passion are disciplined and chastened by recourse to reason, supported by reliable habits of self-restraint. This implies that the instinctual tendency of the powerful and the influential to use influence and forcefulness must be responsibly managed. For power and influence simply *must* learn to embrace considerateness.

In the long run, considerateness is best achieved by that immemorial form of human civilization: *established systems of justice.* But justice does not fall from the sky. It grows. And it can neither grow nor flourish apart from a matrix of temperance. And temperance cannot grow and flourish without a commitment, on the part of the more disciplined members of the moral community, to *fortitude*, to ensure that the training of all the community's members in self-control and self-discipline does not become intemperate itself.

Short of such elementary forms of self-transcendence, humanity ceases to be human. For once again, might does *not* guarantee right. It is most certainly part of humanity's responsibility to accept and welcome power and forcefulness, and to practice the human ability to wield them in a constructive manner. After all, it takes endurance and forcefulness to bend and conquer the often intractable cosmic givens and to shape them in such a way as to draw them into the ambit of human civility. And since the use of power and force is inevitably tied in with passion, it is part of moral maturity to befriend it, not to squelch it, let alone to repress it.

But the uncritical, merely instinctual exercise of power and forcefulness and passion is subhuman; so are unexamined habits of treating class and other power establishments as if they were inherently unquestionable, and entitled to respect and submission as a matter of course [*u*]. So, finally, are ingrained habits of lording it over the

---

[*u*] The Christian West is entitled (albeit with proper theological provisos) to take credit for an enormous cultural, moral, and religious victory, namely, the awareness that the institutions of both class privilege and slavery lack intrinsic moral authority. This insight, which first began to take shape in the high Middle Ages, eventually led to government by the people and the abolition of slavery, at least as a matter of socio-political and moral principle. Small wonder that Hegel, in the final three chapters of part IV of his lectures on the philosophy of history, could extol these developments, which were so dramatically promoted by the Reformation, and made so definitive by the French Revolution and its nineteenth-century aftermath, and especially (so he thought) in the German nation. In fact, Hegel outright enthused about them, and regarded them as the triumph of Reason in history, and even as the fulfillment of what he saw as Christianity's central motif: the liberation of the human spirit in history. This, he thought, was the essence of God's creative activity in the world (*Vorlesungen über die Philosophie der Geschichte*, pp. 492–540; cf. H.-G. Gadamer, *Das Erbe Europas*, pp. 63–64). Of course, in proposing all

outclassed and the outcasts and the lonely and unloved by exploiting them or (worse) by treating them with contempt, calculated neglect, or indifference, as if their predicament were morally acceptable simply because it is a "natural" given [*v*]. After all, it is humanity's vocation *and* responsibility to value all cosmic givens, but only in hopes of turning them into truly humane—*i.e.*, shared—gifts.

[3] It has been suggested that the dynamics of power and influence are closest to cosmic process (§129, 3; 4, a; cf. §117, 5; §120, 3 and a). This means that in the Great Chain of Being they have the lowest ontological intensity. There is comfort in this, for it implies that for all their bluster and despite their enormous capacity for destruction, cosmic forces are the easiest to transcend and to turn to constructive purpose. For one thing, they are often chaotic; they are weakened by their own randomness and multiplicity. More importantly, the human ability to transcend them is built right into humanity's instrument of cosmic power and influence, namely, the human body—relatively undifferentiated and thus highly adaptable, and besides, endowed with superior manual skills and backed up by an infinitely re-

---

this, Hegel is taking, in characteristically Protestant fashion, far too anthropocentric a view of the Christian faith (cf. §20, 2). Still, let us pardon him for now, if only for the following reason. In criticizing the systemic abuse of power in bygone ages, Hegel is accomplishing something that some contemporary Catholic German theologians opposed to liberation theology would seem to have difficulty imagining even as a possibility, *viz.* practicing liberation theology without having read, let alone having been inspired by, Karl Marx. I owe this observation to Gustavo Gutiérrez.

[*v*] Neither the defeat of class as an entitlement to power nor the abolition of slavery marked the end of the systemic abuse of power, of course. This is due, in large part, to the fact that class, race, and sexuality (more broadly, influence, inclusion, and intimacy) give rise to "endless permutations, combinations, and interferences" (cf. §98, 4). This leads to an insight of wide application. *Wherever and whenever just conditions in the area of inclusion (and in particular, race) and in the area of intimacy (and in particular, sexuality) are lacking, human beings, no matter which side they are on, are apt to resort to cosmic means: they will try to force justice and love by dint of unjust and even violent forcefulness and ditto power structures.* Examples of this, too many to mention, come to mind. Off-hand, we can think of the justification of warfare and systemic racial discrimination to maintain and enforce the superiority of one ethnic group over another. We may also think of the systemic reduction of the life of affection to a function of male needs for dominance, which tends to reduce women and children to cheap labor and even to property. The latter evil is often bolstered by immoral forms of "civilization" such as the forcible confining of women to harems and the practice of widow burning (*satī* or *suttee:* cf. *ER* 14: 128–29), and even by the infliction of debilitating mutilations, such as clitoridectomy (cf. *ER* 3: 535–37) and the "golden lily" feet forced in childhood upon countless Chinese women, from around the tenth century till well into the twentieth. The practice of elective abortion, too, comes to mind. Eventually it will be argued that the proposition formulated in this footnote has a wider application.

sourceful mind (cf. §115, 9). In humanity's bodiliness, therefore, cosmic process, that matrix of all forcefulness and capacity, naturally and spontaneously aspires, first to self-discipline, but then also to deliberation, and ultimately to the glorification of God.

[4] But for that reason it is also true that wherever human beings choose to live largely by power and influence, they condemn themselves to frustrating their native aspiration to transcendence over infra-human cosmic process. That is, those who live by power do violence to their deeper selves, with their own hands. Thus the life governed by the lust for dominance is essentially self-consuming. This, too, is a matter of experience. Leading a life enslaved to power and influence requires an enormous expenditure of libidinous energy. Playboys will play harder and harder to convince themselves that they are still playing and not doing something more injurious.

In due course, living by passion and power will ruin the self-esteem human persons and communities owe to their deeper selves. For indulging in habits of power, influence, and violence vis-à-vis otherness on a regular basis is impossible without grave self-abuse. No wonder living by passion and power typically leads to self-contempt.

> All this the world well knows; yet none knows well
> To shun the heaven that leads men to this hell."[61]

[5] Self-abuse. Self-contempt. These words lay bare once again the profoundly self-contradictory (that is, ultimately, *sinful*: cf. §113, 3) nature of the life governed by what Augustine called "lust for power" (*dominandi libido*: cf. §121, 3). On account of their native potential for higher purpose, human beings are natively urged to practice positive regard vis-à-vis one another and the world around them. If they do not follow this inner urge they become self-destructive. When the human zest for life degenerates and becomes an addiction to life (that is, when human beings become so governed and obsessed by fear of diminishment and death that they are prepared to subdue and dominate other human beings and the cosmos in the interest of keeping *themselves* alive), humanity becomes its own worst enemy. Miserably, among the higher animals, human beings are perversely unique in one respect: they will lash out against their own kind, not only instinctively but deliberately as well, and thus bring down upon their own kind the very thing all living beings instinctively fend off: diminishment and death. Even more miserably, human beings dominated by the passion for survival will endanger human beings who offer no appreciable physical threat to the life of others (cf. §115,

1–5): the weak, the marginal, even the innocent righteous (Wisd 10, 2–12). But this ferocity will, of course, only generate more ferocity; for in typically cosmological, retaliatory fashion, mindless violence will provoke mindless violence in return. When thus caught in a spiral of violence as mindless and purposeless as any irreversible chain of cosmic reactions, human life becomes a certain road to death— death for all that is alive, whether human or infra-human.

[a] The Scriptures know this. In and of themselves (*i.e.*, by divine design) sins of ferocity and violence cry out for *retribution*. "Those who shed human blood, their blood will be shed by human hand, for God made humanity in the divine image" (Gen 9, 6; cf. Gen 4, 10; Num 35, 30ff.). "All who reach for the sword shall perish by the sword" (Mt 26, 52; cf. Jer 15, 2; Rev 13, 10) [*w*].

[6] One need not be a benighted puritan or a weak soul to understand (with the entire Jewish and Christian traditions *and* with the great philosophic traditions of the West) that the moral "weaknesses" of lust for power and capitulation to passion are in and of themselves crass moral failures, far below humanity's integrity and native

---

[*w*] The issue of deliberate violence raises, of course, the difficult question of *vengeance* as a moral and theological problem. Christians have to be especially cautious here, lest they give in to the temptation to create odious and untrue (and indeed crypto-Marcionite) contrasts between Christianity and Judaism. Israel's God is the God of love and compassion, *not* the God of wrath and vengeance. In particular, Christians must remember that the New Testament differs from the Hebrew Bible in one very important respect: no New Testament writing is the product of a community that was ever in a position to take responsibility for *public* life and regulate it. Accordingly, the absence, in the New Testament, of theological analyses of, say, just warfare or the death penalty must not be taken to imply that the early Christians simply rejected the two as morally and religiously unacceptable. Most importantly, however, Christians must realize that, in the Jewish Scriptures, and certainly in the wisdom literature, vengeance is viewed as *God's* privilege (Deut 32, 35; Ps 94, 1; Is 41, 14); only God can be trusted to accomplish justice by means of retribution and chastisement. Accordingly, human beings can always pray that God may wreak vengeance on the godless; they can even take delight in their enemies' deserved misfortune (Pss 5, 11; 58, 10–11; 137, 7–9). But human beings themselves cannot resort to retribution and revenge without further ado; both are strictly regulated (cf. *e.g.*, Lev 19, 17f.). In fact, the Jewish Scriptures, starting with David (1 Sam 24, 4f.; 26, 5–12), commend pardon and forgiveness as expressions of trust in God; and finally, in the wisdom literature, we find the outright assurance that God will repay vengeance with vengeance (Sir 28, 1. 7)—a theme Jesus will radicalize by proclaiming unconditional forgiveness and love. From a modern point of view, what is, of course, hardest to stomach in the Hebrew Scriptures is the notion that human beings must, in the service of faith and justice, be the willing, obedient instruments of divine vengeance (cf. §110, 4). Still, while this idea certainly occurs in the Hebrew Scriptures (Num 31, 1–12; cf. 25, 16–17; Judg 14, 4), it occurs relatively rarely; and in any case, it is firmly told apart from murder in the service of self-advancement (cf., *e.g.*, 2 Sam 4, 8–12).

dignity. As such, they are objectively sinful, even if they are often inculpable in particular cases, due to "invincible ignorance" or to the lack of even the most rudimentary habits of discipline and civility.[62]

[7] Two New Testament documents make this very clear: the Letter of Jude and the second Letter of Peter—the latter an early second-century document of uncertain origin dependent on Jude, or rather, a full-orchestra version of it, with a number of variations added by way of reinforcement. The author does not mince words:

The Lord knows how to rescue devout people from their trials, and to hold the wicked for the Day of Judgment, to punish them, especially those who go in for foul bodily lusts and hold the Lord's rule in contempt. Bold, self-important, . . . creatures of instinct, speaking ill of things they do not understand, like wild animals born but to be captured and destroyed, they will be paid in kind, wrong inflicted for wrong done. Enjoying debauchery in broad daylight, they are a shame and a disgrace when they join you in your love meals, wallowing in their fraudulence, with their sights set on adulterers, their appetite for sin never appeased. They will entrap unsteady souls, their hearts are well-versed in greed, children of God's curse that they are. . . . These people are wells dried up, clouds blown about by a storm; deepest darkness is being kept in store for them. They make noises as hollow as they are high-sounding; by dint of bodily lusts entrap people who have only just escaped from among people living in error. They promise them freedom even while indentured to destruction themselves—after all, anybody mastered by anybody else is his slave. For, having once escaped the world's pollution through the knowledge of our Lord and Savior Jesus Christ and then again caught and conquered by it, their final condition is worse than their initial. For it would have been better for them never to have known the way of righteousness than to know it and then turn away from the sacred commandment handed on to them. They have become cases in point of the proverbial truth: "A dog will back to his own vomit" and "A washed sow will back to the mud to roll in it."

(2 Peter 2, 9–10. 12–14. 17–22)

[8] Yet there is an even deeper misery that besets individuals and communities that thus live on the edge of human life, captives of the power of passion and oblivious of the freedom of either the mind or the spirit. Due to their dependence on the world and the flesh, the cosmos itself loses its grandeur to them and the life of the senses its verve; both cease to carry them up and away, in the direction of a transcendent God (cf. §102, 8). But humanity's native orientation to God remains ineradicable, so the sensual and the influential typically develop habits of obsessive, quasi-religious attachment to, and reliance on, the instruments of violence, the possession of impressive material wealth, and the intense enjoyment of the lower functions of the sentient life. Not infrequently, this is accompanied by the wor-

ship of painfully subhuman *idols* (cf. §114, 4). Small wonder the
New Testament (and the Pauline corpus in particular) can equate
the life of power and passion with idolatry.

[a] A telling example of this is found in the Letter to the Christian
community in Philippi (Phil 3, 17–21). Availing himself of a Jewish idiom that occurs with great frequency in most of the New Testament traditions, Paul raises the question, How are we to "walk"
(Gk. *peripatein*; cf. Heb. *hālakh*)? Thus, what is at issue is *life style.*
Paul begins by recommending *mimēsis.* The Christians at Philippi
are to learn from example, both his own and that of other
Christians who have learned from him: "Join in imitating me, and
observe those who walk in the manner you see us exemplifying."
To enhance this exhortation to shared Christian conduct, Paul
brings up a contrasting example, namely, the dissolute behavior
with which the Christians in Philippi can be taken to have been familiar from contacts with their pagan neighbors: drinking to excess, carousing, debauchery, licentiousness (cf. Rom 13, 13). Numerous influential voluntary associations in the Roman cities, including Rome itself, were only too well known for these forms of
intemperance, and for the seditiousness that regularly accompanied them. Paul does not mince his words: "Their end is undoing;
their God is the belly and their glory is in their shame; [in short,]
they are earth-minded" [*x*].

[b] Several observations are in order here. First, the middle section of this tirade is a parallelism, in which "God" and "glory" (Gk.
doxa) are semantic equivalents [*y*]. Secondly, the reference to the
belly *(koilia)* certainly connotes the lower passions and instincts,
whereas "shame" *(aischynē)* may very well refer to the sex organs.
Both idioms derive from the Hellenistic understanding of the hier-
archy of parts and functions that prevails in the human body as a
whole. The body's members and organs are more eminent according as they are situated higher, away from the earth, or less "weak"
—*i.e.,* less tender to the touch. Thus the eye is more eminent than

---

[*x*] In writing this, I am endorsing the interpretation proposed by my friend and
colleague Wendy Cotter, who persuasively argues that it is highly improbable that
Paul's denunciations are aimed at either Judaizers or gnostic Christians. Cf. her
"Our *Politeuma* is in Heaven: The Meaning of Philippians 3. 17–21."

[*y*] In the vast majority of cases, the Septuagint renders Hebrew *kabhōd* ("glory")
by *doxa.* In the Hebrew Bible, *kabhōd* is often a metonymy for the divine Name.
This makes it tempting to interpret *doxa* in the present passage as a metonymy for
"God." In any case, *doxa* occurs in close association with the word "God" in many
places in the Pauline corpus, especially Romans and 1 and 2 Corinthians.

the ear and the hand more eminent than the foot; the head is nobler than the chest, and the chest nobler than the belly, which in turn is nobler than the genitals [z].

Thus our text shows that the pursuit of power and the objects of passion are potential idols. To realize this, all the Christians in Philippi have to do is to look at the immoral life style current in the many other voluntary associations in town, where people, uncouth and without sufficient status, join forces, so as to secure for themselves the sense of worth and the influence that is so hard to come by in any urban environment patrolled by an imperious military.

[9] We must wind up. Those who live mainly by power and passion live in a cosmos that constantly reminds them, one way or another, of the very thing they live in constant dread of: *finitude*. All cosmic combinations and ventures, including human ones, must obey its laws. In the biophysical and psychophysical world, finitude concretely means: *life is precarious, death is certain.* The life dominated by passion and power is, therefore, inherently marred by a bitter irony. For what the worldly, sensual life passionately, and indeed desperately, struggles to delay, defy, and deny is worldliness's and sensuality's only assured end: death (cf. Rom 6, 21).

The old connection: sin and death.

---

[z] In the first Letter to the Corinthians, Paul uses this analysis of the human anatomy to teach the Christian community that in order to bring about *unity and equal standing for all* in the Body of the Church Christians must practice *affectionate attention and studied inequality.* The more fortunate members in the Christian community are to extend to the less fortunate care and concern in reverse proportion to their lowly position, and they are to do so freely and generously. Only in this way will they succeed in reassuring those of low status that they are members of the Body as fully as they themselves rightly assume they are (1 Cor 12,12–26; cf. §150, 6, a).

CHAPTER 16

Reason, Judgment, Prejudice: Deliberation and the Moral Life

ALIENATION, DELIBERATION, VIRTUE, JUSTICE, CONSCIENCE

[§134] THE LIFE OF DELIBERATION AND VIRTUE

[1]   No identity without alienation, it was proposed (§122, 1, b). But alienation is not a black-and-white proposition; it involves us in a dynamic *process* with many shades of grey (or rather, perhaps, more happily, numerous shades of color).   And since we are not just cosmic but also human, alienation reflects the whole range of dynamics inherent in *humanity*. That is to say, it occurs at various *levels*—cosmological, anthropological, theological (cf. §126, 5, b).

The previous chapter focused on our engagement with otherness as it operates at the cosmological—*i.e.,* biophysical, psychophysical, sentient—level. At this level, human beings live by dint of *cosmic mutuality* (§115, 8).   They not only draw life and growth from cosmic otherness; they also contribute to it; and they do so not only by depending on cosmic otherness or by facing it down and forcing it to comply with them, but also by letting it depend on them, and even by submitting to its forceful impact. At this level, our *sensibilities* are formed, and indirectly, our *mentalities*.

The present chapter is devoted to the next level of the dynamics of alienation. Here the issues are properly anthropological. How does engagement with otherness operate in the distinctively human, *deliberate* life—the life of emergent rationality and free choice, of growth and development in humanity proper, and thus, of *morality and* (at least by implication) *immorality*? Let us begin with a brief sketch.

While holding the appalling capacity for a subhuman life governed largely by passion, life in cosmic alienation naturally has a positive prognosis (§122, 1, e). It lends itself to the characteristically human life—a life not only disciplined and civilized, but also positively and deliberately moral. If things go well in our growth and development, the nurture and the discipline with which others sustain and fashion in us will awaken in us, in due course, an awareness of our own place in the community. This will help bring to the surface specific character traits and sensibilities both individual and communal; these will in turn support reliable habits of self-discipline as well as lay the foundation for properly *chosen* commitments. Beyond this, the care freely offered to us by others will inspire in us an emergent sense of self, along with a first awareness of an individual (or rather, personal) *conscience*, mainly in the form of a developing moral sense.

This conscious self (which is a conscientious self as well) is elusive —hard to pin down and observe. It also has an odd way of surprising us as we develop. It will surface, sporadically perhaps but unmistakably, in memorable experiences of self-identity and responsibility, but also, less intelligibly, of confusion about and discontent with ourselves. If and to the extent that we really mature, this deeper, mysterious self will even manifest itself habitually, often by way of a basic, wordless sense of contentment with how we are turning out and who we are, especially if we are fortunate enough to find ourselves surrounded, affirmed, guided, and corrected by the affectionate attention shown us by morally mature others (cf. §95, 6). Thus enabled and cheered, we will find ourselves moving, whether gradually or by leaps and bounds, from craving to authentic desire, from fantasy to creative imagination, from self-maintenance and self-assertion to self-acceptance and self-possession, from absorption and immersion in otherness to positive regard for otherness. We will grow in detachment, habitually rise above passion, and attain levels of serenity and *apatheia* (cf. §111, 5) at which our moral sense is increasingly animated by a deep, liberating sense of duty (cf. §105, 3–5). Thus we will reach levels of maturity at which other-regarding, humane love becomes a real option, or even a fairly reliable habit. Accordingly, we will find ourselves empowered to prize other things in their distinctiveness, and other persons even more so; to the extent we do so, we will also discover our truer, more genuine selves. This in turn will greatly enhance our native, distinctively human ability to transcend passion and narrow self-interest. Encouraged by a curious, hard-to-put-your-finger-on love that feels like a deep-seated desire for goodness, we will find ourselves *shaping ourselves* in a truly deliberate, responsible fashion. In short, we are becoming deliberately "self-actualizing" persons, capable of both deep self-acceptance *and* loving regard for all that is other.[1] In practice, this willing formation of self takes the form of the quiet, constant pursuit of an array of consciously and freely acquired habits of enjoyably responsible living: *virtues*.

[a] Ever since the dawn of Western civilization, and specifically in the classics of Greek philosophy, virtues have been *classified*—variously, of course. Naturally, such classifications satisfy the human need for coherence and order in *understanding*. But they do much more than that. They tacitly convey that the responsible life, both communally and individually, is *a life of dynamic coherence*—that is, of coordination and harmony forged by the human spirit out of the relative randomness and multiplicity of alienation. Put differently, classification conveys that *living morally is living harmoniously and wholesomely*. One commanding classification in the theological tradition of the Christian West (and one deeply indebted to Aristotle) is found in Part II of Thomas Aquinas' *Summa theologiæ.*

[b] In the *prima secundæ*—the first part of Part II of his *Summa*—Aquinas deals with the *fundamental* aspects and qualities of "virtue." Chief among these, perhaps, is the fact that (human nature being what it is) "virtue" is to be regarded as simply synonymous with *human* virtue; accordingly, acts are moral inasmuch as they are human and *vice versa* (cf. §115, 2, [a]).[2] But in this context Aquinas also treats such basic issues as the relationship between virtue, which is spiritual and deliberate, and passion, which in and of itself is neither.[3] Even more importantly, in the *prima secundæ* Aquinas lays the foundation for the detailed *system of virtues* to be developed later, in the second part of Part II of the *Summa*—the *secunda secundæ*. He does so, for example, by first distinguishing between intellectual and moral virtues, the former being habits of understanding, the latter of will. (The distinction, he explains, is inadequate; there are moral elements in intellectual virtue, and *vice versa*.[4]) More pertinently, Aquinas goes on to identify four "principal" virtues: *prudence* (which is essentially intellectual), *justice, fortitude* and *temperance* (which are chiefly moral). Virtuous living of any kind turns on these four. This is why they are traditionally referred to as "cardinal" virtues (from Lat. *cardo*, "pivot" or "hinge": q. 61). Finally, he explains, the moral and intellectual virtues must be told apart from the theological virtues—faith, hope, and charity —on the ground that the latters' object (*i.e.*, God) surpasses the natural capacity of human reason (q. 62).

When, in the *secunda secundæ*, he develops his detailed account of the virtues (and of the vices opposed to them), Aquinas proceeds hierarchically. He opens his treatment with the "theological" virtues: faith, hope, and charity (*qq.* 1–16, 17–22, 18–46) along with all their permutations of good and evil—purity of heart, apostasy, timidity, mercy, and scandal, to name but a few. He then moves on to the intellectual and moral virtues and vices, which he treats in a descending order of moral maturity. Prudence (*qq.* 47–56) gives him an opportunity to discuss things like as craftsmanship, good counsel, shrewdness, and negligence. Sixty-seven questions—more than half the total number dedicated to the cardinal virtues—deal with justice (*qq.* 57–122); they raise issues like discrimination, mutilation, theft, false witness, fraud, and usury, but also prayer, devotions, restitution, tithes, swearing, oaths and vows, and sacrilege. The subject of fortitude (*qq.* 123–140) gives rise to treatments of, among other things, martyrdom, penny-pinching, perseverance, generosity, and vainglory. Finally, temperance (*qq.* 141–169) brings up, among numerous other things, shame, the proper use of food and drink, fasting, as well as a whole gamut of sexual issues, but also humility and pride, eagerness to learn, and (charmingly, as a subspecies of modesty, which is the habit of acting becomingly) the attractive little virtue of *eutrapelia*: a knack for play, a sense of humor, and a facility for wit,[5] as Hugo Rahner has reminded us, in an elegant essay.[6]

[c] It is hard to decide what more to admire in Aquinas' extraordinary display of erudition, discernment, and experience. It is deeply inspired by an unwavering, firmly religious and theological dedication to the pursuit of the highest forms of virtue. But it also recognizes the breadth and subtlety of the human capacity for both maturity and perversion (and along with this, for the endless twists and turns of human motivation and behavior). Most of all, perhaps, what is striking is Aquinas' kindness in appreciating the many forms of genuine virtue accomplishable by human beings habitually living their lives this side of moral perfection.

[2] Our treatment of passion, temperance, and fortitude in the previous chapter (§§127–133) has already suggested that human development toward mature virtue is apt to remain deeply beholden to the matrix from which it emerges: the sentient, passionate life and its powerful dynamics. In fact, one crucial experience in the mature deliberate life is precisely the following. Whether by leaps and bounds or gradually, we simply have to become conscious of the extent and the depth to which the deliberate life remains tied in with passion and the senses. And it is part of moral maturity not not only to learn to accept this, but also, and especially, to take responsibility for it. In

Plato's vivid image, only if the charioteer—the soul—knows how to curb the horse that is unruly will he succeed in getting the whole team of the horses of instinct to take him where he wants to go.[7] We cannot live without passion and sense, so we realize as we mature; but if we live largely by them we will find ourselves mindlessly craving, not only to *live*, but also to *secure life* at all costs. Worse, we will find ourselves fighting to secure life by hook or by crook, regardless, against all odds and against all comers. Only on the basis of this sobering piece of self-knowledge can we make the much-needed efforts, not only to discern the difference between the impulse of vital passion and the life of the mind, but also to act on that discernment in such a way as to integrate sense and sensibility into life of deliberation in a balanced fashion. And conversely, only to the extent that we succeed in creating this balance will we also begin to plumb the depth of humanity's inclination and even preparedness to place its powers of deliberation mindlessly at the service of passion and sensuality. Thus a good sign of growth in the direction of our true (if always to some extent presumed) integrity is this: that we find ourselves consciously noticing as well as acknowledging the extent to which we are beset by a clutter of confusions and imbalances inherent in alienation—confusions and imbalances giving rise to concupiscence at the sentient level (§113, 3, b). And on the other hand, should we find ourselves habitually judging and taking action rashly and inconsiderately (that is, on the basis of passion, imbalance, sensibility, and the waves of concupiscence), we would do well to take this as a sign of personal and moral misdevelopment; for we would be allowing ourselves to be led by the instinctual, the agreeable, or (at best) the merely convenient, rather than by the reasonable, the normative, the conscientious, the truly *humane.* This invites close analysis and elaboration.

[a] Let us start with a note about the *expository procedure* to be used in this chapter (cf. §7, 2). We will begin our inquiries with some preliminary theoretical observations with a very broad scope; they will take up the remainder of the present section. These observations concern the relationships between the two elements of moral experience just outlined: the pull of our involvement in the world of otherness and the inner voice of our own conscience (cf. §105, 4 and [e]). These matters are treated ahead of everything else in this chapter for the following important reasons.

[b] Like the treatment of the passionate life offered in the previous chapter, a crucial focus of our treatment of the deliberate life

in this chapter will be *moral development*—its nature, its potential, its hazards, and its failures. That is, a vital organizing principle of the treatment to follow will be the dynamics of that distinctively anthropological feature of humanity: *moral consciousness*. Any treatment of this theme must, of course, include a treatment of the things which moral consciousness enables: deliberate moral action of the incidental and the habitual kind—*i.e.,* virtuous *acts* and *habits* of virtue.

This can also be put differently. In line with a commitment undertaken and formulated long ago (cf. §23, 7, a), the treatment of the deliberate life about to be offered will endeavor to do justice to the connection between systematic theology and *ascetical theology*. This will become especially prominent later on, toward the end of this chapter (§§139–140).

However, this firmly personalist theoretical focus makes it imperative to underscore, right from the start, that *the essence of the moral life does not lie in personal deliberation alone,* as Max Scheler— himself a personalist of true stature—has explained with such authority.[8] The reasons for this are twofold: (1) conscience is not the privilege of an individual (nor even of a closed social group), and (2) conscience is not wholly unrelated to otherness and objectivity. The consequences of this are twofold, too. Firstly, any analysis of conscience as a moral authority must be placed against the horizon of *humanity* regarded as both a *biophysical* unity and a *moral* community (or at any rate, as a global community consisting of particular moral communities). Secondly, conscience must be placed in the context of that permanent matrix of responsible human living: the *cosmos.* Let us put this differently. Both the mature concience and the conscientious, responsible life are essentially beholden to *otherness* in all its forms, and specifically, to the *values* objectively inherent in whatever is other (cf. §136, 1; cf. also §115, 11, a, [n]) [a].

[c] This can also be phrased differently. The deliberate life does, of course, tend toward (and indeed require) individualization and

---

[a] There is a secondary, specifically Catholic reason why this point is made so forcefully here. For centuries, the chief goal of the theological study of the moral life was: the training of candidates for the priesthood in the practice of hearing private confessions. This favored concentration on individual sins, virtues, and motives in moral theology. Matters related to communal morality were largely regarded as belonging in the sphere of homiletics and (in religious communities) ascetical exhortation. Over the past century and a quarter, the Catholic treatment of social and systemic sin and virtue as *shared moral concerns* (initiated and sustained to no small extent by the social encyclicals of Popes Leo XIII, Pius XI, John XXIII, Paul VI, and John Paul II) has sought to correct this traditional one-sidedness.

personalization. Morality involves human transcendence over the pressures of both instinct and the immediate situation; hence, it is a matter of *choosing*—of making *decisions* in a conscientious manner. In that sense, every single moral act, being conscientious and self-directed and in that sense autonomous, is genuinely *personal.* However, the human capacity for self-differentiation and conscientious decision and action is only the *formal,* constitutive element in the making of moral choices. The *material* element in moral decision-making is supplied by life *in alienation*—that is, by issues and choices that arise in the course of human life as it is concretely lived, inexorably tied in with otherness—other persons and other things. Without this *material* element, our conscientious choices would be purely formal and hence, without moral substance. Not even in our most personal moral decisions does our conscience, no matter how self-directed and self-motivated it may be, have only itself to consider or to live up to. Immanuel Kant was genuinely mistaken in thinking that the conscientious and deliberate life is wholly reducible to personal autonomy and freedom.

[d] This raises *a basic issue in moral theory.* It was claimed earlier on that "the responsible life, both communally and individually, is *a life of dynamic coherence*—of coordination and harmony forged by the human spirit out of the relative randomness and multiplicity of alienation" (§134, 1, a). What was argued a moment ago points in the same direction: far from being an exercise in individual moral self-suffiency, the conscientious life simply has to be, one way or another, an integrated whole—a combination of increasingly mature interior discernment and increasingly deliberate engagement with exteriority. This thesis implies two related propositions: (1) there must be, both in us and among us, an active principle of *unity* "beyond virtue" that holds together such particular virtues as we can call our own, and (2) this active principle is inconceivable except as a reality that positively relates us to otherness—*i.e.,* to *multiplicity.*

The Stoics—the recognized ethicians of the ancient world—endorsed the former of these two truths with great insistence. In fact, they were prepared to claim that the various virtues are not just *interconnected,* but simply *one;* for a person to be wise, they taught, is the same as for that person to be possessed of each and every virtue—a position not unknown in the New Testament, where the Letter of James explains that offending in one point of the law is the equivalent of not keeping the law at all (Jas 2, 10).

In a lucid essay, John P. Langan has shown how Augustine, who took the Stoics very seriously, clearly found this scriptural text a bit of an embarrassment: while it safeguarded the inner unity of the moral life, it did so at the expense of an obvious moral fact, namely, that there is such a thing as growth (and decay) in the virtuous life.[9] He opted, therefore (also with the support of Scripture), for *charity* as the principle both of the coherence among the various virtues and of growth in them. In so doing he guaranteed the two propositions set forth a moment ago. While many in number, the virtues must be interrelated if the moral life is to be of one piece, yet living persons can never escape the demand for growth in at least some virtues. Consequently, moral imperfection, while unacceptable as a matter of *principle*, is acceptable in practice, as long as Christian people *mean* to live by the love of God—that is, by charity.

Augustine's synthesis is elegant, yet (so Langan explains) it is purchased at considerable cost.[10] Firstly, in due course, the stated primacy of virtuous *intention* over virtuous *action and accomplishment* was not only to be used as an excuse for much moral mediocrity; it also helped encourage the view, so widespread in the modern era, that moral integrity is a matter of pure interiority after all. Secondly (and at least as importantly in both Augustine's day and our own), by founding the classical virtues on the explicitly Christian virtue of charity, Augustine (anxious as always to keep his distance from the culture of imperial Rome; cf. §121, 3) suggests that the virtues of the pagans are unreliable—part of ordinary human family instinct at their best and deceptive (because implicitly self-serving) at their worst. This position, already unacceptable to Augustine's own "Pelagian" contemporaries is liable to be equally unacceptable to modern Christians and particularly to post-Vatican II Catholics, who have come to recognize and admire God's Holy Spirit at work outside the limits of the visible Church.

This explains why some twentieth-century Catholic moral theologians, among whom Alfons van Kol deserves special mention, have argued in favor of the moral virtue of *humanitas* or "humaneness."[11] *Humanitas* is *mature human kindness* or "friendliness" (*philia*). Although it is "merely natural" in theory, in practice it is always a matter of graciousness freely given (cf. §95, 5, [*pp*]); there is no sound reason why it could not be called "charity" understood as a *moral* virtue with a implicitly transcendent dimension and orientation (cf. §154, 4, [*oo*]). This conception may very well have been unknown to Aquinas, who lived in a professedly Christian commonwealth and thus could be content to endorse Augustine's position; but it is highly relevant in the post-Enlightenment world we live in. *Humanitas* is the habit of natural concern for *each and every human being;* at its core lies the recognition that *human beings as such* are entitled to respect and positive regard (cf. §95, 4). In our own day, the world community is beginning to understand that human beings are *in and of themselves* subjects of "human rights." *Humanitas,* therefore, must extend beyond the narrow circle of each and every particular moral community. It must take the form of kindness to all other human beings; of readiness to understand and be open and generous to them; of readiness to bear with others and forgive them; of being disposed to give alms, share wealth, or otherwise assist the poor and the disadvantaged; of preparedness to be of assistance to other human beings *as such,* and consequently, to be actively concerned about global injustice.

[e] Mature *humanitas* defines both the extent of justice and its horizon. Let us elaborate. On the one hand, *humanitas* will seek to manifest itself in many *particular works of justice;* on the other, it will never be satisfied with these works, since the human family as a whole will always be larger than any single, particular moral community. In other words, while a present moral imperative, *humanitas* cannot stop short of *global* humanity's truly *common* good, even if —theologically speaking—this truly common good should turn out to be unattainable this side of the new heavens and the new earth.

[f] So, before turning our attention to the development of *personal* freedom, to its decadence, and to the dynamics by which the moral life of individuals can become sinfully degenerate in its entirety (§§137–140), we must elaborate the positions just formulated.

We will first undertake, under the rubric of the cardinal virtue of *justice,* some basic inquiries about *structures of alienation* as essential determinants of the deliberate, conscientious life (§135). Following that, we will engage in a first round of reflections on the critical subject of *conscience* (§136)—one which will be matched as well as complemented by a second round in chapter 18 (§155).

[§135] SYSTEMS OF JUSTICE

[1] To enable us to focus on the structures of alienation in the deliberate life, let us return to some important themes touched on more than once already.

First of all, *we live together humanly—that is, morally—by living within systems (i.e., structures) of justice.* This can be approached and clarified in a more general manner as follows.

Humanity is finite; more specifically, it is cosmic. Cosmic indeterminacy and tension are the matrix of both humanity's promise and its precariousness, of both its capacity and its weakness. Accordingly, human existence is marked, to an appreciable degree, by dynamic pressures seeking resolution and balance. Ineluctable, permanent tension prevails especially in the force field created by the dynamics of the three basic issues of human life in the cosmos: *influence, inclusion, and intimacy,* along with their endless permutations, combinations, and interferences (cf. §129, 1, a–c; cf. also §98, 4; §137, 7–8; §154, 1). Here if anywhere, the instantaneous goods are apt to be the enemy of the lasting; the dynamics of these three dimensions of cosmic alienation and the instinctive urges connected with them must be brought within the ambit of human self-transcendence. Accordingly, everywhere in the world, humane attempts at civilization and morality consist in large part in the management of the dynamics of power, association, and affection, in hopes of turning the considerable energies resident in them into humane values while reducing their explosive capacity for confusion and chaos. The result is the construction of a variety of socio-cultural systems and institutions structuring the dynamic processes unleashed by the pressures of influence, inclusion, and intimacy; in this way particular moral communities attempt to ensure broadly acceptable levels of humane interaction, in the interest of the common good. This structuring is indispensable on pragmatic and moral grounds, but even more on symbolic ones, since reliable socio-cultural systems and institutions signify higher, less palpable goods as well. Think of basic human safety, the benefits of living with dignity and in peace, and the blessing of living in the divine presence. Small wonder we frequently find such systems supported by religiously significant narrative (cf. §123, 7). However, even though the universal and religious significance of justice and the common good is far from negligible, systems of justice first of all need the *moral* support of all those they are designed to benefit; only on this condition can they be practically effective and meaningful. It follows that something focal and fundamental is required of all in the moral community: the cardinal *virtue* of justice.

[a] A caution is in order here. The matter-of-fact phrase "construction of . . . systems and institutions" in the preceding para-

graph might suggest that justice *as a virtue* is just a matter of compliance with the stated provisions of a social contract intentionally, rationally, and consensually arrived at. As a matter of fact, however, the patterns regulating the pervasive dynamics of power, trust, and *erōs* are to a significant extent a matter of something far broader and deeper than contract and consensus. They are the embodiments of a moral community's *praxis* and wisdom. That is, systems of justice are not merely practical or rational, but largely traditional and cultural; not uncommonly, they are equivalently immemorial. That is, they are frequently experienced as being simply there— wise, self-evident and self-justifying; in that sense, they are valuable cultural prejudices. Accordingly, existing patterns of power, trust, and *erōs* are seldom experienced as wholly reducible to rationality; once again, they tend to be experienced as *symbolic*. The justice they embody, therefore, is understood as surpassing merely rational criteria, even though appeals to reason are often used, not only to commend existing patterns of power, trust, and *erōs* and to maintain them, but also to criticize and adjust them. And such criticisms and adjustments are often undertaken not only on practical and deliberately moral grounds, but also for transcendent reasons.

Discerning individuals and communities have, of course, always realized that systems of justice are not purely rational, but "conventional." They have also understood that they are contingent; that is to say, they know that all socio-cultural systems are replaceable, *in principle*, by other configurations and structures. Yet those same discerning people have also been *practical*; they have by and large felt that the actually prevailing system is *in practice* "as good as any." After all, what matters is not so much that a social system is better than others (let alone "the best of all"—an undemonstrable claim often made by politicians attempting to exploit the patriotism of their audiences to get their votes); what matters is that the system is *good and wise*. No social system, including our own, is without imperfections; some of these imperfections can be corrected; the remaining are to be endured with fortitude; but in any case, this particular social system is *ours*, as well as ours to cultivate and refine; that is what matters. Thus, not even the most traditional systems of justice are neutral and simply disciplinary; they are authoritative because they are actively and even proudly (even if unthematically) *owned*. This means: systems of justice tacitly appeal to freedom of choice, and hence, to civility and virtue; in that sense, they inspire *loyalty* (or, in cases, its opposite). Thus (if we leave aside the discontent of opponents), any social system's inherent vulnerability to criticism and disapproval is balanced by cherished tradition and the felt attractiveness of the wisdom accumulated under its aegis.

[2] A second realization has already been touched on: *no system of justice is perfectly balanced.* Influence, inclusion, and intimacy are fields of experience inherently beset by imbalance and lack of resolution; accordingly, even the most settled system of justice is liable to be at least least somewhat unstable. The causes of this are twofold.

Firstly, the powerful dynamics of influence, inclusion, and intimacy strike most people as inseparably associated with the concrete structures of socio-cultural life within which they occur: existing traditions about class, race, and sexuality, not uncommonly of such long standing that they are experienced (at least by the majority) as "natural" (cf. §129, 1, a–c). Still, these given patterns tend to look more stable than they really are. Often they are quite volatile, and hence, intractable. This is the case because, in typically cosmological fashion, they are balancing acts: they contain—*i.e.,* they *both* harbor *and* keep in check—immense reservoirs of latent biophysical and psychophysical energy, and hence, of potential *passion.* To direct (or redirect) the forces of power, trust, and *erōs*, therefore, all rational systems of justice bent on self-correction must take on pre-existing arrangements that are widely (as well as anxiously) held to be sacred. Hidden fears of instability and anarchy help make prevailing social systems quite resistant to efforts at modification and refinement.

The second reason why all patterns of justice are somewhat unstable is connected with the first. All systems, while creating conditions for the pursuit of harmony and the common good, are *simplifications.* Deliberate ("rational," "artificial") social structures have this in common with prevailing ("given," "natural") ones that they set boundaries, definitions, and canons, whereas the dynamics that they must manage exist on a continuous range. Social systems not only regularly fail to accommodate exceptions; they occasionally make even the ordinary course of justice look like an imposition. They typically err in the direction of overcontrol and overregulation. It is clear that issues involving up/down, in/out, and close/far involve very palpable (and in that sense objective) goods and evils; yet in practice these issues are always matters, not of black and white, but of more and less. This means that concrete instances involving issues of control, association, or affection, even when judiciously as well as peremptorily adjudicated, never quite cease to be experienced as *relative* (cf.

§137, 13 and [*k*]). The moral life (like human life *tout court*) resists reduction to rigid rule and regulation.

Rational systems of justice that appreciate all this will, therefore, be flexible; they need to be kept flexible; to an appreciable extent, they must be open to practical accommodation; they will be humane; and since *summum ius summa iniuria*,[12] they will not insist on being absolutely principled. That is to say, in order to prevent the letter of the law from violating the prevailing sense of justice and the common good, they will mix justice with *equity* (often referred to by Catholics, especially in the context of canon law, as *epikeia*).[13] Good social systems help individuals as well as communities lift themselves above arbitrariness and chaos, but they stop short of pretending to perfect harmony; while fashioning real opportunities for justice, they refrain from claiming to embody kingdom come. Even at their best and wisest, they retain inequities; even more ominously, they remain open to manipulation and abuse.

Thus the very qualities that lend authority to systems of justice also serve to limit their authority. Patterns regulating control, association, and affection are means to strike a moral balance—no more and no less; while offering expedients to transcend the pressure of raw cosmic process, they institutionalize not perfection but the golden mean (§123, 2–4). This, of course, is the same as saying that the transcendence over raw process they achieve is imperfect; like the dynamics they regulate, even the best systems of justice remain part and parcel of humanity's situation of alienation (§123, 2–4), of its cosmic predicament (§115, 5). This has two consequences.

[a]   Firstly, the practice of justice is not self-authenticating, and thus, not self-supporting. For one thing, *systems of justice* depend on habits and dispositions that run deeper and are hard to prescribe: cooperation, friendliness, *humanitas*, love (cf. §134, 2, c–e; §154, 4, [*oo*]): all must *concur* in creating room for the claims and aspirations of all. For another, to be effective as well as fair, the virtue of justice must rely on the three other cardinal virtues. At an elemental level, all human beings without exception should learn and cultivate individual and communal *temperance*; to ensure basic humanity, the impulse of passion must be tamed, and moderation in the pursuit of aspirations and claims to influence, inclusion, and intimacy must be ensured. Furthermore, beyond temperance, there is need for *fortitude*—typically the virtue of the practical and of those growing in moral experience. It involves the willingness to work for

the common good while sustaining the frustrations inherent in the deliberate pursuit of it, amidst the conflicting and often instinctual claims and aspirations of the many. Finally, lest the system of justice become an end in itself, as well as onerous by dint of strict justice fanatically applied, any moral system needs the long view, in the form of *prudence*—typically the virtue of the more reflective and mature among the moral community's members. The latter must see to it that norms and regulations are intelligently conceived, reasonably interpreted, and flexibly applied, and make sure that cases not clearly covered by the system are intelligently, fairly, and compassionately adjudicated (not rarely by quietly letting them be).

[b] Secondly, all systems of justice typically protect against breakdown, not only those living under its aegis, but themselves as well. Very concretely, they develop means to put *pressure* on members who consistently fail to cultivate the virtue of justice in accord with the accepted patterns of justice. This pressure occurs in all forms and at all levels of association (family, household, church, community of work, and so forth) as well as by a variety of means (house and company rules, exercise of oversight, the threat of disciplinary measures). Further down the line, such instruments of pressure enable moral communities to resort to judicial structures. That is, *legal* forms of justice are necessary in order to ensure a minimum common good, and *forensic* enforcement of laws is needed to insure, among other things, that conflicts meet with just judgment and fair treatment, and non-compliance with fair punishment.

Here we have reached morality's lower end. Here the troubling question arises if there exists a point where humanity and morality (cf. §115, 2, [*a*]) simply degenerate into the sub-human and the irretrievably a-moral. Faced with this extreme, moral communities must develop patterns of justice to deal responsibly with its morally dysfunctional members—some stuck at pre-moral levels of development through no fault of their own (§129, 1; §130, 1, f), others regressed to them, others unwilling (or so it would seem) to lead minimally moral lives (cf. §128, 2, a–b).

[3] The third realization: *in practice, even the most responsible systems of justice are biased.* Such biases favor those enjoying positions of advantage in the fields of influence, inclusion, and intimacy. This fact (of which the Jewish and Christian traditions have long been aware and frequently severely critical) can be explained and understood as follows.

Like all socio-cultural structures, systems of justice are susceptible to change. In typically anthropological fashion, they embody *particular* intellectual and moral *choices*. Consequently, the case for their adjustment, refinement, and revision is never closed. But, as already explained, the roots of their instability run deeper than the anthropological level; it is with good reason that this section has alluded more than once to "passion" and "raw process." Human culture and morality are never wholly protected against the relatively unfocused impulses that characterize the infrahuman cosmos; accordingly, socio-cultural change of any but the almost imperceptible kind is hazardous. To the detached, free-thinking mind the possibilities of cultural and moral arrangement may seem legion, and changing the system may look like an interesting thing to undertake. But persons who are realistic (that is, practical because wise), will not be so naive. They appreciate humanity's cosmic condition; consequently, they are apt to be aware just how easily *form*—that vital prerequisite of all morality—can be overwhelmed by instinctive habit and passion. They also know that in the long run not every form "works" equally well.

All this becomes manifest when cultural and moral arrangements are altered, and not just when they are altered erratically or violently, but also in rational, responsible ways. Visceral reactions will abound; a vast amount of passion, not all of it constructive, is released—passion of craving as much as passion of temper (§127, 2–5). To think that moral communities achieve (or can achieve, or should achieve) systemic adjustment, refinement, and revision by deliberation and sweet rationality alone amounts to a frightful failure to appreciate the precariousness of the higher goods that human communities know they somehow represent, but often do not see their way to representing in a satisfactory manner.

Still, despite the cosmic odds and the uncertainty of human accomplishment, the demanding task of developing systems of justice is (certainly in the Jewish and Christian traditions) a *human* responsibility—part of the management of an unruly cosmos and a *ditto* humanity. Accordingly, Jews and Christians can never regard any cultural or moral systems as *perfect*—that is, as transcendently protected against the pressures of the very dynamics they seek to govern. In doing so, they recognize the following obvious fact of social life. In "the real world," those who enjoy positions of advantage (those in control, those at the center of the action, those assured of affection) normally have a bigger stake in the functioning of the socio-cultural balancing act than the weak, the marginal, and the lonely and unloved; consequently, the influential, the pivotal, and the well-liked must carry a heavier load of moral responsibility on behalf of *all*. "All" here really means "all." It includes all those whom the Hebrew scriptures graphically lump together in the phrase "the widow and the orphan"— that is to say, those whose well-being, in God's eyes, is the real touchstone of the caliber of a community's *humanitas*, and hence, of the quality of its structures of justice.

Still, even well-balanced socio-cultural systems (that is, systems in whose construction and maintenance the powerful, the insiders, and the loved have made a point of resorting to reason and putting impartiality and the common good ahead of self-interest) are biased by the very dynamics they are meant to manage. All people wish to secure the goods held out by the dynamics of influence, inclusion, and intimacy; consequently, the many who are inadequately involved in the construction of the social system (as well as the many who *feel* they are inadequately involved) are apt to be at least somewhat dissatisfied (rightly or wrongly, but then again, who determines, conclusively, who is right and who is wrong?) with the share of the goods that comes to them under the system that currently channels the dynamics. Thus, not only is every moral community is liable to stop short of the truly common good (and hence, liable to divine judgment), but also continuously open to destabilization from within, on squarely moral grounds. *The moral credibility of social systems and established practices of justice is intrinsically limited; justifiable moral discontent is and remains inherent in the concrete deliberate life.* This realization has consequences both moral and theological.

[4] The construction, maintenance, and reconstruction of systems of justice is part of humanity's responsible stewardship on behalf of itself and the cosmos (§98, 5). This stewardship task is obviously never completed. Finitude and alienation are here to stay. Consequently, the moral life never provides total relief from the neuralgic ambiguities connected with the search for balance and the golden mean (cf. §123, 2–4). For this reason, particular systemic arrangements or even complete systems, held by some (or even by many) to be reasonable, just, and liberating—equitable embodiments of the common good—will be judged arbitrary, biased, or confining by others.

This means that the dynamics of influence, inclusion, and intimacy will perpetually raise new ethical issues, which will test existing systems as well as the moral commitments they have helped shape. At times, this will result in systemic change, brought about by activity of the discerning or undiscerning kind, whether individual or communal. But every activity (just like all discernments) will in turn be to some extent affected, positively or negatively, by existing patterns, by the preferences and prejudices of the main change agents, not to mention the happenstance inherent in the dynamics of influence, inclusion, and intimacy. This means that not even the most responsible, humane social change is ever impartial. The common good—that ideal of the moral life—turns out to be elusive. *No social system regulating control, association, and affection can entirely succeed in channeling these forces in a morally definitive fashion.* In the end, ethical systems are no more self-sustaining or self-justifying than justice itself.

This has consequences. Social systems have this in common with positions: they implicitly connote alternatives and thus invite comparison with them (cf. §108, 1; 4). In that sense, they are "weak." They do have strengths, but these strengths are partial; they will show up as strengths only if and when the system as a whole is discerningly interpreted. But this raises the fundamental, distinctively anthropological issue of *analogy*. All socio-cultural systems are *relative* and thus, *comparable*, and it is only *in the comparison* that they will reveal, not only their characteristic strengths, but also the degree of their congruence with, and openness to, other cultures—that is, their capacity for *inclusiveness*. Socio-cultural systems that despise or resist such comparisons (and they usually do so by setting themselves up as superior, incomparable, and practically absolute) condemn themselves to sclerosis. Worse, they also become systems of *discrimination* and *prejudice*, not only in regard to the outside world, but internally as well. And to the extent they do so, they become *inhumane*. We will have occasion to come back to these themes later on (§137, 7–13).

[5] Sooner or later, the fact that *all* social systems, without exception, are mutually comparable, and hence, *relative*, will drive home a further realization: socio-cultural systems tacitly appeal to realities beyond themselves—that is, to realities of a transcendent nature. In other words, the dynamics of power, trust, and affection, being both pervasive and never quite resolved, naturally end up appealing to the religious imagination. This implies that the moral life enjoined by the social system demands that it be placed in the perspective of ultimate meaning, in the manner it is recognized as authoritiative by the moral community. All structures of justice, therefore, implicitly demand that they be both interpreted and examined in the light of these higher realities—that is, interpreted and examined *theologically*.

[a] Polytheistic cultures do so largely mythologically. In them, the ceaseless play and interplay of influence, inclusion, and intimacy is the manifestation of superior cosmic forces. These are hard to resist, often impersonal, ultimately intractable, a-moral, forever at loggerheads with each other, and hence, dividing humanity. As a result, in such civilizations, human beings and communities tend to find themselves permanently locked into fixed alliances, not only with higher powers, but also with a segment of humanity, namely, "their own kind" (which obviously is taken to be, by definition, civilized). By the same token, they find themselves at odds with certain other powers and with certain other segments of humanity, namely, "the other kind" (which they take to be, by definition, barbaric). In seeking to be moral in such a framework of meaning, human communities and the individuals in them often imagine themselves to be involved in a struggle of cosmic proportions, in which different spheres of influence, inclusion, and intimacy are pitted against one another. This implies, in the end fatalistically, that humanity's moral responsibility in every relevant sphere of life is sharply limited. After all, if local biases and prejudices are sustained and ratified by superior powers, the scope of the religious imagination is sharply limited by accidents of birth and circumstances of time and place. No wonder the great universalist moral philosophies of the ancient world, notably Platonism and Stoicism, could insist so firmly that human freedom and fulfillment were attainable only by those who succeeded in relinquishing or transcending these busy, partial, and frequently divisive powers, and made their home in the realm of timeless Truth or transcendent Reason (cf. §27, 4, a).

[b] By contrast, the tradition of Jewish and Christian monotheism has accepted these powers, in struggling faith and hope, as part of God's unfinished creation—that is to say, as part of an undomesticated cosmos and a wild and even wayward humanity, to which the One True God is nevertheless no stranger (cf. §79, 1–4). Accordingly, it has regarded the dynamics of control, solidarity, and *erōs*, along with their inherent imbalances and perpetually unresolved tensions, as fundamentally good and positive. Hence, it has considered them emancipated *in principle* from the invisible powers. This belief stirs the religious imagination. To the eye of faith, far from lacking perspective or ultimate purpose, the struggle for justice here and now has an infinite scope. The dynamics of power, trust, and affection, intractable as they are, *can* help *all* of humanity move

in the direction of the living God, who alone is all-powerful, all-embracing, all-loving (cf. §98, 1; 4, a–c; 5).

Still, like all created things, the dynamics of influence, inclusion, and intimacy lead to God by embodying not perfection but finitude, by offering not instant resolution but ceaseless ambiguity, by symbolizing not the definitive state of humanity and the cosmos but a provisional one—that is, one suggestive of transcendence yet substantially unresolved. This state of irresolution invites the practice of disciplined, mature, realistic human responsibility. Clearly, the life of power, trust, and intimacy must be reliably organized. But in the last analysis, responsible human stewardship can transform raw energy into morality and harmony only if it is done so at God's behest and in behalf of God (§98, 5).

Thus, ultimately, the human struggle for justice must orient those who participate in it to God, by way of faith, hope, and loving self-abandon. This will enable them to accept and embrace the relentless dynamics of influence, inclusion, and intimacy; this will permit them to channel and humanize them carefully, imaginatively, patiently. Humanly speaking, only by virtuous living can power, trust, and *erōs* be genuinely meaningful and productive (cf. §115, 10). Only in this way, too, will those who *are* civilized and just become a credible and indeed attractive portrayal of the transcendent God (cf. §75, 2), to whom they owe everything and to whom, ultimately, they offer themselves, along with their moral attainments.

[6] This, however, is a never-ending task, for, like power, trust, and affection themselves, the structures of justice which human beings forge in order to regulate these dynamisms will invariably remain inconclusive. For while it is true that worship of the living God lacks integrity if it is not verified in responsible moral conduct, it is also true that the structures that embody and support responsible moral conduct are and will always remain incommensurate with God's mystery. Even the most virtuous behavior and the most sacred structures of the good life are part of a universe that remains imperfect (cf. §44, 2; §45, 2). As such, the authoritative structures that regulate the dynamics of influence, inclusion, and intimacy are (to restrict ourselves to the Christian faith perspective) part of Christianity's "transitional" state (§76), even though they are eschatological in orientation.

At their best (that is, when they succeed in turning potential for chaos into the kind of liberating harmony that does at least substantial justice to all involved) structures of justice are virtually sacramental. Normally, they do not cease to be the stuff of ambiguity, struggle, concupiscence. At their worst, their limiting features stifle the liberating ones; when that happens, the morality they embody and commend becomes "closed," as Henri Bergson has splendidly explained in *Les deux sources de la morale et de la religion* (ET *The Two Sources of Morality and Religion*). Systems of justice, in other words, can become so dense and impenetrable that they no longer leave room (in Lonergan's phrase) for the "insight" that makes structures of limitation habitually discernible as vehicles of the human attunement to the Transcendent (cf. §137, 9, a).

[a] This raises an important theological issue of a practical nature. The Jewish and Christian traditions occasionally claim, by means of both narrative and affirmation, that certain authoritative patterns and institutions (whether immemorial or historic) that regulate the dynamics of power, trust, and affection are the result of revelation —that is, of "direct" divine intervention or commandment. In light of what has been explained (cf. §§94–95), such statements are best interpreted as expressions of the community's collective theological imagination; they express the experience that such human arrangements are born out of faith and authorized by God, and thus canonical; but they *can* be canonical only because they are *symbolic*, and hence, *transparent*. This transparency is vital, for taken *by themselves*, even the most sacred systems of justice are not conclusive (cf. §137, 10, and a–b) [*b*]. At their best, they are quasi-sacramental, divinely graced and assured instruments of *humanity's moral and*

[*b*] Instances far too numerous to mention support the thesis that stable structures of influence, inclusion, and intimacy, which the Jewish and Christian traditions regard as divinely authorized, are so regarded on *discretionary* and *symbolic* grounds. That is, while they do render God and God's will present, they are not as absolute as, say, "One Lord, one faith, one baptism" (Eph 4, 5). To use a catholic idiom, they are "sacramental." This implies that they are not immutable in an absolute sense. Thus both the biblical account of Israel's history and the biblical and post-biblical history of Judaism show a great variety of bearers of sacred and moral power and authority, a great variety of definitions of inclusion in the community of life and worship, as well as a great variety of laws regulating affective relationships —sexual, marital, and familial. All these different determinations reflect, not absolute uniformity, but differences of time, place, and circumstance, as well as (most of all) different stages of faith-development. Yet *all* the determinations are certified and enforced, with varying degrees of acceptance and permanence, by appeals to divine authorization. The record of the Christian community's history reflects the same discretionary process. Internally most of all, but also in regard to the outside world, the Christian community has never regarded as divinely warranted only one single form of community authority, one fixed set of conditions for community membership, and one single form of the life of affective intimacy.

religious self-management. Accordingly, those who live by them typically value them and feel responsible for them. As a result, they will be imaginative, discerning agents of their (re)construction; they will search for rules of conduct that secure impartiality and balance —those emblematic attributes of justice—in the service of the common good of the moral and religious community.

[b] However, there is an ominous alternative to transparency: *prejudice.* Wherever and whenever sacred structures of power, solidarity, and affection are taken for granted or become ends in themselves, they turn opaque; they harden into structures of unexamined living; that is, they turn not only inadequate but also unjust. As a result, they begin to divide the very people they are meant to unite as a moral community. Custom has a lot to do with this sort of sclerosis. Still, not infrequently is it less a function of sluggish custom than of latent passion; most commonly in the form of collective fantasies inspired by prejudice of the type that leads to loss of realism and vision—a subject to which we must come back (§137, 13, b). For now it suffices to observe that immobile social structures, including sacred ones, are apt to lose their symbolic value. They stop representing not just divine Transcendence but also human freedom. Instead, they turn into limitations placed on human intelligence and responsibility, both morally and theologically. No wonder such patterns and institutions of justice are widely experienced as obstacles to human persons' access to their better moral selves *and* to the living God. In Paul Tillich's pointed idiom, they become "dead symbols."[14] Such structures are in need of responsible reappropriation, and maybe even more of fundamental reform.

[7] So far, we have dwelt at some length on the *material* element of the deliberate, responsible life, namely, the structures of alienation. Now we must turn to its *formal* component: conscience and its uses.

[§136] CONSCIENCE

[1] Conscience is elusive. It is not a fixed, solid entity within us that readily offers itself to observation and study. This is not surprising. Conscience is a function of humanity's transcendental attunement to all that is, and thus, ultimately, to God. Like this attunement itself, conscience can comes into felt, effective existence only by emergence —a lifelong process. Like the transcendental attunement, too, conscience can become an "object" of understanding only by *reflection*

(cf. §112, 2). But then again, what gives rise to this reflection is none other than the experience of conscience itself, both in others and in oneself. But since the mature experience of conscience is a function of the developing moral life, conscience offers itself for reflection only to those learning to live conscientiously [c].

We are driven to the conclusion that conscience comes into its own only in alienation. That is, the *formed* conscience arises through and within concrete *situations*—situations involving objective, "material" values "out there," which shape the given, distinctively human talent of moral responsibility. Thus, while arising from the depth of the human spirit, conscience never ceases to be beholden to otherness, as to the matrix of its own emergence. Conscience's highest function, the sense of duty, will not emerge in us apart from a reliable, realistic, fairly articulate, ever-developing moral sense (cf. §105, 3–5).

This moral sense derives almost entirely from otherness, of course. It results from behavior enjoined on us or suggested to us or exacted from us or drawn forth from us by "outside" factors: early training and conditioning, familial nurture, religious and cultural formation, and many other forms of discipline, challenge, invitation, and precept. The moral sense also results from the demands made upon our sense of duty by the values spontaneously felt to be objectively resident in otherness—other persons, other things.

It follows that positive, situational data, past, present, and to come, are conscience's starting capital as well as the stuff of its continuing activity and development. External facts and objective values, in other words, remain pertinent to us even in our deepest moral maturity; at no time can conscience afford to stop appreciating, recounting, evaluating, and reevaluating them.

It also follows (as Max Scheler has so admirably shown in *Der Formalismus in der Ethik* [ET *Formalism in Ethics*], and as his admirer, Pope John Paul II, has recalled in his encyclical *Veritatis Splendor*) that the genuinely mature conscience is not the individual conscience that claims to have successfully emancipated itself from the matrix of its emergence, which is otherness. That is to say, the mature conscience is not simply autonomous, responsible to nothing and nobody but itself, and hence, purely formal and autonomous (as the Enlightenment tended to imagine, foolishly). Rather, it is *the conscience that has*

---

[c] This thesis remains to be complemented by its counterpart: conscience, when worn down and stifled by habits of moral apathy and sin, will move toward effective non-existence; it will then, of course, elude reflection as well. Cf. §140, 5.

come alive, thanks to the developing sense of duty deeply resident within itself (that is, ultimately, the sense of God), *to the objective conditions of its own ongoing emergence*. These "objective conditions" consist of life as it is lived in practice, day after day. The mature conscience, in other words, results (in the words Plato attributes to Socrates) from the practice of

. . . raising questions, on a daily basis, regarding the nature of virtue and regarding the other things about which you can hear me talk with others and scrutinizing both myself and others.[15]

[2] In mounting this argument, we have, very importantly, uncovered the first and fundamental use of conscience. *Conscience represents, within our own selves, ourselves as essentially responsible subjects* (cf. §105, 4, [e]). By keeping us alive to moral issues that face us, our conscience represents, to each of us, the "better self" that we have become; it also represents to us the "better self" that we are not or not yet, yet are natively called to be.

Let us term this use of our conscience *self-representative*. We avail ourselves of our conscience in a self-representative manner whenever we have recourse to it as the inner impulse that both prompts and enables us *to take responsibility for ourselves as free agents*. Let us phrase this more descriptively. We use our conscience in a self-representative manner whenever we scrutinize, test, and appraise our own lives and the lives of others with whom we are connected by bonds of community, with a view to both amending our own lives and enhancing their moral quality. This occurs at two levels.

[a] More obviously and perceptibly, by taking stock of our behavior, we test and examine our actions (and thus indirectly ourselves) *by existing norms*. These are offered to us by our concrete *moral sense* —that is, by such prevalent moral norms as we recognize as conscientiously binding on ourselves. In doing so, we at least implicitly regard these norms as equally binding, as a matter of ordinary justice, on other members of the moral (and religious) community or communities of which we are members. Conscience understood as moral sense is what enables us to examine our lives and ourselves, so as to reveal to us our moral standing, both in our own eyes and (presumably) before the tribunal of the particular moral community to which we belong and presumably are content to belong.

[b] Yet more unobtrusively and basically, conscience enables us to test our actions *and* ourselves by reference to a decisively higher tri-

bunal, *viz.*, our *sense of duty*—the drive for goodness residing within us. (Incidentally, while deeply personal, our sense of duty is hardly ever a wholly individual experience: we are usually aware of sharing it with trusted friends and associates.) Conscience understood in this latter capacity represents, at the center of our day-to-day lives, the "perfect selves" we natively aspire to being, at least implicitly, before God. This boundless aspiration is superior to any *particular* moral norm, no matter how conscientiously accepted and followed; accordingly, it essentially transcends the limited norms by which the moral community is used to test itself and its members. For *the true measure of the moral caliber of our "cause"*—that is, of our human lives as encompassing projects—*is* (not law but) *never-ending desire.* It alone sets the ever-receding standard of excellence that keeps alive what is deepest in us: the ceaseless quest both for moral integrity and for the transcendent Goodness that beckons us beyond all moral integrity.

Socrates, who knows this and who makes this quest a matter of daily practice, explains that it springs from "the familiar oracular impulse of the divine spirit" in him. This spirit not only warns him away from what he should not do; it is also the "manifestation of the god"—the mysterious divine presence deep down within him, about which he finds it impossible to "keep quiet" without "being disobedient to the god."[16]

No less than Socrates, John Henry Newman is familiar with the experience of transcendence as integral to the experience of conscience; he can even turn it into an argument for the existence of a transcendent God (cf. §105, 4–6 and [*e*]). But he is equally concerned to regard the moral sense—that yardstick of objectivity and adjustment to otherness—as an integral part of the experience of conscience (even though he rightly holds that particular duties enjoined by the moral sense are legitimately subject to change, and hence, so we may infer, to responsible debate: §105, 3).

[3] Thus, for Newman as for the great Tradition of the West, conscience is that mysterious reality within us by virtue of which we *mediate*, more and more responsibly as we grow, *between the living God and the whole range of values resident in the universe, including humanity.* Little wonder that, in a splendidly indignant passage, Newman can turn this double conviction into a sharp indictment of the way in which modern liberalism has confused conscience with autonomous, wholly self-regarding, heedless self-will:

. . . now let us see what is the notion of conscience in this day in the popular mind. When men advocate the right of conscience, they in no sense
mean the rights of the Creator, nor the duty to Him, in thought and deed,
of the creature; but the right of thinking, speaking, writing, and acting, according to their judgment or their humour, without any thought of God at
all. They do not even pretend to go by any moral rule, but they demand,
what they think is an Englishman's prerogative, for each to be his own master in all things, and to profess what he pleases, asking no one's leave, and
accounting priest or preacher, speaker or writer, unutterably impertinent,
who dares to say a word against his going to perdition, if he like it, in his
own way. *Conscience has rights because it has duties;* but in this age, with a large
portion of the public, it is the very right and freedom of conscience to dis-
pense with conscience, to ignore a Lawgiver and Judge, to be independent
of unseen obligations. It becomes a licence to take up any or no religion, to
take up this or that and let it go again, to go to church, to go to chapel, to
boast of being above all religions and to be an impartial critic of each of
them. Conscience is a stern monitor, but in this century it has been super-
seded by a counterfeit, which the eighteen centuries prior to it never heard
of, and could not have mistaken for it, if they had. It is the right of self-
will.[17]

[a] In the last resort, therefore, conscience is oriented away from
self and toward both otherness and Transcendence. This explains
why the great Tradition has recognized a second, more self-transcendent, and hence, more admirable, use of conscience: conscience used in the service of *representation of the other.* Let us express this in different words. The Christian conscience continues
the Jewish tradition of acknowledging that certain obligations are
incumbent on us simply because the inherent worth of *others*—other persons, other things—demands that we do justice to *it.* This vital issue, largely overlooked by the Enlightenment and its aftermath, must be examined and pondered at some length, in chapter
18 (§155, esp. 4–9).

[4] For the present moment, however, it is time to move on. So far,
our treatment has explored the two basic components of the deliberate life. The first was alienation and its structures, along with their
hopes and liabilities (§135); the second was conscience and its dynamisms, as precarious as they are promising (§136). The two—otherness and conscience—meet in humanity, that is to say, in living, active, struggling human communities and individuals.

This realization must set the scene for the controlling theme of the
following sections: the dynamics of the deliberate life understood as
a whole—of its growth and its development, of its degeneracy and its
sinful decay.

SIN AS FAILURE IN HUMAN DELIBERATION

[§137] THE DELIBERATE LIFE BESET BY FANTASY AND PREJUDICE

[1] Let us begin at the beginning. From the outset, human experience is shot through with the sense, not only *that* we crave and *how deeply* we crave, but also that we must *learn what we can crave effectively*. There is a catch here. Even as we grow in consciousness and freedom, we discover that we remain significantly affected by everything that otherness in all its forms has permitted (or urged, or forced) us to want, and often continues to do so, whether we like it or not. But this implies that our emergent consciousness and freedom remain at all times relatively inexperienced and somewhat irresolute guides to action. For, as our world opens up, we find ourselves called to wider, deeper forms of truth and goodness. That is, time and again we find we are surprised by moral challenges which our past experience has only very partially prepared us to meet.

Thus, in the area of *desire* (§127, 2–3), our present consciousness and freedom never wholly assure us that what we want here and now is what we genuinely, "authentically" want. Could it be that we merely have been, or are being, *made* to want pleasurable things, by training, habit, convention, circumstances, the authority or the manipulative skills of others? Worse, we cannot even be sure that what we have been, or are being, made to want by others is what those others want for themselves; could it be they just want *us* to want it? In that case, in being agreeable and in practicing what we assume to be *mimēsis*, we are not really associating with others who are on our side; we are merely submitting to the desires of those others who have succeeded in making us dependent on them, even for our very lives and lifestyles. We never outgrow our need for dependence; so is there anything at all that I can be sure *I* want? Who really wants what? Important issues like this can be substantially unclear (cf. §150, 8).

Our predicament does not improve when we resort to *temper* (§127, 4), take charge, and endeavor to gain what we want by being forceful. For, come to think of it, are the things that we want to accomplish by force, here and now, genuinely, "authentically" the things we want? Or are we, in being forceful, merely overcompensating—masking a momentary or habitual lack of clarity and resolve on our part? And once we have, by dint of forcefulness, secured what we figured we wanted, do we still want it? Or does what we once *seemed* to want turn out to be something we were merely *being induced* to want, chiefly by the social censure we encountered and which made what we pursues

so forcefully look attractive (cf. Rom 7, 7–11)? And is the rival-creat-
ing "I" that we asserted and established in the act of being forceful
genuinely the "I" we habitually care to be?

No wonder that, as we mature, the life of continued dependence
on, and contest with, otherness will cause us to feel *consciously* torn
between an "inner" life and the challenges and demands thrust upon
this inner life from the "outside" (or so it would seem). But the moment we say this, we must recall: any "outside" we experience is really
part of *us*—that is, of our "inner" life. Being human means: to be a
self in alienation; this implies we have no choice but to experience
ourselves as *inwardly divided* in some way and to some degree (§122,
1, b; e). No wonder we feel torn, on our way to maturity, between a
fuller, authentic "self" and an incomplete, inconsistent "ego."

Of the fuller, authentic self we can be *deeply* aware, if only obscurely
and intermittently. By contrast, we far more readily experience our
ego, yet always as a function of our engagement with otherness. And
because otherness is forever in flux, the experience of our ego—our
observable, or at least discernible self—is quite inconstant and inconsistent [*d*]. Small wonder the morally mature among us feel chroni-
cally inadequate to their deeper aspirations and responsibilities. No
wonder, therefore, that even as we become freer and more deliberate
in engaging otherness (that is to say, even as we mature morally), the
experience of our emergent selves is compounded by an amalgam of
"mental passions" [*e*].

[2] The vehemence and directness of passion, it is true, is liable to
abate as we mature, grow in detachment, or simply age (or, less ap-

---

[*d*] For a fundamental philosophical and theological treatment of these topics, cf.
Louis Dupré, *Transcendent Selfhood*. Readers of Martin Buber's *Ich und Du* (ET *I and
Thou*) may have heard echoes in this paragraph as well. The "incomplete self" just
mentioned is the "I" which Buber, in the first part of his book (pp. 30–31; ET pp.
73–75) treats as the "I" that is correlated with "It"; it is the "I" that regards itself as
a defined subject *over against* objects—*i.e.,* as separate from them. Far from being
the original "I" (the "I" natively correlated to "Thou"), this is the "I" that arises *after*
we learn to tell ourselves apart from otherness—the *nachichhaft* "I." This latter "I"
is typified by self-regarding experience and use *of* the other, rather than by other-
regarding encounter *with,* and presence *to,* the other (cf. §56, 12, a and [*h*]).

[*e*] Let us hasten to stress that the turmoil of mental passion is not inhuman, let
alone immoral; in and of itself, it is natural and morally indifferent. Still, lest it run
away with us, it must be integrated—that is, accepted, moderated, and channeled.
That is, human passion, both of the instinctive and of the mental kind, invites *formation* by dint of both discipline and reason informed by discerning faith-commitment. This formation is normally made available to individuals and smaller social
units by the accumulated wisdom, both narrative and practical, of the larger, more
encompassing moral and religious *communities* of which they are part (cf. §123, 7).

pealingly, as we find ourselves drawing a firm circle around ourselves and settling for the stale comforts of Easy Street: stagnation, mediocrity, embattled ego). As discipline shapes us, by dint of growth, nurture, training, and culture, both our appetites and our passionate responses are apt to be shaped, ordered, differentiated, and even rearranged, and thus eased, tempered, sublimated. We acquire habits, some convenient, some virtuous, some dubious. And through and in all of this, a character and a personality are fashioned (if always to some extent mis-fashioned, too).

But neither habits, whether sound or questionable, nor a firmer personality, nor even a deeper sense of identity, will shelter us from the challenges of otherness (unless, again, we should settle in the sty of contentment, where we will die the slow moral death of mediocrity or self-ensconced ego).[18] As long as we are alive, therefore, we will keep on *being shaped*, for better, for worse, from the outside; otherness will keep on affecting us, willy-nilly. Underneath and alongside such personal stability as we have acquired, we will continue to encounter fairly unenlightened, unspiritual, clumsy, jumbled, haphazard modes of development, thrust upon us by "the slings and arrows of outrageous fortune."[19]

All this implies that we will never be wholly emancipated from passionate experience, nor should we be. We remain affected, vitally as well as mentally, positively or negatively, soothingly or menacingly, overtly or more subtly, by touch, nourishment, odors, fragrances, and aromas, physical closeness, sexual intimacy, telling looks, knowing glances, suggestive intonations, playful interchanges, prized possessions, socio-political and intellectual encounter, and the many challenges ordinary life offers to our biophysical selves and to our ego. In fact, much to our surprise, we may find ourselves, in our maturity, *seeking* to be affected in all these ways! Involvement with otherness, and hence, passion, also penetrates the more rational processes that mold and shape us: socialization, acculturation, skills appropriation. Most disconcertingly, alienation and passion turn out to infiltrate that (arguably) most spiritual of humanity's cultural attainments: the use of language [*f*].

[*f*] Language is, of course, a prime source of stability as well. It is mainly by virtue of the *fairly stable representative power of words and idioms* that language enables us (who live by it) to transcend particular situations and their inconclusiveness (cf. F. J. van Beeck, *Christ Proclaimed*, pp. 87–88). Yet in every kind of language-use, including writings and printed texts (including the one you are reading this very moment), there remain persistent elements of semantic instability, *and hence, of mental*

Also, if we keep maturing (again, without settling down into routines) we may find ourselves taking sharp turns, even in maturity; we may even find ourselves throwing caution to the winds and deliberately putting ourselves in the way of the possibility of a "big change." Either way, we will find ourselves changing in unanticipated ways. That is, we will stumble upon novel ways in which otherness turns out to stir up passion in us; we will find our need for both gratification and control shifting to new, unfamiliar areas of desire. Surprised, we will mutter: "Live and learn." Thus the experience of alienation continues, as long as we live; so does the experience of mental passion. This is, we discover, what life is like. We change, and we keep changing, and the one sure difference we can make even as we change consists in accepting change rather than resisting it and thus making life harder, both for us and for those around us. To the extent we accept change, we will find that it harbors both wisdom and freedom, and that it opens for us that deeper resource for changes truly deliberately chosen: an increasingly stable (*i.e.*, flexible) sense of identity.

But alienation and passion will continue to spell ambiguity—that is, at least some lack of both intellectual focus and moral resolve. This makes even the most satisfying experience of growth and development (and thus, the exciting search for authentic identity) perplexing to the end. Life in alienation, full of potential as it is, is also rife with puzzlement: selfhood and otherness, identity and alienation, authentic desire and wishes forced on us by otherness in all its forms are intertwined, almost inextricably. If we must negotiate for life (and we must), the terms of negotiation (so we discover) are never

---

passion. This is often overlooked, especially by readers of *texts*, particularly of printed texts. The reason for this is that the *appearance* of permanence and objectivity of printed texts disguises the deeper instability that underlies them. The latter manifests itself in the form of *ambiguity*, brought about by uncertainty of semantic reference, prestigious but fraudulent idioms (both well-worn and novel), and "fissures" in the web of textual meaning, where layer upon layer of unstated prejudice and ideology can hide out and lie in wait ("subtexts"). These linguistic ambiguities are, of course, as confusing and infuriating as the experience of the divided self, yet (like it) they are not intrinsically negative; the evocative power of, say, lyrical poetry and liturgical prayer (and even of theological language) substantially depends on the constructive use of ambiguity, to say nothing of the opportunity for patience and silence they create, along with latitude for freedom and deep eloquence. Accordingly, the largely negative interpretations put on the ambiguities of language by certain forms of nominalism, existentialism (cf. §11, 1, [*l*]), and deconstructionism are unconvincing; they would seem to arise out of a repressed (rationalist?) demand that language should be what none of those who speak it and live by it can ever be: wholly transparent in intention and expression, and thus, fully in the clear about identity, as well as insured, in advance, against mishap and manipulation.

wholly plain, and consequently, neither are our options. There is something ludicrous about this. Accordingly, this is where a sense of humor becomes part of moral maturity.

[3] Step by step, our analysis of the deliberate—that is, the *moral*—life has taken us into the realm of the *mental* experience of life in alienation. Once again, let us observe that here, too, the natural prognosis is positive (cf. §122, 1, e). Stimulated by otherness, we are apt to find ourselves actualized and enhanced; otherness tickles our fancy; it stirs our imagination. From our first toys and trinkets on up, we find ourselves invited and encouraged to turn otherness into the stuff of creativity, identity, and interpersonalness. Yet at the same time (as we have seen) mental life is hardly all clarity and freedom; even as habits of mature self-control transform the ways we engage otherness in action and interaction, we never cease to be moved by passion, even in our minds. One form of this (and one to which the moral life is profoundly and often painfully subject) must occupy our attention at some length: *fantasy*.

[4] It has already been suggested that we are moved by passion even in our deeper, "mental" selves. This is neither surprising nor alarming; catching our inner selves *reacting* passionately to otherness *out there* is well within the range of a life inspired by both reason and morality. This is especially true if on occasion, in the wake of a passionate experience, we come to an understanding of what went on inside us, and even more if, looking back, we are satisfied that our inner turmoil was broadly proportionate to the occasion. All the turbulence, we may thankfully notice, did not make us lose our minds, or, what amounts to the same, our connectedness with reality.

However, we experience in our minds a different variety of passion as well. We experience turmoil that is to an unsettling extent *interior* and *unconnected with objective realities*. The difference becomes obvious once we notice that, while the passionate mental episodes of this latter kind are often *triggered* by identifiable outside occurrences, the turmoil we experience is either disproportionate in intensity or unrelated in kind to the occasion that triggered it. This becomes even more obvious when we notice that the turmoil often occurs without being attributable to any occasion at all. Our minds, we thus discover, are affected, agitated, and (more ominously) swayed by *fantasy*.

[5] Fantasy usually takes the form of mental representations of the outside world, others, and ourselves, with a strong emotional impact on our conscious selves. If we pay attention to ourselves, we will find

our inner worlds teeming with such events, as long as we live. For all
minds are home to fantasy. It is part of moral maturity to learn how
to transcend fantasy, not by squelching it (a vain enterprise anyway),
but by accepting it and living with it, in a discerning manner.

And heaven knows we need discernment here. For fantasy is a Tro-
jan horse. On first inspection it is fascinating, but it shelters an army
of intractable adversaries. It is often dazzling. It can simulate, in a
thousand compelling ways, a life of emancipation, independence,
and freedom—the stuff that dreams are made of (and daydreams
even more). Fantasy has a way of generating a spate of exciting new
combinations of old images; this creates the illusion of creativity and
authenticity. The problem is, of course, that fantasy gives us little or
no *actual* otherness to deal with; exciting as the world of fantasy may
be, it is largely fictitious.

This has consequences. We are to develop morally, but we can do
so only by engagement with genuine otherness—otherness that is
really out there. But fantasy is only tenuously connected with *actual
otherness*. This means that it runs counter to moral development;
acting on fantasy as if it were reality is characteristic of the morally
immature, the narrow-minded, and the undiscerning.

Only real otherness can stir our emergent rationality and freedom;
by contrast, fantasy disrupts, discourages, and blocks development; its
hallmark is mental fixation and compulsion. This becomes clearer if
we look at our own experience: we will recall how fantasy can be a
source of apprehension, fear, and horror; it can create (again, in a
thousand dazzling ways) a world of emergencies, hazards, and men-
aces. Clearly, we must make substantial moves beyond the life of fantasy to attain moral maturity. (But this is precisely where the plot
thickens again, for the world of fantasy within us is very resilient. Fantasies have a way of punishing us for our attempts at keeping them
down in the interest of realism and self-control; they will come back
with a vengeance, to haunt us worse than ever before.)

[6] Since suppression of fantasy is of no avail, we must opt for the
way of discernment and self-knowledge. For what goes on in the life
of fantasy? Unconsciously, we keep alive, in our minds, the raw busy-
ness of past experience of life in alienation, along with its hazards
and its anxieties, and thus, with our own passionate reactions to it.
Fantasy, in other words, is a function of the human mind inasmuch
as it remains preoccupied and prepossessed by past engagements at
close quarters with otherness, and by the passions tied in with such

encounters. Out of this vague backlog of half-integrated and uninte-
grated experiences of past otherness (of both the purely cosmic, random kind and the human, deliberate kind), fantasy fashions *illusory
alternatives to present otherness.* Instead of enabling us to take the cues
for our engagement from *actual* ("out there") situations that invite
engagement and appropriate responses, fantasy prods us ("in here")
to bring into play an arsenal of available stock responses. This explains why people habitually guided by fantasy can claim, with infuriating aplomb and candor, that they are acting on their "experience."

Somewhat paradoxically, these stock responses are a matter of both
impulse and *routine.* (The latter, by the way, often creates the illusion
of seriousness; routine somewhat resembles deliberate, studied regularity; its underlying lack of freedom is often masked.) Fantasy, in
other words, prompts us to live by passionate, largely *conditioned* responses *as if* they were measured, *intentional* ones. No wonder that
fantasy, being emotional and sentimental in origin, is not only regressive, but also deeply prejudicial. Minds moved by fantasy shun interest, observation, focus, empathy—those typically human, mature, and
moral ways in which the free, reasonable mind inspired by *humanitas*
seeks to engage otherness. Let us pause and elaborate.

[a] But first, an important conceptual and terminological clarification. Fancy, imagination, and fantasy are not synonymous; they de-
note three different things. *Fancy* is a function of straightforward,
unprepossessed, ingenuous *memory;* by fancy, we *combine* random
episodes of life in alienation by *playing* with them. By contrast,
imagination is a function of *the human spirit proper;* by imagination,
we *constructively* work with the stuff that fancy merely plays with.
That is, we turn the stuff of fancy into the stuff of *symbolic vision and
creative freedom,* of the kind that transcends passion and befits and
develops authentic identity. By imagination, therefore, we become
better attuned to otherness and, ultimately, to God.[20]

Fantasy is utterly different. First of all, it is characterized by *passivity.* It is typical of the life of fantasy that *it* plays with *us;* fantasies
have a way of haunting us. Fantasies are things we *submit* to: we allow the stuff of fancy and the passion tied in with it to run away
with our minds. For fantasy is that "part" of the mind where we are
driven by the force of past involvement in cosmic mutuality (§115,
8), with little or no *present* support from our native, spiritual transcendence. When this happens, *we are not necessarily to blame.* For
not infrequently, fantasies are the aftereffects of cosmic disasters

and simple mishaps; quite often, they are the repercussion of encounters with human beings who have touched us without proper
respect for our transcendence—or, for that matter, their own.

But culpability and blame are not at issue here; here what matters
is understanding. The point is this: while imagination both feeds
on and fosters spiritual freedom, responsiveness, responsibility, and
(ultimately) faith,[21] fantasy both feeds on the cosmic, purely reac-
tive element in us and fosters it, at the expense of self-transcendence. In other words, fantasy turns alienation into something we
merely *tolerate*—we do not really accept it, let alone embrace it for
our growth and development. Phrased differently, fantasy allows estrangement from our truer selves to get the upper hand over our
identity. An early symptom of this spiritual illness is a certain weariness with regard to truth and reality. Living (like Sybil Greeves in
Muriel Spark's short story *Bang-Bang You're Dead*), in a world of ambiguity and make-believe, we tend to forget that "the price of allowing false opinions" is "the gradual loss of [our] capacity for forming
true ones."[22] On that basis, we are liable to develop a vague kind of
"worldliness" and (worse) a lack of inner freedom. Eventually, a
curious lack of interest in cultural and spiritual matters may take a
hold of us, leading to various forms of superficiality to the world of
humane otherness. Even worse, habits of fantasy may lead to insen-
sitivity to what is distinctively human, in the form of either aggression or passivity [g].

[b] Fantasy is activated, first and foremost, by an excess of biophysical and psychosomatic experiences of novelty, shock, instability,
and uncertainty; accordingly, it fosters in us, as a matter of mental

---

[g] What has been explained in the last two paragraphs can be better understood
by making use of a distinction proposed before: fantasy is to imagination what
estrangement is to alienation (cf. §122, 1, e, [f]). One author who sharply realizes
the crucial importance of responsive and responsible realism in the mature life is
Herbert Fingarette. In *The Self in Transformation*, he convincingly argues that psy-
chotherapy remains incomplete as long as persons merely come to an *understanding* of the debilitating perceptions and attitudes they have come to adopt (and indeed, cherish) in order to cope with repressed past emotional injuries. The reason
for this is that capacity for realism is not fully restored as long as we use the *knowledge* of our emotional handicaps to excuse ourselves; not until we find ourselves enabled to *take responsibility for them* are we fully cured. — On liberation from fantasy
as a precondition for moral virtue and other-regarding love, cf. Iris Murdoch's pertinent observations on *realism as a moral accomplishment* in *The Sovereignty of Good*,
pp. 65–67; the present treatment is deeply indebted to this lucid little book. Incidentally, Miss Murdoch's many novels are in many ways demonstrations of the labyrinthine difficulties that beset us as we search for realism as a moral accomplishment. Cf. also her more recent *Metaphysics as a Guide to Morals*, esp. pp. 316–37.

habit, an impassioned anxiety about ourselves and our well-being. Proximately, this anxiety takes the shape of *temper*. Thus, fantasy is apt to cast anything that is other in the role of the *rival* (cf. §127, 4). Fantasy will egg us on to stay ahead, to push, to gain the upper hand, to disagree, to attack—whatever will ensure that we get to enjoy and keep the attention and the comfort of what we want, without getting hurt by what we do not want. Relentless, fantasy will insist: "You never know." "You've *got* to teach 'em, or you'll be dead." Living by fantasy means living by an aggressive mental appetite for advantage powered by anxiety.

But deeper down, fantasy has a less active, but (on reflection) far more telling face: resistance—even to the point of total fixation. Quite regularly, fantasy takes the shape of day-dreams—lively, one-act plays automatically shown in the mind, as repetitious as they are irresistible. In them, I typically find myself (or "us") at the center of the action, either winning big or losing big, either the focus of much-deserved attention and care or, very unjustly, the target of disregard and disavowal. This shows that, deep down, fantasy measures everything that is other by its potential for reassuring my anxious ego by *gratification and indulgence* (cf. §127, 3).

[c] Noticing things like these gives us clues as to how fantasy proceeds. Fantasies prod us not to *respond appropriately* to otherness, but merely to *react* to it, largely with reference to our own self-interest and our immediate security needs. Thus, fantasy moves us to act impressionistically, on the spur of the moment, with little or no regard for the actual occasion. It may even force us to the point at which we will act out, either by instinctively seeking out occasions that fit our fantasies, or (worse) by actually creating such occasions, regardless of the situations we find ourselves in. To the extent that we give in to this obsessive dynamic, the motive behind our reactions and actions will not be choice, let alone realism, but the pressure of images and self-images and schematized memories and "ideas" carried over from situations we no longer recall, recycled and reconfigured for further application (or rather, mis-application).

The observation that these mental images are repetitive implies another observation: fantasies are typically *standardized*. This is dangerous, for recurrent fantasies, while only residually related to the real world, have a tendency to become utterly compelling. With them, we are liable to habitually fill the vacuum caused, not only by the novelty or intractability of the situations in which we find ourselves, but als by the lack of inner clarity and resolve we ourselves bring to such situations. As a result, mere probabilities in the real world may stir up in us old, deeply-established fears and prejudices. The latter will posture as certainties and convictions about other persons and things so formidable as to leave us virtually no choice. Without allowing us to discern whether our perceptions are reliable or deceptive, fantasies will appeal to the (alleged) past and insist: "This is simply how things are." "We see it this way." "This is just like them." "This is the way I am." "Never mind." "Do it anyway." "You have to do what you have to do." Thus, to the extent that we live by fantasy, we miserably deliver up our powers of deliberation to the chances of chronic mental passion.

[d] Fantasy's close affinity with passion is further evidenced by the *compulsions* it encourages. These compulsions have a counterpart in fantasy's construal of the outside world. To those living by fantasy, otherness appears in the semblance of a whole world of undeniable, alien *powers of inclusion and exclusion*—an array of menacing masks that haunt the world and play perilous games with it. Not surprisingly, therefore, fantasies embody deeply rooted forms of instinctive *conformity* and *non-conformity*. Even less surprisingly, such fantasies are *contagious*. This implies that *fantasies both feed prejudice and are fed by prejudice, at least indirectly*. That is to say, fantasies betray their true nature in that they have a clear affinity with the infectious dynamics of cosmic mutuality (cf. §115, 8); put in sentient terms, they live off the herd instinct and even reinforce it (cf. §122, 1, e, [g]; §126, 1, b, [a]).[23] No wonder that living by fantasy regularly takes the form of that parody of genuine *mimēsis:* purely imitative behavior deliberately, willfully, and often obstinately undertaken as if it were the right and moral thing to do. Thus people driven by fantasy will insist that what they are doing is what they *intend* to do ("Can't I do what I want to do?"). In fact, however, what they are doing is living lamely, at the mercy of (that is, in dread of) the powers that control the "mental atmosphere." Like all powers and authorities, such powers come in kinds: family "traditions," tribal prejudice, witless fads, mass media routines, unexamined stereotypes, the mood of the moment, popular rages, accepted rationalizations, including fashionable ideologies masquerading as thought —even as original or "critical" thought [h].

---

[h] This analysis analogously applies to the higher, often fantastic powers that populate the mythologies and fables of traditionally polytheistic cultures. In many

[e] What has just been explained implies that fantasy is apt to have social ramifications and consequences, and hence, that it can lead to systemic and institutional moral degeneracy. It does so by fostering discriminatory prejudices. This observation brings us back to the fundamental moral issues of human sociality: influence, inclusion, and intimacy, as well as the systems of justice that "contain" them (cf. §135, 2). These systems have already been treated at some length (§98, 4; §129, 1, a–d); they will come up again in the next section (§138):

[7] The dynamics of influence, inclusion, and intimacy are cosmically rooted; that is to say, passion is integral to them. Thus it should not come as a surprise that they are a fertile breeding ground for fantasies. The same holds true for the social patterns that harness and channel them—not only the "given" (or "natural") structures of class, race, and sexuality, but also the more deliberate socio-cultural structures that shape and modify the given.

Still, lest we should take a purely negative view of power, trust, and *erōs* (which would be unbiblical as well), let us begin by recalling that these forces, however ambivalent they may be at the sentient level, are not just food for fantasy. They naturally have a positive prognosis (cf. §122, 1, e). The ambiguities and tensions inherent in alienation are capable of striking our fancy, stirring our imagination, and especially (in what is easily the most distinctively *anthropological* fashion) appealing to our capacity for reasonable evaluation and discernment. After all, the passions inherent in power, trust, and sexuality naturally lend themselves not only to play, but also to sublimation and refinement. As human persons and communties succeed in transcending passion and the needs of the moment, they learn to perceive, in humanity and the cosmos, opportunities for something nobler—something beyond cosmic vicissitude, mutuality, and change. That is, they begin to appreciate what Aquinas calls "the gradation found in reality" (§102, 2 [l. 74]). Put differently, they will have the experience of *analogy*. Things cosmic and especially things human, so they will discover, no matter how riotously entangled and indistinct and competi-

---

instances, familiarity with these powers is taught from early childhood on; they often stir the moral and religious imagination; hence, mythology often educates and civilizes human communities and attunes them to the world of invisible values. But this same familiarity can also mis-shape a culture by dint of fantasy: enslavement to "traditional values" and dread of the unknown can morally cripple countless human beings who live by mythology. Morally and theologically responsible inculturation involves crucial and very demanding elements of *discernment* (cf. §98, 1–2).

tive and dissimilar they may be, are not wholly incoherent, let alone completely estranged one from the other. They turn out to be naturally related and even adjusted to each other. The "region of dissimilarity" (cf. §113, 3, e, [k]) turns out to be knit together by deep *systemic resemblances and affinities*. Little wonder the discerning, ordering mind can feel at home in it. For it finds that reality does not consist in a congeries of powerful monadic units of massive cosmological density forever vying with each other for the right to exist (as Spinoza suggests: §106, 5, c, [n]). Far from it, for creation is a "universe": an *all-inclusive* whole, existing in open structures characterized by truth, goodness, beauty, and worthiness of notice; the rough-and-tumble of evolutionary process has yielded *form*—albeit at the cost of immense failure and suffering, as Pierre Teilhard de Chardin so keenly realized (cf. §117, 5). In the mind's eye (implicitly operating on its affinity with God's transcendent, all-encompassing vision), all that exists holds together, even though, admittedly, unity remains forever laced with multiplicity, and distinctiveness and specificity of form remain inseparable from indeterminacy and alienation (cf. §102, 10; §115, 5, c, [e]). Furthermore, the dynamic edifice of the universe is not in the last place so meaningful and appealing because it is ordered *hierarchically*. That is, the discerning mind finds itself exquisitely transported, by form upon analogous form, through (and beyond) the world's finitude as well as its own—toward what must be the transcendent, limitless Form of truth, goodness, and nobility.

[8] Enlightened and stirred by this dynamism toward the Transcendent, the human mind finds itself directed to more intermediate, typically anthropological goals as well. Humanity is to come into its own by means of action (cf. §87, 2, a)—by engagement with cosmic otherness. Human beings (and the Christian community in particular) are in dramatic transition from the God-given order of nature to the God-given order of grace (cf. §76, 1), but they can reach their goal only by traveling a road: they must interpret and transform, and thus humanize, all that is within their ken: humanity itself and the cosmos. While trying to reach the heavenly City, the Church travels and re-travels a world being made holy by its very act of pilgrimage" (cf. §36, 3). To the fertile human imagination, therefore, the given structures of humanity and the world (both the natural and the cultural) always invite further, deliberate ordering.

This ordering must attempt to conceive and create structures that are integrally *humane*. At a first, basic level of deliberation, this involves the development of structures that transcend the immediate pressures of cosmic action-and-reaction. That is, human beings must fashion an environment in which (1) brute cosmic process as well as the natural evils that are its by-product are controlled, and (2) a first-level moral community in which passion and the life of the senses are disciplined and intemperate, uncivil behavior is appropriately tamed (cf. §131, 1).

But humanity's moral horizon extends beyond the imperatives of what is immediate and passionately pressing. Finding itself within the broader dimensions of the world and history, humanity owes it to itself to develop forms of order and coherence that truly appeal to the *discerning mind*. By intelligence and patient resolve (cf. §120), human beings are to put *humanitas* to work: they must develop structures that secure justice beyond the here-and-now of immediate involvement. These structures must enhance and ennoble things human and cosmic to the point where they begin to disclose a wider reference as well as a deeper transparency. To the extent that this undertaking is successful, the given structures of humanity and the cosmos, and particularly those of class, race, and sexuality, will be creatively and responsibly adjusted to achieve fully human, meaningful, *moral* purposes. That is, they will be adjusted to *the common good*, now finally understood in its ideal definition, namely, as including, as a matter of principle, not just what is immediate and at hand, but all that is human anywhere and at all times.

Thus the vision of a new, more capacious and more permanent order of justice arises—one in which trials of strength give way to offers of intelligent and voluntary association and cooperation. On the way toward this higher justice we will deal with otherness in a maturer manner—that is, not just by dint of close yet disciplined involvement with others, but by intelligent, dispassionate, long-term vision and appreciation as well. Thus the focus of our moral attention will shift, away from influence and power and discipline, and toward inclusion and trust and mutual understanding. Nobler, more humane, more civilized structures of justice will be conceived and enacted. These structures will deal with the forces of connection and separation not by simply controlling and taming the push and pull of differentiation, but by embracing differences and even cultivating them. They will deal with fear, not by eliminating discrimination but by refining it into critical, discerning appreciation. They will seek to accommodate the many varieties of human existence and experience in such a way that *both their distinctiveness and their mutual relatedness* are prized and displayed to advantage. In this way, they will facilitate forms of truly humane (that is, mutually civilizing) *mimēsis*, leading to the exchange of cultural and moral goods, to the potential enrichment of all the communities participating in the exchange. To the extent that this comes about, appropriate, attractively varied, just (or at least relatively just: §135, 2) structures of influence, inclusion, and intimacy will come about. These will inspire rather than dispirit the human mind, and transform its trepidation into ingeniousness and high hopes. As such structures themselves become more fully human, they will become more transparent as well: they will more reliably attune the mind to God, in whom

> All things counter, original, spáre, strange;
> Whatever is fickle, frecklèd (who knows how?)
> With swíft, slów; sweet, sóur; adázzle, dim[24]

find not only their source, but also their ultimate coherence.

[9] Living (whether explicitly or implicitly) in the light of such a faith-perspective, moral people and *ditto* communities will not fear to acknowledge and accept, *as a public fact*, the tensions between their deep, native attunement to transcendence and the limitations and impasses inherent in the life of influence, inclusion, and intimacy. They will readily acknowledge the anxiety inherent in living not just with imperfection and provisionality but also with sin and its consequences. They will be regularly suffering from it. Yet they will be neither fascinated nor enthralled by them. They will neither suppress their anxiety nor exect it to be eliminated; rather, they will quietly try to have it transformed, by faith (cf. §16, 6; §126, 5, [*b*]; §142, 12, [*c*]). The structures of power, association, and affection, both the more given and the more deliberate, will, of course, always be beset by ambiguity, relativity, tension, and even abuse. But these frameworks of finitude, imperfect as they are, and often less than just and badly in need of correction, *will turn into stepping-stones*. Rather than accentuating the gap that necessarily exists between the particular and the transcendent, such structures will be expected to bridge it. That is, they will be valued, *as a matter of principle*, and in characteristically anthropological and fundamental-theological fashion, not just as useful means and measures to ensure law and order, but also (and far more importantly) as *symbols* that connect and unite.

[a] A fundamental ingredient of this appreciation is (to borrow Bernard Lonergan's term) "insight." Insight is one of the forms of authentic (that is, *analogical*) understanding of the world and hu-

manity. The test of any structure's insightfulness is that it enables and brings about the sort of in-depth understanding that conveys that the human beings are immanently attuned to the Transcendent. That is, insight is capable of conceiving and interpreting particular, concrete structures of limitation in such way that they start mediating between those living by them and the Transcendent. Insight, in other words, enables the human mind to view the patterns and marks of finitude in the perspective of Mystery, which includes the acknowledgment of their inherent ambiguities and tensions and imperfections as (sometimes) painful tests of faith. Sustained by faith-commitment, individuals and communities living by insight will succeed in living by sound, flexible (that is, always in some way inconclusive and provisional) socio-cultural traditions. In fact, they will support them, find them positively meaningful, and often participate in shaping and reforming them.

[10] However, if our analysis of the human situation is to be adequate, we must become self-critical once again. So let us turn away from the positive capacities of the human mind and remember some of its liabilities.

It has already been suggested that in our imperfect, fallen world insight and judgment (and thus, justice and moral equilibrium) are always in jeopardy. Unsettling fantasies will suggest that engagements with reality that go beyond the accustomed and the convenient are hazardous, and that the thirst for wider, more inclusive horizons is an unreliable guide to a better world. Such fantasies are apt to make all of us nervous. They will scramble the analogical imagination and inhibit the human ability to envision something yet unknown and unattempted, say, a more and more inclusive moral order—that is to say, a common good worthy of the name. Taking advantage of the precariousness of human understanding and of the defects of each and every structure, fantasy will terrify persons and whole communities with the prospect of chaos and loss of identity. It will insist on self-maintenance and self-assertion; it will foster prejudice to the point at which any wider vision gets effectively blocked (cf. §137, 6, a–e). Individuals and communities dominated by fantasy and prejudice will insist on obstructive moves in the name of fairness and equilibrium, and under the banner of justice. Typically, they will appeal to ethnicity, nationality, and customs of long standing (which they are incline to call "tradition"). To boost their obstructionist posture vis-à-vis otherness in all its forms, cliques of self-appointed insiders will arise within the community, and seek to establish both themselves and their prejudices as morally normative. Claiming to be the core of the moral community as a whole, these righteous, militant tribals will insist on disregarding alternative positions and countervailing trends; they will rage against what they regard as marginal elements, which they will depict as disloyal; they will be blind to that all-encompassing moral community (or rather, to that community of moral communities) which is humanity at large. The justice they insist on pursuing will fit only their own preconceived visions and values; being of the narrow, mostly self-regarding, largely *closed* kind (cf. §135, 5–6), this justice will eventually betray itself as inhumane and unjust.

No wonder that the prejudiced, guided by mental passion as they are, will rarely commend the forms of equilibrium and justice they advocate by appealing to their intrinsic attractiveness or moral significance. Instead, they will simply declare that the structures of justice they favor are causes that must be "defended" (or, as the case may be, "resolutely pursued"). In practice, this frequently means they want their cherished values aggressively enforced, by recourse, not to reasonable public norms, but to naked power, undiscerningly, and regardless of any human or moral appeal, not to mention consequences. Discerning people will immediately realize, of course, that such advocacy of power to enforce what can only be embraced by free appreciation proves that the causes of the strongmen are prejudiced, and in all probability morally flawed as well (§133, 2, [*v*]; cf. §128, 2, b). All this invites some very careful further analysis.

[a] The dynamics of influence, inclusion, and intimacy are persistent, pervasive, and entwined. Not surprisingly, therefore, anxious individuals and groups, or in cases even whole communities, will be keen not just on controlling these dynamics, but on seeking total relief from them. They are apt to do so by trying to "freeze" them— that is to say, by trying to bring them to a halt, by adopting very definite structures of power, association, and affection. Typically, when it is suggested that the rightness of structures of justice is a matter of interpretation, discernment, and human responsibility (cf. §125, 5, c), and hence, of discussion, they will intensely object. In their eyes, there is no real discussion about systems of justice; what is really needed are assertion and execution—law and order. Typically, too, they will advocate the upholding and enforcing of very definite moral codes (mostly of the conventional, but at times also of the radically unorthodox kind) in regard to class, race, and

sexuality; these codes, they will insist, are plainly the right "solutions." Unfortunately, the main thing these "solutions" will accomplish in practice is canonizing as satisfactory and final (and thus as simply normative) are very particular, often intolerant forms of interpreting and organizing influence, inclusion, and intimacy. Such forms may well suit the preconceptions and even the moral and religious convictions of particular groups, but on a wider perspective and from a basic moral and religious point of view, they are at least debatable, often dubious, and sometimes even wholly unacceptable morally.

Authorities often attempt to justify such prejudicial canonizations of closed structures of justice and morality by appeals to "mystery." Appeals of this kind are invariably unconvincing. Of course it is true that socio-cultural arrangements and institutions are not just operational and pragmatic. They are *significant.* They represent higher, transcendent values. This means (once again) that they are *symbolic,* and in that sense they do involve a dimension of mystery. But precisely for this reason, acceptance of socio-cultural institutions is a matter of appreciation, discernment, and voluntary commitment. Thus, institutions are best *commended* to the moral community, not forced upon it. Authoritarian appeals to mystery, however noble they sound, are usually nothing but attempts at *mystification* [*i*]. This requires further clarification.

[b] On the one hand, we have the human spirit's native desire for transcendent goodness, along with its inseparable companion, humanity's "unstable ontological constitution" (§112, 5). On the other hand, there are the structures of justice, which must help the human spirit actualize its aspiration to transcendence by channeling the life of influence, inclusion, and intimacy. But, as has already been noted, these structures are inherently beset by limitations and impasses. No wonder tension necessarily arises between aspiration and conformity. Still, it was observed, the tension is often felt to be acceptable (and indeed, meaningful); this is because the shared experience of confinement inherent in living within social struc-

---

[*i*] Mary Frohlich defines mystification as "a largely unconscious but nevertheless pervasive effort to obscure the fundamental anxiety of human existence by falsely resolving it in a worldview structured by hierarchical dualisms" ("From Mystification to Mystery," p. 176). The present paragraphs are much indebted to this insightful essay, which succeeds in putting some of Bernard Lonergan's key intuitions to constructive use in the exploration of the theological significance of human sexuality.

tures is redeemed by the fact that the latter provide a *shared experi-ence of symbolic coherence.* This experience, it was added, is most ef-fectively brought about by shared faith-traditions (§137, 9).

For, in the last resort, the acceptance of social structures cannot be coerced, certainly not on a large scale or for a protracted period of time. Yet the issue is never a matter of black and white, since change—some of it as quiet as it is wide-spread—*will* occur in socio-cultural and religious traditions. Structures that were once shared, appreciated, and authoritative sometimes turn out to have imper-ceptibly decayed. Traditional worlds of symbols are apt to be shak-en. As a result, the tension between aspiration and conformity will increase. And while this is happening, the tensions inherent in the prevailing structures of civility, justice, and public morality will be-come increasingly difficult to accept as a matter of course.

This translates into another tension—one very different from the ordinary and liable to cause deep divisions within the moral com-munity. Forms of justice, it was stated, must at least unthematically be integrated into wider, ultimately transcendent perspectives that are *shared;* what will happen when these perspectives become elu-sive—a matter, not of broad, unthematized consensus, but of the-matic, disparate opinion? (Here Christians of every stripe do well to remember that Christianity is no longer the normative intellec-tual and moral climate in the modern world; cf. §106, 1, c.) The first effect is: many of the prevailing frameworks of justice and forms of morality become unconvincing, to the point of being ex-perienced as almost arbitrary. In such a situation, a creeping sense of general moral maladjustment is apt to get the upper hand, along with a lapse of morale. The socio-cultural options which the com-munity has had at its disposal to give shape to the dynamics of in-fluence, inclusion, and intimacy are widely felt to be arguable—even implausible; the available structures of justice are widely felt to be so partial, so contingent, and (morally speaking) so ambiguous that they are perceived as incommensurate with "the way things should be"—even if there is only the vaguest sense of what the lat-ter expression might refer to. Dissociation is occurring; disintegra-tion is on the horizon.

Throughout this process of dissociation, however, the dynamics of influence, inclusion, and intimacy continue unabated; in fact, they are liable to be all the stronger for operating in an increasing socio-cultural and moral vacuum. This will cause floating anxiety, which in turn will add fuel to the fire of instability and concupiscence. Understandably under the circumstances, low public morale will be compounded by a lapse of public morality. This situation creates an opportunity for the forces of authoritarianism. As individuals and groups find themselves nervously attracted or repelled by a variety of half-convincing moral options, calls for law and order are apt to arise. Rather than patiently suffering through the prevailing maladjustment and working toward *inclusion* by way of a new moral and symbolic consensus, impatient groups will insist on certainty and assurance, achieved by dint of *exclusion*. They will seek to impose and enforce very specific, very partial patterns of justice as exclusively normative. They will attempt to idealize them; in any case they will try to justify them; but they are liable to do so mostly by mystification (cf. §137, 10, a and [*i*]). But engaging in mystification amounts to not dealing with an existing maladjustment so as to resolve it; it is an attempt at perpetuating it, by driving any opposition ("the others") underground.

Our analysis implies not only that mystification divides. It also implies that (like the moral chaos it tries to quell and exorcise) mystification it is powered by the dynamics of *concupiscence*. And like concupiscence, mystification takes two principal forms, and fantasy is inherent in both. This invites explanation.

[c] A first, basic form of mystification is as *natural* as concupicence itself (cf. 113, 3, b). It flows from the quandaries naturally inherent in human life in alienation; accordingly, it occurs mainly on the threshold of morality, even though it may look clearly immoral to outsiders. Many human communities are still living largely by undesirable cultural and moral arrangements of long standing, often undisturbed by encounters with alternatives. Such communities unwittingly suffer from an anthropological disadvantage: lack of otherness as a present leads to lack of imagination. Custom, after all, is comfort, even if it is only half-civilized; and long-standing customs, whether civilized or not, are apt to lead, imperceptibly, to incapacity to imagine, let alone striving to achieve, structures more adequate to integral humanity—say, moves in the direction of genuine equality of opportunity for the poor, for the racially different, and for women and children. So when encounters with other cultures and other arrangements of justice do occur, such communities *naturally* find themselves upset, depressed, even bedeviled.

In such situations, deep-seated worries about the unknown will arouse fantasies of chaos. Accordingly, the "naively prejudiced" will

cast outsiders in roles of lasting moral irresponsibility: "the poor
are lazy"; "colored people are as a rule less talented"; "women are
too weak and too emotional to be in charge." (Incidentally, their
opponents in the moral community, typically equally prejudiced,
and often mesmerized by visions of total breakdown of custom, will
often, on the rebound, idealize outsiders with a similar lack of realism, also rooted in fantasy: "only the poor know real selflessness";
"people of color are the ones who have real integrity"; "women, not
men, hold the key to life's mystery.")

Such prejudices are all the more contagious for being (in characteristically fantastic fashion) out of touch with reality. This renders
them liable to obstruct the exploration, not to mention the introduction, of alternative arrangements of justice—which is exactly
what suits the conventionally minded and the quietly prejudiced.

The second form of mystification is far more insidious; it is deliberate and for that reason genuinely immoral. Here discriminatory
forms of civilization and morality are positively, deliberately, and often perversely canonized as incontrovertibly just. The community
resorts to (in Lonergan's idiom) "scotosis"—the systematic, often
deliberate darkening of the human intelligence, and thus, the ban-
ishing of distinctively humane insight from consciousness, especially from *public* consciousness. When this occurs, insight is displaced
(again in Lonergan's terminology) by "myth."

In Lonergan's conception, "myth" is any system of thought that
blocks self-knowledge and self-transcendence rather than inspiring
or enabling them.[25] In this sense, myths are forms of sinful concupiscence, which induce deliberate attempts at preserving or establishing not just unsatisfactory systems of justice, but situations of
downright systemic sin. Applied to the present context, myth is the
kind of fixity of public opinion that will allow communities held together by prejudice to salve their common conscience and so to
ease their sense of moral responsibility. Now since it is characteristic of sin to wear a religious mask (§114, 4; cf. §125, 3; 5, e), the
sinfully prejudiced will embrace as reasonable and "realistic" largely
mythological fantasies that distort and demonize outsiders. Typically, too, they will defend and even advocate fantasy-based structures of injustice and inequality by arguing—usually in an authoritarian fashion—that they enjoy transcendent authorization [j].

---

[j] Sadly, among Christians, this often takes the form of appeals to "orthodoxy."
The latter in turn often take the form of the rehearsal of biblical quotations taken

[11] Our reflections on the deliberate life have led to an insight. Rigid systems and stereotypical notions rooted in private or collective fantasies of self-preservation and aggressive (often passive-aggressive) self-defense are apt to develop structures, not of truly inclusive justice inspired by the experience of analogy, but of *discrimination and prejudice*. The result will be cultural and moral conceptions and institutions that systemically divide humanity as a moral community in unjust, abusive, and hence, sinful ways. This should concern all those who cherish the deliberate life, since it involves an unacceptable reduction of humanity's God-given responsibility on behalf of itself to something less than fully human.

That is, discrimination and prejudice have immoral consequences at the *anthropological* and *theological* levels. It is humanity's distinctive privilege to be attuned to *all* of reality, and in and beyond it, to God. By excluding certain segments of humanity and the cosmos for the sole reason that they are inconvenient to patterns of moral contentment enjoyed at the center of a moral community, human beings not only do others (namely outsiders) a glaring injustice; they also condemn themselves to a less than fully human stature. This is not in the last place the case because any refusal to include other human beings by properly engaging (or at least respecting) them amounts to a refusal to enhance them; and theologically speaking, any refusal to enhance others is tantamount to a refusal to cooperate responsibly, both with God's creative activity (§122, 1, c–d; cf. §98, 5) and with God's universal salvific will (cf. 1 Tim 2, 4). The same point can be made by observing that some form of engagement with otherness is, for all human beings, the only way to authentic identity (§122, 1); by willfully refusing to treat others, whoever they may be, both as genuinely human and as genuinely other, the prejudiced cut both themselves and their victims off from the blessing to which all human beings are natively oriented: moral integrity and authentic identity, and even more importantly, a transcendent destiny. Fantasy-based, prejudiced structures of systemic discrimination, therefore, are sinful, as

out of context and interpreted as immutable, normative truths sanctioning the *status quo*. Some examples: "The poor you will always have with you" (Mt 26, 11; cf. Deut 14, 11); "the Jews ... killed both the Lord Jesus and the prophets, and have persecuted us, and they displease God, and they are the enemies of all, as they keep us from preaching to the Gentiles so that they may be saved; thus they are constantly filling the measure of their sin; but then again, [God's] wrath has descended upon them, for good" (1 Thess 2, 15–16); "Christ is the head of every man, and the husband is the head of the wife, and God is the head of Christ" (1 Cor 11, 3).

are habits of deliberate estrangement from others; if not abandoned and repented of they will kill humanity as a distinctive (that is, moral and spiritual) presence in the cosmos.

[12] Systemic forms of injustice that gain acceptance have a fateful *cosmological* significance as well. This can be understood as follows. Structures of justice that are *de facto* unjust differ from individual acts of injustice in one important respect: they tend to discredit the responsible life publicly. That is to say, they help call into question in a public, official way humanity's position of primacy in the cosmos and its transcendence over the powers that hold sway in the cosmos. It has already been observed that the prejudiced passionately want to have structures of systemic injustice in the areas of inclusion and intimacy enforced by recourse to power, undiscerningly (§137, 10). But, in Iris Murdoch's words,

. . . the victims of power, and any power has its victims, are themselves infected. They have then to pass it on, to use power on others.[26]

That is, the passion that drives privileged insiders into habits of domination is apt to contaminate their victims as well, and by association, those sympathetic to the victims. They all find themselves turned by force into marginalized outsiders. But once marginalized, such outsiders are liable to conclude that appreciation, openness, deliberation, and virtue are obviously of no use in the building of a just society, or at any rate, that only the powerful and the insiders can afford them, since it is clear as day that justice is *effectively* established only by power, and if necessary, by violence. Whenever and wherever this sentiment takes root in a community, humanity is well on the way to forfeiting its intellectual and moral transcendence and regressing to the politics of mere passion, as suggested not long ago (§137, 10).

[13] This invites further analysis and elaboration. Let us start with some points already made.

At the *sentient, instinctual* level, passion of temper is the normal and, indeed, indispensable expedient for survival in the world of otherness. Without contest and self-assertion, human beings, particularly in the early stages of development, cannot mature as they need to. They will fail to achieve self-differentiation vis-à-vis otherness. As a result, they are unlikely to learn the vital art of self-definition (§127, 4).

But what is appropriate and indeed promising at elementary biophysical and psychophysical levels may well be regressive and even downright immoral at the level of the responsible life, especially if deliberately adopted. Yet this throwback is precisely what fantasy will encourage. Human beings driven by fantasy will habitually spoil for a fight (or, what amounts to the same, habitually anticipate defeat). Put differently, the prejudiced will regress to the point where they will deliberately and systemically aim to fend off and attack all otherness as a potential threat to themselves. But what most decisively adds to this tragedy and makes it virtually unbearable is this: *human willfulness and deliberation in the area of aggression lack the instinctive restraint that typifies the use of force at the purely sentient level.* In the animal world, especially at the higher echelons, moderation typically prevails even in the realm of rapacity, and violence is rarely (if ever) wanton. Within the same species, the stronger seldom prey on the weaker; killing and havoc for the sake of killing and havoc hardly (if ever) occur.

By contrast, human beings turned aggressive are habitually poised to adopt *habitual rivalry* as their *deliberate* strategy for engagement, not just with the cosmos at large, but even with other human beings. They are willing to fight otherness not just needlessly but also with a vengeance. Thus they will habitually fail to practice that most human of human abilities: the art of discerning otherness spiritually—that is, of interpreting otherness in terms of *analogy and resemblance.* They will stop *relating.* Standoff becomes a way of life.

This will utterly bedevil human life in alienation. For, to adopt a terminology used before (§122, 1, e, [*f*]), for those habitually governed by the instinct for rivalry *alienation will degenerate into estrangement.* Human beings (and indeed entire communities) will turn fundamentally distrustful. Accordingly, they will misconstrue whatever is other and different as alien and hostile. That is, they will systematically misinterpret *relative* differences in *exclusionary* terms. As a result, they will live by *polarization and division* rather than by a sense of *relativity and relatedness* [*k*]. Habitually incapable of discernment, they will be incapable of sizing up strangers, possible opponents, or seemingly adverse cosmic forces realistically. Accordingly, they will also be

---

[*k*] Mary Frohlich argues that, strictly speaking, sexual differentiation is "neither fundamental nor wholly systematic"; it occurs on a *spectrum.* Measured against humanity's "central form," male and female must be understood as *relatively,* not irreducibly, different ("From Mystification to Mystery," pp. 182–84). Women and men, therefore, are essentially relatives, not rivals. We will come back to this in chapter 18. Still, in anticipation, the present treatment is already suggesting that the point made by Mary Frohlich holds good for class and race as well. Much as social chasms separate the rich and the poor, the victors and the victims, and the masters and the slaves, they are all relatives, not total strangers. And much as cultural chasms separate tribe from tribe, nation from nation, and people of color (whites included) from other people of color, they are all relatives, not mere insiders and outsiders.

unable to engage them in a *reasonable, measured* fashion. This effective loss of distinctively human rationality will give rise to neuralgic, often debilitating social and socio-political impasses, both within human communities and among different human communities—impasses kept alive by fantasy-driven forces of mutual prejudice and discrimination. No wonder the responsible exercise of moral judgment, not to mention human freedom, is habitually obstructed.

In cases, however, these very impasses and standoffs and stalemates, impossible to admire as they may be, turn into blessings, after a fashion. In the face of imminent violence of the worst kind, they *can* act as a deterrent—at least provisionally.

[a] Still, cultural stalemates have enormous potential for horror. Typically, the forces of fantasy will impel those whom they dominate into taking action, *any* action, in hopes of breaking the deadlock in their own favor by acting forcefully and deliberately, and "if necessary," violently.[27] In their blind self-absorption, they will justify the use of force by insisting on interpreting the situation in moral terms, and even religious terms, ignoring the fact that God is the God of all at the expense of none (cf. §155, 11). Contagious fantasies will now posture as a summons to moral responsibility. They will suggest that there are times and places when the "will to power" simply *has to* replace conscience, discernment, and mutual regard as the "effective moral law" of the deliberate life. Masquerading as moral principle, grandiose fantasies turned infectious will now encourage the view that "under the circumstances" public moral impasses can be resolved only by the intentional use of naked power, and even by premeditated violence (cf. §133, 2, [*v*]; §137, 10). When this happens, human beings become a threat to human life as well as a force for cosmic evil.

[b] Still, if we are to fathom fully what is involved in this fatal dynamic, we must take an even more painful step. For beneath the will to power and the recourse to deliberate violence lurks an even more regressive dynamic. Here, it is useful to recall that at the instinctual level the urgency of temper is rooted in the passion of desire. Also, it is in the experience of elemental *desire* that the dependent human being experiences its critical need for otherness and its craving for relief from the threat of death—a relief only otherness can provide. In the most elementary stages of growth and development human beings are dominated by need and craving (cf. §127, 2–3).

This provides us with a clue as to what underlies that blight of the deliberate life, namely, the fantasy-based habit of the prejudiced to misconstrue all otherness as alien and hostile, and thus, to resort to deliberate violence as a matter of course. It is nothing but a throwback to the infantile craving for an otherness that must unconditionally meet the infant's every wish and be prepared to indulge it. This impotent yet imperious posture of blind self-regard, which is so typical of the prejudiced turned violent, suggests that deep down they demand to live their lives surrounded by indulgence and connivance. Deep down, that is, the violent live in a scarcely differentiated world. In that world, everything must be agreeable with everything, and measured *mimēsis* has retrogressed to mindless mimicry —that is, unconditional conformity. Thus the misconstrual of the other as an enemy that must be defeated at all costs serves, in the end, to gratify that most primitive of all cravings: the self-centered wish to live by feeding off the totally indulgent other, absolved from the need (and indeed the fundamental human imperative: §122, 1) to risk establishing an identity in encounter with otherness.

This is the world in which the thug and the coward call the tune. Prejudices parading as structures of justice will arouse collective fantasies of the most primitive kind: dreams of furious destruction as the only viable alternative to fantasies of death. When human beings act out such dreams, they will regularly claim to be inspired by a holy indignation in the service of a cause deemed just; in reality they are just displaying the human capacity for that most painful degeneracy of human deliberation at the cosmological, biophysical level: willful, ferocious, murderous violence—the transmogrification of the infantile temper tantrum. Again, when this happens, humanity becomes a deliberate threat to human life itself as well as a force for cosmic evil (cf. §115, 10, a–b; §117, 2; 3, b–c).

[14] It is time to move on. Our exploration of the impact of fantasy on the dynamics of inclusion and discrimination demands that we pay special attention to one very specific moral issue. It is one which no one venturing to live morally and religiously in North America can overlook, let alone ignore. Yet its significance is well known elsewhere in the world, for example, in the Near East and on the Malaysian Peninsula—areas where human beings have met on the field of coin and cannon (cf. §11, 6) for centuries. And in any case, the globalization of Western culture, begun in the sixteenth century and exponentially intensified in the twentieth, has given it a deep moral ur-

gency, and will doubtless continue to do so for a long time to come: *race* [*l*].

[§138] RACE, PATTERNS OF INCLUSION, PRUDENCE, AND THE MORAL LIFE

[1] In the previous chapter it was proposed that *class*, being the most elementary, "natural" structure of *influence*, is the prototypical representation of all that is involved in the dynamics of power and the passions associated with it. It was also argued that the dynamics of influence have unmistakable affinities with cosmic process, which suggests that class and the social structures associated with it are characteristically *cosmological* (cf. §129, 2–3).

We must now make and elaborate an analogous suggestion in relation to *race*. Racial differentiation, it will be argued, is the elementary, biophysically based (and to that extent "natural") form of the dynamics of *inclusion*. As such, race has an exemplary significance in

---

[*l*] One way to appreciate this claim is to recall two things. Firstly, the English-speaking world of the past three centuries has typically used prose fiction as the outstanding literary vehicle of its exploration of pressing moral and religious issues. Secondly, the theme of what is arguably the earliest piece of novelistic writing in English is a community that has forged harmony out of differences of class and race. *The Isle of Pines*, by the radical republican and alleged atheist Henry Neville (1620–1694), appeared in London in 1668; French, Dutch, Italian, German, and Danish translations soon followed. The book purports to be the account, written by a Dutchman, of the recent discovery, by the crew of a Dutch vessel driven off course near Australia, of an island population of about two thousand, going virtually naked, yet speaking English. They are the descendants of a group of five survivors, shipwrecked in 1569 A.D.: George Pine, his master's daughter, two servant-girls, and a black slave-girl. After initial hardship, they had found that the island was a little paradise. Naturally enough, this discovery had prompted George to enjoy his four women companions—though, in the case of the slave-girl, only at her solicitation, only in the dark ("my stomach would not serve me"), and only rarely, for the sole purpose of procreation. Having little else to do but while away the time with the women, in arbors especially built for the purpose, George (whose description of the community's origins is now in the hands of his grandson William, the "Prince" of the present community and its spokesman) ended up fathering as many as forty-seven children, who in turn married and multiplied. Now divided into four clans, the community has lost much of its former innocence and religious fervor, though they have kept up their regular Bible reading and prayer gatherings. They live in reasonable harmony only because their lives, and especially their sexual and marital mores, are regulated by draconian laws. We get a taste of the tension when, as the Dutch are about to set sail, the ribald leader of the clan whose matriarch was (who else?) the black slave-girl imperils the community's tenuous social order by "ravishing" a woman of a lily-white tribe, thus causing a brawl. Chaos erupts, but the Dutch, at the Prince's request, quell the disturbance by dint of firearms. In the end, the visitors from the West depart, satisfied that they have saved from ruin, by thoroughly modern means, this fetching attempt at starting a human society from scratch.

the realm of mutual trust and association, and (as will become clear) in the practice of *discernment* required by it.

Issues of inclusion and discernment have, of course, an unmistakable affinity with the deliberate (that is, the distinctively *human*) life. Not surprisingly, therefore, the social structures connected with inclusion and discernment—that is to say, language and manners (or "culture")—raise *distinctively anthropological* issues. All these propositions require analysis and argument.

[a] First of all, there are good reasons to think that the dynamics of inclusion are at one more remove from cosmic process than the dynamics of influence.

It was stated before (§117, 5; §120, 3 and a; §129, 4, a) that class, power, and influence have an affinity with the *multiplicity* and the (relative) happenstance typical of cosmic phenomena. Differentiation in the area of influence consists in countless natural forms, all of them broadly analogous, yet also relatively undistinctive and uncoordinated, and thus, often hard to identify and tell apart. At the other end of the range, there are good reasons to suspect that the dynamics of intimacy have a close affinity with humanity's native orientation to God—a proposition to be examined in due course (cf. §160). Why? In the area of intimacy, differentiation *by elementary, biophysical, natural forms* occurs along the lines of *the lowest possible multiple,* which is two: maleness and femaleness. Not surprisingly, the two are also deeply analogous: in each species, while the sexes are so dissimilar as to be virtually inconfusible, especially while sexual maturity lasts, they equally unmistakably belong together.

These observations raise a host of heuristic questions. Could it be that the dynamics of *inclusion,* whose elementary, "natural" form is humanity's differentiation by race, figure halfway between those of influence and intimacy? That is to say, could issues of inclusion be roughly equidistant, so to speak, from (on the one hand) humanity's sentient participation in cosmic process and (on the other) its direct affinity with God? And in that case, could it be that issues of association and dissociation (that is, of inclusion and exclusion) affect humanity far more deeply than issues of power and influence? And thus, could it be that they constitute the single most urgent challenge to the distinctively human capacity for mediation between the cosmos and God (cf. §117, 5; §122, 1; §96, 3; §2, 1)? If influence should turn out to be *the* cosmological issue in the deliberate life and intimacy *the* theological one (which at this point remains to be seen, of course), could it be that inclusion is *the most characteristically anthropological?* Let us follow these leads.

[2] We begin by repeating something already alluded to in passing (§138, 2), namely, that racial differences rarely come singly. Typically, they are accompanied by marked differences of tongue and civilized manners (including, in many cases, religious observances) as well as reinforced by them. Let us, then, briefly compare the otherness involved in race, tongue, and manners with the otherness involved in class and the power-structures related to it [*m*].

[a] As explained earlier, structures of power are both countless and inescapably present. They occur everywhere and all the time; all human beings are forced to deal with them, and thus have first-hand familiarity with them. They also occur on a broad range of intensity. While this makes quite a few of them almost wholly unmanageable, many of them are relatively easy to face, especially since the readiness to face them is built right into humanity's biophysical and mental makeup (cf. §115, 9). But then again, confrontation is hardly optional; it is a matter of survival. Controlling and managing alien forces is a vital necessity, whether they are unleashed by the cosmos at large, or come in the form in which human beings meet with them, not only among one another but also within themselves. Thus the dynamics of influence leave human beings absolutely no choice but to strive to transcend them (cf. §129, 5–6).

[b] By contrast, natural ("given") structures of inclusion and exclusion are not nearly as numerous. Patterns of racial differentiation (and of the linguistic and cultural differences usually associated with them) are *relatively* few and far between, whereas the "common cultures" naturally marked off by them are often sizable. In

---

[*m*] Note that "tongue" encompasses both "speech" and "language"—or, in Ferdinand de Saussure's terminology, *parole* and *langue.* The experience of linguistic otherness is incomparably more vivid when perceived by the ear than visually—in writing or on the printed page. Accordingly, actual foreign speech is a far more direct invitation to inclusion or exclusion, or to openness or resistance, than the experience of foreign languages as alien literacy systems. Yet even the latter's ability to inspire associations and conflicts according to cultural and linguistic divides is considerable. On the North American continent, the language situation in Canada comes to mind. And to limit ourselves to only one other example out of many, while Serbs and Croats speak the same language, they are separated by different alphabets, Cyrillic and Roman respectively; this not only serves to reinforce the difference between Orthodoxy and Catholicism, but also creates two cultures that militantly insist on being different.

many places, serious racial, linguistic, and cultural strangeness is a fairly distant phenomenon; the lives of substantial segments of humanity—many millions of people, in fact—are virtually untouched by genuinely unfamiliar forms of race, tongue, and manners. Our world is marked by increasing horizontal mobility, of course, of both the voluntary and the violent kind; as a result, the number of these people is shrinking. Still, it remains true that patterns of association and problems of inclusion and exclusion do not occur with the ubiquity and the persistence typical of structures of power and issues of influence.

However, when and where inclusion and exclusion issues do occur, their intractability turns out to be directly proportioned to the comparative infrequency of their occurrence. Many human beings (and *their* number is running into many millions, too) live in circumstances that make it impossible for them to ignore or avoid human beings who are significantly different—racially, linguistically, and culturally. This makes the making of decisions regarding association and dissociation inescapable, and often a matter of daily experience. In such cases, issues of inclusion and exclusion turn out to be surprisingly engrossing, intense, explosive, as well as *very* divisive. Something else becomes clear as well. It takes more than straightforward, well-intentioned natural resourcefulness and forcefulness (of the kind fruitfully employed to control forces of the merely cosmic and instinctive kind) to settle the impasses that will arise between race and race, language group and language group, culture and culture. In fact, they frequently end up making matters worse.

[3] There is another (and, on reflection, very characteristic) difficulty whenever and wherever issues of inclusion and exclusion arise: a curious sense of futility and pointlessness, which may turn into utter frustration. Another comparison between the dynamics of influence and those inclusion will bear this out.

[a] The frustrations inherent in tests of *strength*—that is, in human attempts to manage the dynamics of power and influence—are very real. Taking on the impersonal, undeliberate cosmic and biophysical forces at work in the environment, in human communities, and even within human individuals is often a matter of mere survival. Human beings simply *have* to face and control these forces. The exercise may not be pleasant; it may even fail altogether; it may divide people into oppressors and oppressed. Yet the vital impor-

tance of the struggle itself is hardly ever in doubt. For people who feel and know they are surrounded and pervaded by the odds of cosmic surprises and instinctive urges the struggle for life is *necessary* for survival, and thus, part of life itself.

[b] By contrast, it is far from clear why it is a *necessary* requirement of human life that we should deal with the perplexing differences created by race, speech, and manners. Why should these barriers be an issue in the first place? In the midst of race riots, language conflicts, and cultural clashes one can hear it said, by average people sick of the physical and mental violence caused by prejudice and discrimination yet unable to get beyond it, that "this is not the kind of thing we should be fighting about," or that "there is no *need* for this." In other words, strife of this kind as well as the prejudicial fantasies that provoke it, are viewed as "unnecessary." But the very realization that these standoffs are unnecessary helps make it obvious just how difficult it is to find ways to resolve them. That is, human beings are quite confident they know *why* they *have* to take on the forces of nature and instinct, and they are ingenious in devising ways to overcome them. But when it comes to differences of race, speech, and manners, they find themselves stymied. Why?

All of us intuit that our sense of mutual alienation is *strictly human* in origin. We are both naturally interested in *human* otherness and put off by it. The familiar and the familial may be essential to us; they also make us prejudiced and wary of human beings that look, speak, and act in unfamiliar ways. With them, we face crises of *humanitas*. We do not exactly know what to do, but we do know that failure to deal with them puts our common *humanity* to shame.

[4] Why is it that we cannot simply *live* with strangers, without having to *deal* with them? Why can we not "leave each other alone"? Curiously, human beings at odds with each other about race, tongue, and manners never succeed in leaving each other alone. No matter how intensely they find racial, linguistic, and cultural conflicts pointless, human beings will not settle for mere survival in a closed environment or an isolated culture. If there is something in us impels us beyond *cosmic* barriers, human strangers leave us even less at peace. Whenever we are faced with other human beings, neutrality about inclusion and exclusion, association and disassociation, is not a viable option. With other human beings, *we cannot not communicate* (§95, 2). Curiously, so we discover, failure to communicate with other humans, perplexing as it is, militates against *humanitas*.

Here we stumble once again upon the distinctively anthropological phenomenon that has demanded our attention many times already. While the dynamics of cosmic process involve us willy-nilly, we know that they are largely neutral. There is no such neutrality in the human world. The simple givenness of a person, it was pointed out long ago, is never neutral; it is invariably a moral fact. In and of themselves, human beings constitute intellectual and moral situations for each other; human beings intrinsically demand to be responded to; factual availability to each other for response establishes a moral responsibility (§95, 4). No wonder the barriers between human races, tongues, and cultures are experienced as forbidding; precisely because the humanity *behind* the barriers, alien and disgusting as it may look and sound and smell, cannot be ignored. What is behind this?

Human otherness, both individually and communally, has features so distinctive as to reveal a dignity and a personalness that refuses to be disavowed. Much as aliens "make sense" only to one another, they command acceptance and communication on the part of all, without exception. Their faces, especially their *eyes*, convey *presence*. They *appeal* to us for understanding. Without ado, human beings, weak and defenseless as they may be, convey that they are meant to be encountered. In and of themselves, they demand that they be dealt with fairly, not coerced, let alone overpowered. *Humanity, in and of itself, involves an unconditional moral imperative.* Accordingly, each and every human being resists being reduced to a *thing*. No human being is to be used, let alone disposed of. Accordingly, none of us succeed in treating others as if they were purely cosmic, equivalently infrahuman phenomena. The mere *countenances* of human beings demand that *justice* be done to them, deliberately, as Emmanuel Lévinas has so insistently taught in our own day, in the wake of the Holocaust. No wonder it takes a moral (or rather, immoral) effort to commit deliberate violence on other human beings. Executioners, to show they are human, must wear masks; they have to save not only the face of human justice, but their own face as well.

All of this has an immediate consequence. All attempts to disavow, control, or subdue the humanity of racially, linguistically, or culturally dissimilar others, *on the precise ground that they are dissimilar*, involves, on the part of those making such attempts, acts of deliberate self-dehumanization—that is, self-debasement to subhuman levels and varieties of consciousness and activity. In its very irrationality, therefore, failure in the area of inclusion is a profound *moral* embarrassment. It offends and wounds the human conscience far more deeply than loss of (self-)control or abuse of power could ever offend and wound it. For this reason, those who *deliberately* apply force to others simply because they are different *commit moral evil*, not only against the humanity of those they violate, but also against their own human-ity—by failing to avail themselves of their native capacity for intelli-gent and moral encounter, and by misusing it in such a way as to treat other human beings as if they were *things* (cf. §95, 1–4, esp. [*nn*]; cf. also §94, 6, a). This thesis is nothing but the personalist for-mulation of a proposition stated earlier (§133, 2, [*v*]; cf. §137, 10; 12–14; §138, 6, a): the brute, willful, undiscerning, and hence, dis-proportionate exercise of power and physical force in the interest of bringing about or maintaining unjust conditions in the park of inclu-sion (and of race in particular) is inherently unjust.

[a] The critical issue in situations of mutual discrimination among human beings, therefore, is not anatomical and cosmological but cultural and anthropological, even though in such cases of conflict the latter are inseparable from the former. Accordingly, human beings spontaneously intuit that the road to resolution of conflicts in this area is not biophysical, psychophysical, or technical, but in-tellectual and moral. That is, it is the road of *understanding and ap-preciation.* Thus, wherever human beings and communities find themselves unable to understand each other *as human beings,* peace is to be expected not from force but from insight (cf. §137, 9, a) and deliberation. Accordingly, it is crucial that differences of race, tongue, and manners, real and tangible as they are, be *interpreted by discernment—i.e.,* in *relative,* not exclusionary terms (§137, 13 and [*k*]; cf. also 6, d; 10, b). While indubitably creating embarrassing impasses, these differences embody a compelling appeal, inherent in human consciousness as such, to the *analogical imagination.* Only the human spirit, availing itself of its affinity with everything that is, can learn that the troubling varieties of race, tongue, and culture constitute a natural invitation to that most distinctively human thing: *self-transcendence, both of the personal and the communal kind.*

For this reason, race, tongue, and culture are far more of a moral challenge than the huge variety of power and influence. No won-der that communications across racial, linguistic, and cultural di-vides are so deeply rewarding if and when these challenges are met.

[b] At some level most cultures are aware of this. The hard-won comforts of life in the safety of a homogeneous community and of a controlled and benign environment are a major source of the

firm sense of identity and mastery over nature that is typical of stable, civilized human populations. The comforts, after all, produce a deep sense of security, belonging, and contentment. Those who enjoy the comforts of homeland and of home, sweet home *know* they are a blessing. Yet at the same time the same people are apt to know intuitively that their blessings are mixed. Deep down, they know that being *confined* to a single habitat and to a single community is humanly (*i.e.*, intellectually and morally) unsatisfactory [*n*].

[5] Deep discontent with the comforts of mere security and belonging (that is, of inclusion too narrowly or too definitively conceived) is not only mentally sound. It is also supported by a discerning analysis and interpretation of the *physical* features of racial, linguistic, and cultural differentiation. Race, tongue, and manners are not nearly as impenetrable and definitive as they might appear at first blush. In other words, they are *relative*. A few phenomenological observations to illuminate and substantiate this.

[a] It has already been explained that racial and ethnic divisions are usually accompanied as well as reinforced by marked differences in speech and civilization. Yet rarely if ever do tongue and civilization entirely (let alone "naturally") coincide with race. The manifestoes of racists, purists, and nationalists of every stripe notwithstanding, the "natural" links between ethnicity, language, and culture are quite loose. Solid correlations between the three can indeed be shown to exist, but they are largely a matter not of "nature," but of human cultivation and effort, chiefly of exploration, commerce, and warfare (cf. §11, 6)—all of them matters of *choice*. To appreciate this, let us take a moment to reflect. We will do so by taking the three elements just mentioned into consideration, one after the other: ethnicity, language, and culture.

[b] *Cultures* (even those most admired and revered for the naturalness, harmony, and distinctiveness of their manners) often overlap

---

[*n*] One literary genre that explores both the hazards and the rewards of this itinerant type of self-transcendence is found across a wide variety of cultures: tales of *voyages*—mythical, legendary, historic. Homer's *Odyssey* is the classic example in the West. In the *Iliad*, the chief issues are power and dominance (which may well explain its wider appeal); by contrast, the *Odyssey's* theme is humane and subtler. Its hero is "resourceful" (*polytropos*) rather than powerful; he is a wayfarer who, in the wake of the fall of Troy, "found himself moved hither and thither" (*planchthē*) in a world of strangeness, in painful search both of his own identity and the companionship of others: "He saw the towns of many people and got to know what they thought; but at sea, he also suffered many afflictions within himself, while seeking to secure his own life and the return of his companions" (*Odyssey* A, 1–5).

with neighboring cultures; more often neighboring cultures with "bleed into" each other. Racists, purists, and nationalists will insist, of course, typically withhout any documentation, that cultures are genuine only to the extent that they are "pure." Accordingly, they will regard the natural vagueness of cultural boundaries as "unnatural," and indeed, as instances of outright "contamination." Yet their customary loudness proves, *ex contrario,* that their views are hardly likely to stand the test of history and anthropology.

[c] Analogously, it is important to realize that the complex structures that make the great *literary languages* as most of us know them so different are not "natural." They have been developed and canonized (and thus made impressive) by bards, poets, prophets, and writers, who have also made the structures *sound* and *appear* spontaneous and natural. Scribes and grammarians have made their contribution to this process by *pre*scribing structures of speech and language patterns under cover of *de*scription. As a result, both native speakers and foreign students are now mostly unaware that developed languages are to a considerable extent cultural constructs [*o*].

[c] But how about *racial differences?* These are, of course, certainly linked with genetic, physiognomical, and physiological traits that *are* observable and measurable (and in that sense objective). Still, we must quickly add that even these traits are relative, not absolute.

First of all, "on the ground," racial features tend to blend into each other; truly significant physical differences rarely occur cheek by jowl; *natura non facit saltus.*[28]

Secondly and far more importantly, while it is true that human beings can often readily identify others as racially different, this is a matter, not of unbiased, quasi-photographic observation of measurable physical features, but of *perception.* But human perception is never a purely passive, let alone objective, recording process; rather, it is a *structuring activity.* We perceive in *Gestalts*—that is, in *unified perceptual constructs.* In perceiving other human beings, we se-

---

[*o*] "On the ground," therefore, there are no sharp language boundaries, except those enforced by culture. Most linguistic units are bordered and connected by largely oral, very flexible "inter-languages," *linguæ francæ,* "pidgins," and "creoles" of one kind or another. Educated people living in cultured societies imagine that foreign languages (which they tend to view as closed systems) are acquired only by immersion or schooling or both. In doing so, they overlook the existence, from time immemorial, of *interpreters,* many of whom have been *illiterate.* Like the "languages" they speak, these linguistic go-betweens operate in that paradise of *ad hoc* oral performance: the everyman's land *between* culture languages—the area that some writers and practically all grammarians consider a mere jungle.

lectively settle, as a matter of unconscious habit, on some features rather than others as distinctive and racially relevant.

Thirdly and most importantly, *Gestalts* are inseparable from *tastes* —that is, from clusters of mostly implicit and unthematically held preferences and aversions shared within the confines of particular cultures [*p*]. It is mostly by virtue of such prevalent tastes that some characteristics of race (our own and others') strike us as desirable and others as undesirable, some as attractive and others as repugnant. Equally implicitly, of course, we tend to feel that traits we find attractive and desirable create the presumption of cultural, intellectual, or moral superiority, and *vice versa*.

For these reasons (as well as other, scientific ones, too many to elaborate here) the notion that racial differences are unequivocal and completely objective is wrongheaded. So is the view that specific racial features are indicative of less tangible, yet equally objective mental and spiritual characteristics (whether positive or negative). Such judgments are nothing but culturally induced prejudices. This is confirmed by the observation that racial features tend to become less and less relevant in everyday human encounter and communication according as those who live in racially diverse societies end up disregarding racial dissimilarities and adopting the received speech and the standard manners of a common culture.

[6] Nevertheless, the observations just made do not imply that the bridging of racial, linguistic, and cultural divides is uncomplicated. Nor is it implied that we should find it easy. For, as a matter of historic fact, all human accomplishments are and will forever remain a most demanding cultural and moral challenge. Precisely because each and every form of shared civility and polish, even the most modest, is a hard-won accomplishment of human transcendence over cosmic process and of human self-trancendence, it is intrinsically inter-

---

[*p*] Consequently, *de gustibus non est disputandum:* it is pointless to engage in disputes over tastes. Like most things cultural, tastes are mainly understood by participative knowledge (§63); their value is proved by the humane enjoyment they give access to—not by argument, and certainly not by the fact that they prevail over other tastes. (After all, poor taste quite often carries the day.) Still, tastes (or rather, those who live by them—the insiders) *can* yield their secret to outsiders, if only on condition that the latter try to understand them appreciatively. And, interestingly, once insiders feel that their tastes are appreciated by outsiders, they are often prepared to acknowledge that tastes—including their own —are relative, partial, and not without shortcomings. This shows that tastes, once properly appreciated, tend to open those formed by them to the attractiveness of other, different tastes. Of course, it also shows that "fusion of horizons" does not come naturally, let alone automatically; it is and remains predicated on *deliberate* mutual understanding.

esting and precious to those whose sensibilities and mentalities and tastes and aspirations are shaped by it; most of all, it is *symbolic*—it embodies and takes the measure of their essential humanity. Engaging in transcultural, interlingual, and interracial transactions, therefore, requires a lot of intelligence, deliberation, and sensitivity—all of them inspired by *humanitas*. For the more common the "common good" is, the harder it is to define and achieve in ways that are acceptable (and, indeed, enjoyable and enriching) to all involved.

This holds especially for situations in which cultural, linguistic, and racial minorities—"sub-communities" with their own "sub-cultures"—have reason to be concerned about the mutuality of acceptance. In such situations, sub-communities are apt to feel threatened. They are liable make efforts to present a united front to the prevailing culture. They will draw firm boundaries around themselves—boundaries likely to be firmer and more rigid according as those within feel less secure about their acceptance by the majority. Inside those firm boundaries, a unified sensibility will be fostered, one way or another, to the point where it will feel like second nature—an alternative way of being human, enjoyed at a carefully calculated distance from "the others out there." This can create an emphatic, militant, sometimes downright intransigent sense of shared identity, which, of course, is liable to tempt other sub-communities to cultivate equally high profiles. They, too, will start insisting on their distinctive manners and habits of speech; they will even exaggerate them for good measure. Wherever this dynamic arises, sub-communities are liable to end up defining themselves by defending their sub-cultures rather than enjoying them. That is, rather than enjoying themselves, they will be defending themselves against allegedly established majorities or against other, allegedly undependable minorities. Nervous confrontation will displace more constructive forms of communication. Societies in such a state of crisis will be marked by palpable (if often mostly unacknowledged) tensions. Anxiety will keep everybody on edge. People will be living in an atmosphere resembling an unstable chemical compound. Infighting and skirmishes will always be around the corner; open conflict and outright violence will always seem imminent. In such situations, the cultural and moral challenge to come to a reasonable determination of the common good, both for the sub-communities and for the common culture, is uncommonly hard to meet.

But even outside such situations of high tension, cultures and sub-cultures are potent determinants of a sense of identity that is fundamentally *defensive*, both communally and individually.[29] For whenever and wherever shared manners, a "native" tongue, and characteristic physical features occur conjointly (or at least are perceived to do so), they will unite people on the strength of a unified sensibility so familiar and so comfortable that it imperceptibly becomes second nature to those who share in the experience. Such a unified sensibility will help give individuals and sub-groups in any community a deep, secure sense of belonging. They *know*, of course, that their shared experience is imperfect, but they will still *feel* proud to be part of it; characteristically, they will demur when outsiders try to point out them the very imperfections they themselves recognize as true. In this way, even harmless forms of cultural pride will breed prejudice. All those who feel they thoroughly "belong" tend to forget that the sensibility they live by is a product not of nature, but of culture—a culture they have gotten used to taking for granted as natural, and long ceased to regard as a matter of past choice. For these reasons, even the members of relatively open communities tend to exhibit insufficient personal and collective self-awareness, self-criticism, and a sense of the relativity of their contentment. Even where there are no standoffs and conflicts, sub-communities tend to think, mistakenly but without ado, that the sensibility of outsiders is simply strange—alien, unnatural, and on that score somehow less humane.

For these reasons, transcultural understanding and communication are challenges in *all* situations where human beings live together. It was pointed out in the previous chapter that the dynamics of power and influence are quasi-cosmological (§129, 2, a); that is, they depend in large measure on circumstances of place and time. By contrast, the dynamics of inclusion are operative, one way or another, in *human* situations *as such.* That is to say, whether human beings find themselves at home or abroad, or whether they are insiders or outsiders, cultural, linguistic, and racial boundaries will *in and of themselves* face the analogical imagination of *all human beings* with formidable obstacles to the practice of openness toward others and realistic self-knowledge. At home, insiders of every stripe will experience their culture or sub-culture as "normal" and as something almost foreordained, and thus, as natively meaningful and superior to unfamiliar alternatives; at the very least they will regard it as so enjoyable and so worth while that it deserves to be carefully cultivated and deliberately protected against contamination and diminishment. And conversely, outsiders to that same culture or sub-culture will be cool to it, have stereotypical notions about it, and note its inadequacies and limitations and joke about them. In this way they show that they will find it not only alien but also anomalous—if, indeed, they do not positively ridicule it, belittle it, shrug their shoulders at it, or (worse) attack it as inferior and a danger to humanity [q].

All of this leads to four conclusions. Firstly, the deliberate, responsible life is impossible without a careful balance between inclusion and exclusion. Secondly, this balance is hard to strike. Thirdly, since only human deliberation can strike it, only *painstaking discernment* can discover it. And fourthly, since inclusion and exclusion are part of the *dynamics* of human life together, all such discernments must be treated as provisional, not definitive.

For, on the one hand, human civilizations inherently cultivate cultural, linguistic, and racial distinctiveness. This results in countless forms of human culture, at every level of association. While this entails limitations for each culture, the multiplicity and variety is constructive and healthy, as well as morally legitimate. Thus it is both natural and right for families, towns, schools, neighborhoods, corporations, trade unions, regions, countries, to foster a common culture or sub-culture. After all, each and every form of human association is a concrete shape of human self-transcendence and thus, a revealing embodiment of *humanitas*. Let us put this differently. Sound human associations and the goods they cultivate are limited and in that sense exclusive, but basically, the limits are not a function of *intentional* exclusion of otherness; they are simply needed to create room for, and give play to, that deeply human gift which is *creative mastery of form.* Far from being something negative, therefore, cultural selectiveness is a precondition for mastery; *in der Beschränkung zeigt sich erst der Meister,* the German proverb says.[30] Humanity as a whole is *called* to engage all things cosmic as well as all things human, but it *can* do so only selectively, in place and time—that is, in such a way as to make *particular, selected* parts of itself and the cosmos humanly (*i.e.,* spiritually) significant. And in the last analysis, the human capacity for form is designed to enable human beings to engage other things and other persons in such a way as to bring out and enhance the world's and humanity's transparency toward the transcendent God, at least here and there and now and then (cf. §78).

---

[q] By way of illustration, one small biblical example out of countless. An early psalm can proudly declare Israel's ethnic (and cultic) identity by marking it off against the Egyptians', who are characterized as an *'am lō'ēz:* a "clan" or "breed" with gibberish for a language: Ps 114, 1 (cf. §97, 3). And what comes to mind in our own day, three thousand years later, is that ominous tale by William Golding: *The Inheritors.*

This significance and this transparency, however, are never assured, let alone final. Let us make this clearer by means of a parallel. Recall that the moral sense, with all its detailed norms, is reliable only to the extent that it is guided by the sense of duty, which is drawn to ever higher moral pursuits by its own immanent dynamism (§105, 5–6). Analogously, even 'the most sublime *forms* of human culture remain vulnerable, and to some extent unsettled and ambivalent. Authentic humanity is attuned to all that is real; its desire for the true and the good and the notable is boundless; natively, no human individual or community is capable of being satisfied with anything short of the absolute. "Our hearts are restless until they rest in you."[31] Accordingly, even the most precious cultural goods are provisional and thus in some degree precarious, made so *by their own particularity*. In this regard, all cultures share in and reflect humanity's "unstable ontological constitution" (§112, 5): attuned to everything that exists and ultimately to God, cultures must either become self-transcendent or turn inhumane and even inhuman. Being special, cultures are invariably tempted to grow too definite, too self-sufficient, and too self-regarding. Taking themselves for granted, they will get self-absorbed and triumphalistic, or (worse) overstated to the point of fanaticism.

In this sense, cultures are *structurings of the common good* (cf. §§10–11). This implies that, like religious faiths (which themselves are structured as religious cultures or at least sub-cultures), cultures must naturally (and often nobly) compete or die. But unless *in measuring themselves against* other cultures they also *open themselves to* them, they will stop renewing themselves (cf. §91, 3). They will lose their transparency and turn opaque. Instead of stirring the analogical imagination of those who are part of it, they will stifle and even kill it.

Ever so many cultures (including Christian ones), we know, have lost their luster and faded away. At one time or in one particular situation, they embodied, in a distinctive manner, a community's immanent ability to take on the world of otherness and thus to give form to its sense of identity and self-transcendence. Many cultures do indeed attract the unwelcome attention of invaders and are wiped out; but many, too, suffer the death of overdefinition—that is, inbreeding and asphyxiation. What once was a community's cherished heritage ends up obstructing *that same community's* capacity for engagement with other cultures in *their* distinctiveness; thus, what was at one time the source of a community's pride turns into an barrier to its self-understanding. While it is true that cultures can flourish only within certain limits, it is no less true that they can *stay* flourishing only if those limits are kept shifting.

Let us conclude. Cultures and sub-cultures *in and of themselves* harbor an impetus for self-transcendence and for exploration of the unknown and the unfamiliar—that is, for *change by dint of exchange*. Cultures are the product of the dynamics of inclusion, and of exclusion only insofar as inclusion can flourish only within limits. These dynamics are ceaseless. Accordingly, cultures and sub-cultures will ignore them at their own peril; to flourish, cultures must be open, discerningly, to neighboring cultures and even to what lies beyond. Cultural communities that define themselves too narrowly (*i.e.*, exclusively) will end up choking themselves off. Among human beings, it has been argued, neutrality is morally impossible, and treating others as morally neutral is a form of violence. Similarly, cultural communities turned self-preservation societies will become a threat to other, more vital cultural communities. For, like human individuals, cultures cannot *not* communicate (§95, 2–4). That is, like human individuals, cultures can in the long run be distinctive only by putting their distinctiveness on the line; unless a culture risks its life, it will die the slow death of self-impoundment. This of course means that the limits within which cultures must flourish (that is, within which they must establish their identity) are extremely hard to negotiate, if for no other reason that they keep shifting.

The preceding obviously implies that not every cultural development, not even the most consensual one, is morally positive. Not every structure of inclusion gives rise to a genuinely humane society. Cultures can degenerate; instead of being expressions of the human attunement to all that exists and, beyond that, to God (cf. §102, 6), they can become structures of obfuscation and, indeed, *estrangement* (cf. §122, 1, a; cf. also §58, 2, a; §91, 3, a; §100, 5, a; §108, 5). For this reason, existing cultures must be challenged and shaken to stay alive; they must get their integrity regularly tested; they need internal critics and antagonists; they need examination by outsiders (cf. §46, 4; 2). For, in Emmanuel Lévinas' pregnant words,

Every rational institution implies being uprooted. The establishment of a genuine society is a matter of being uprooted—it marks the end of an existence where 'being at home' is an absolute, where everything comes from inside.[32]

Humanly (that is, morally) speaking, therefore, only those persons and communities that make deliberate efforts, both realistically and imaginatively, to appreciate and understand the distinctively other (and indeed, the strange and the downright alien) will deepen their understanding and appreciation of what is distinctive about themselves, both positively and negatively (cf. §95, 7–8). By contrast, wherever there is failure to understand and engage the distinctively other, human reason and the cultural shapes that incorporate it will find themselves decaying into mere custom. In the long run, the moral contentment inherent in being distinctive will deteriorate; this in turn will regularly (though often imperceptibly) lead to the cultivation of trite preconception and lazy prejudice; it can also lead to various forms of belligerent fanaticism and fundamentalism. Forms of civilization are distinctively human; consequently, they must obey the law of right reason, and this they can do only if none of them are allowed to be humanity's definitive form.

By way of summary, let us sum this up in different words. Wherever human sociality and inclusion are too narrowly conceived and practiced, self-absorption and fantasy will drive out imagination, and understanding; human communication with genuine others will die. To those imprisoned in such a world, any form of distinctive otherness will loom only as an array of opponents, to be passively ignored or (worse) aggressively excluded.

[a] At this point in our explorations, we must note the important links between the dynamics of inclusion and trust on the one hand and the dynamics of influence and power on the other.

Structures of power and influence, it was stated, typically maintain themselves by engendering cultures of *honor* and *loyalty* (§129, 3, f). There is nothing wrong with this, for power is a fact of cosmic life, and pride, loyalty, and a sense of honor can be, and often are, deeply constructive, humane, and moral. It is only human that valuable forms of human civilization should be treasured and held in high esteem by those who enjoy them; typically and quite appropriately, human beings by and large deem themselves fortunate to be part of their culture. Accordingly, they consider the defense of their cultural heritage, honorably and with united forces if need be, a matter of legitimate self-esteem and self-definition.

Still, just as cultures can turn opaque, self-regarding, and self-absorbed, so pride, honor, and loyalty can become forms of prejudice, fueled by mere fantasy. To the extent that this occurs, those participating in such cultures and shaped by them are apt to consider, in practice, things foreign or alien dishonorable and shameful. This will make them prone to bigotry, and to making aliens the object of stereotyping, caricature, and ridicule (cf. §29, 1–2). By the same token, they will be suspicious of *deviant insiders* who protest against established forms of unidentified bigotry. They are also likely to aggressively shame them into conformity, by means of public derision and harassment, and if need be by judicial action.

In such situations, unholy alliances between power and prejudice are likely to develop. Before long, such alliances are likely to give rise to a phenomenon mentioned before: wherever and whenever human communities and individuals fail to establish just and humane conditions in the areas of inclusion (and in particular, race) and intimacy (and in particular, sexuality), they are liable to maintain the *status quo* by resorting, not to human reason, but to characteristically cosmological means, in the form of unjust and even violent power structures and strategies of immoral forcefulness (§133, 2, [*v*]; §137, 10; 12–14; §138, 6, a). To the extent that this happens, the responsive and responsible regard for otherness in all its forms, which is the anthropological precondition for the responsive and responsible regard for God (cf. §95, 4–10), is displaced by blind self-regard. That is to say, the spectre of blind (*i.e.*, quasi-cosmological: §129, 2, a) force and violence has appeared on the anthropological horizon, beclouding the landscape.

This very alarming development invites further reflection, in two sets of observations, the first more positive than the second.

[7] It is well known that of all *distinctively human* phenomena, culture is the most basic. Even the scantiest evidence of burial customs is evidence for the presence of humanity. Humanity is inseparable from civilization, and thus, from knowledge, freedom, and morality.

This has momentous implications of a moral and religious nature. It is clear why this is so: once two human cultures have drifted into each other's ken, power is no longer the only issue. It will remain significant, of course, but, certainly in the long run, it is not the most significant. *Self-consciousness is.* That is to say, in any human encounter, inclusion and exclusion, trust and the limits of trust are *the* issues: they go to the heart of what it means to be *human*: we make demands on each other. What kind of demands? Looming large behind questions of trust and inclusion—and all the larger for doing so unthematically—are the great, precarious themes that make us human: understanding and morality, and along with them, even more unthematically, religious faith and practice. These central anthropological issues are apt to catch human beings off guard, individually and communally. In the encounter with unfamiliar others, we are most keen-ly confronted with our basic selves. We become self-conscious, and (given the unfamiliarity) clumsily so. In fact, anthropological issues turn out to be at least as intractable and volatile as issues of power and influence and often even more so; no wonder they are extremely hard to manage. We ourselves are!

On reflection, this is not surprising. Self-awareness and awareness of other do not occur at the level where the purblind give and take of combining and decombining cosmic forces operates by dint of action and reaction. They occur in the realm governed by the delicate dia-lectics of the human spirit forging *identity* out of alienation.

Let us put this differently. Encounters between human beings with significantly divergent personal and cultural sensibilities can succeed only if on *both* sides there is basic ability, willingness, and resolve to understand and accept; in other words, to be successful, any quest for understanding must be rooted in the more fundamental willing-ness to allow oneself to be understood and to accept acceptance.[33]

Let us elaborate a little. In distinctively human encounters, *under-standing proceeds dialectically:* constructiveness and receptiveness are one another's precondition in ways in which activity and reactivity in the park of power and influence seldom if ever are. For understand-ing and acceptance engage, not just human forcefulness nor even human resourcefulness, but also the far more clearly human capacity for *imagination.* Only the analogical imagination, whose source is *con-naturality and sympathy with the other,* can beget the *participation and in-terpretation* required for mutual understanding and acceptance (§63). Small wonder that all methods to establish the latter (a fascinating object of observation and study for outsiders like anthropologists and social psychologists) are very hard to carry off for those involved in the encounter. And needless to say, their outcome is invariably not hard to predict, but even harder to maintain and follow through on. This is why human understanding and acceptance are forever in process and never definitive, as most of us know from personal expe-rience, often exhilarating, often disappointing [r].

It was explained long ago that the challenge of communication, whether interpersonal, social, or intercultural, largely arises from the fact that, in most human encounters, interactions take the shape of

---

[r] For a stimulating phenomenological investigation and discussion of the dy-namics here treated rather more abstractly and theoretically, cf. William E. Bier-natzki's monograph *Roots of Acceptance: The Intercultural Communication of Religious Meanings.*

transactions that not only involve *things*, but are *also mediated by things* (§95, 1 and [*gg*]). In other words, mutual understanding and acceptance, no matter how spiritual and transcendent they may be in and of themselves, can never cut themselves loose from *things*—cosmic realities and their powerful impact. Yet at the same time we realize something else. If our encounters with really different human beings and communities are to be genuinely humane, we must rise above the very things that play such a crucial role in our attempts to communicate. To adopt a terminology used before, "communication-*to*" can be *humanly* effective and significant only to the extent that its matrix is "communication-*with*" (§95, 1). We forge genuine identity out of alienation only to the degree that we treat the *things which* we exchange and *through which* we communicate as *symbolic*. Accordingly, we must convey, somehow, that the truer sharing occurs at the level of *self-communication* (cf., once again, §95, 1 and [*gg*]).

This demonstrates a vital point: the dynamics of inclusion and exclusion involve our *identities*—again, personal, social, or cultural. For some of the "things" we bring with us into our encounters (and not the least important by far) are the noticeable, observable, incomplete identities on which we have come to rely for our self-definition (cf. §137, 1 and [*d*]), and which we now bring to the encounter, mainly in the form of developed sensibilities and mentalities. But since our identities are incomplete (*i.e.*, necessarily in process), they are by definition *provisional*—that is, neither final nor non-negotiable. This implies that the selves and the sensibilities we bring to our encounters are not completely stable; they will never provide us with an Archimedean point of leverage. We ourselves, our communities, and the cultures of which we are remain exposed to the powerful impact of the forces of alienation and cosmicity, especially in this sense that none of us can communicate with different persons, communities, and cultures without dealing with the unfamiliar *particulars* in which they have reposited their identity. This invites further development.

Humanity never ceases to be radically cosmic (cf. §116, 3). This means that situations in which the dynamics of inclusion and exclusion arise as moral issues are very often *triggered* by purely a-moral and pre-moral forces. These forces occur on a spectrum: they range all the way from the blind play of cosmic and biophysical odds to mindless, heedless human violence. Obviously, this implies that many human encounters are not elective; they are dictated and imposed by forces that are a-moral, pre-moral, and at times downright immoral.

Even more than other animals, human beings have the instinctive ability to ward off alien influences and traditional enemies by means of forcefulness, often by combining their efforts. But like animals, human beings do not always prevail; ordinary antagonists both infra-human and human—"famine, plague, drought, diseases, wars"[34]—often carry the day (§118, 5, b). From time immemorial human individuals and communities have been put under duress by the forces of natural, pre-moral, and outright moral evil; very frequently, they have been driven into exile, out into the wide world—that is to say, into *involuntary* appointments with other human beings and communities and cultures, to whom they had been total strangers.

The details of many of these movements have, of course, receded into the mists of pre-history. But some of the historic migrations remain a matter of fairly reliable record, like the great population migration in Central Asia and Europe in the course of many centuries around the beginning of the Common Era. Among other things, these movements gradually propelled the Germanic tribes into Western and South Western Europe, and almost succeeded in pushing the Celts into the Atlantic Ocean. Even present-day North America is to a significant extent the product of comparable dynamics; only in this case the moving forces have been enormously enabled and intensified, from the mid-nineteenth century onward, by the development of transportation technology, which made the horizontal mobility of very large numbers a human (that is, moral) *option*—even if it was a forced option in innumerable cases. And the phenomenon has continued, at an even more terrifying rate, in this century of migrant laborers and their families, forced displacement of entire populations, and hapless refugees—victims of famine, disaster, and mindless human violence by the millions.

Cosmic and quasi-cosmic forces, it has been stated, have the ability to bring human beings and communities and cultures together. Beneficial cosmic and quasi-cosmic forces can favor constructive human encounters across racial, linguistic, and cultural divides, and even facilitate them. But no cosmic or quasi-cosmic force can *of itself* bring about *constructive* human encounters; the most they can do is bring about *occasions* for such encounters. Accordingly, innumerable human encounters are *at least to some extent forced*. Here it is vitally important to recognize that the capacity to take advantage, in a discerning manner, of such occasions and to turn them into distinctively human encounters lies *exclusively at the anthropological level*. There and nowhere else is transcendence over the forces of cosmic and quasi-

cosmic mutualities a possibility; there and nowhere else is the opportunity *and* the capacity for deliberation—that is, for humanity and
morality—available.

Only significantly free, responsive, responsible, virtuous human beings, communities, and cultures, substantially enlightened and guided by right reason, can advisedly choose to go out of their way so as
to constructively relate to other, strikingly different human beings
and communities, whom the vicissitudes—often violent—of cosmic
and human agency of one kind or another have put in their proxim-
ity. In the harsh climate created by a morally unintelligible cosmos
and the severe impairment of humanity's own ability to act morally,
especially when under pressure, such acts and habits of self-transcendence are very demanding. No wonder they are relatively few and far
between. Many human individuals, communities, and cultures still
have only the dimmest visions and hopes for humanity as a whole.
The notion of a common good that exceeds the bounds of individuals, families, tribes, societies, "sovereign" nations, or cultures of long
standing strikes many of them as a threat to their identity. They believe, rightly or wrongly (but who is to tell?), that they cannot *afford*
any such truly common good—that is, a good that encompasses both
them and others, and even humanity as a whole, in an ever-widening
culture of effective communication. But creative discernment and
knowledgeable appreciation of alien otherness is in short supply everywhere in the world, much to the moral detriment of humanity everywhere. Even the many cultures that like to think of themselves as
genuinely open regularly find the demand for *mutually* transforming
interpersonal, international, and transcultural encounters hard to
tolerate. Much as they proclaim "humanity" as their ideal, they find
that it is easier professed than practiced; when confronted at close
quarters with particular others, they find themselves unable to be sufficiently self-critical; accordingly, trepidation and anxiety prevent
them from meeting the challenge with confidence. Understandably
so, for even the best of one's close neighbors are notoriously more
demanding than all one's faraway friends told together.

"And for all this, human nature is never spent."[35] Humanity's transcendental desire for freedom and identity, which constitutes the
core of its orientation to all that is, is ineradicable. In the last analysis, it can be counted on to continue to inspire a transcultural humanism. For this reason, human beings will always be responding to
otherness by turning their native capacity for analogy and participation into responsible and deliberate action. Broader horizons will

open, if not always gently; wider humanisms will emerge and become attractive, if never without at least some violence. Humanity's yearning for civilization may be wounded; it will not die.

Yet if the promise held out by this cheerful profession of faith in humanity is incalculable, so are the risks. This leads to a final reflection—one distinctly less encouraging and, for that matter, cheerful.

[8] Historic experience shows that cultures that combine appreciable power and influence with considerable intellectual and moral distinction are the only ones that can meet racial, linguistic, and cultural differences confidently—that is, in such a way that, far from inhibiting the pursuit of intelligent engagement with otherness, the differences actually *invite, stimulate, and further* it. But history suggests two other things as well. The first is that such cultures are the exception rather than the rule. The second was intimated long ago, when it was pointed out that "[u]nderstanding is . . . a positive way of initiating the interplay of structures, and one, on the whole, more humane and peaceful than coin and cannon" (§11, 6). We do indeed know from experience that even the most genuine human understanding across racial, linguistic, and cultural divides rarely if ever succeeds in emancipating itself complete from power and even violence. This should give us pause. Why would this be? Are not all human persons and communities natively concerned with all other human beings and communities? Is the desire for deliberate concern with otherness not rooted in humanity's attunement to the world of the spirit wherever and however it manifests itself? Surely such a deep orientation cannot simply go underground?

The unfortunate fact is that our native desire for inclusion and engagement with the cosmos and other human beings, while ineradicable, can degenerate and decay. It can be resisted and suppressed; it can even be positively denied. Whenever and wherever this happens, the results are miserable. One of our most distinctive goods lies in our native desire to relate, positively and from the depth of our human authenticity, to other human beings through the medium of distinctive cultural forms and moral ideals. Yet in practice this desire can turn sour on us, and degenerate into a positive, intensely aggressive evil. This possibility is inherent in the dialectics of inclusion and exclusion.

Aquinas learned this from Aristotle. *Corruptio optimi pessima:* the degeneration of what is highest and best begets not some form of amiable, tolerable mediocrity, but "the worst."[36] How so?

The dynamics of inclusion and exclusion are distinctively *anthropological*. Where they operate, we find ourselves in a sphere different from the world of cosmicity and matter. In the latter, quality is inseparable from quantity, and hence, from growth and corruption; morality and immorality are invariably a matter of *magis et minus,* of more and less. But we are in the realm of the human spirit proper; here growth and decay are, not progressive or cumulative, but dialectical (cf. §54, 5, d; §148, 5, a, [*m*]). Neutrality is impossible here; we are dealing not just with the realm of things and instincts and passions; we are dealing with *persons* (cf. §95, 5). Here, *exitus* and *reditus* can exist only in mutual *perichōrēsis.* Not to engage otherness is to stagnate and to undermine the very capacity for self-transcendence that makes us human; not to grow in identity is to stagnate and eventually to become degenerate. In communities where this stagnation occurs, cherished, constructive forms of living by familiarity of culture, unity of language, and racial balance will get idolized, and the proud visions that once inspired the shared values and upheld them degenerate into false ideals. Perceptions of racial characteristics get simplified and absolutized, habits of speech get reinforced to force conformity, and in-group manners baffling to others are passed off as civilized. No wonder relationships with others turn into exercises in distortion, braced by crude stereotypes and stubborn prejudices that dehumanize the soul and drain it of the milk of human kindness.

In such an environment, fantasy will replace discernment. Posturing, boasting, and propaganda will stand in for understanding. Typically, persons and parties that are least sensitive to justice in matters of inclusion and exclusion will advocate and resort to something they know much better: the use of power and even violence to bring about what they mistake for justice (cf. §133, 2, [*s*]; §137, 10; 12–14; §138, 6, a). In due course, relatively trivial conflicts, frequently elicited by provocation, will set off acts and outbursts of rage and violence all the more mean and vicious for being not only irrational but also deliberate and intentionally disproportionate. Miserably, justice and human "communication" will eventually take the shape of "making examples," calculated vindictiveness, cold-blooded intimidation and terror tactics, "ethnic cleansing," reciprocal slaughter, and even outright genocide—all of them excused and even justified by appeals to ideals that are have obviously become false and inhumane.

[a] This gives rise to a hypothesis. Could it make sense to say that the more significant the role played by *deliberate, historic human vio-*

lence in the *historical origins* of present-day interracial and intercultural confrontation, the harder and more thankless the task of trying to achieve constructive relationships today? This hypothesis would appear to follow from the proposition, quoted in the previous paragraph, that unethical recourse to power is typically a symptom of sinful deficiency in justice in the areas of inclusion and affection (cf. once again §133, 2, [*v*]; §137, 10; 12–14; §138, 6, a).

Examples galore come to mind. Let us review some of the more glaring ones.

The history of the Christian West is punctuated by the violence inflicted by Christians on the racially and culturally different *Jews*. In the Iberian peninsula, they were forced to convert till, in 1492, they were banished. In the eighteenth and nineteenth centuries, after generations had been forcibly denied participation in the ordinary structures of justice and driven into exile, numerous Jews let themselves be coopted by the residual Christianity of the Enlightenment as "Deists with a difference," only to be threatened with complete extinction by the Third *Reich*, which successfully appealed to another completely ideological construct—namely, the purity of the "Aryan" race—to drive millions of Jews into violent deaths.

But the Jews (and the *Armenians* massacred by the Turks early in this century) are far from alone. Historic practices of slavery in the West (such as the systematic raiding of *Ireland* by the Norwegian, Icelandic, and Sicilian Vikings in the early Middle Ages, and of the coastal regions of *South America* by the Portuguese in the sixteenth century) typically targeted victims both sharply different racially and living at significant distances from the homelands of those doing the capturing and the trading of slaves. All this taken together suggests that the combination of geographical distance and unmistakable racial differences has often been considered sufficient reason to view the prisoners as subhuman "savages"; this plainly served as a "moral" rationalization for the use of inhuman force. The gratuitous justifications of the violence inflicted, in the course of the *Conquista*, on the *native Americans* of South and Central America, would appear to be another example of this phenomenon (cf. §62, 1, b, *g*]). A similar dynamic must have been at work in the case of the violent abduction of hundreds of thousands of black Africans into slavery in the New World, especially in what what was to become the United States. The geographical distance that separated the Negroes from the slave traders and the racial gap (both the real and the perceived) between them, combined with the notion that they were humanly inferior, apparently sufficed to allow the traders to suppress the sense that they shared a common humanity with the Negroes they captured and traded. This helped make the slave trade a mere feasibility proposition—that is to say, a strictly pragmatic undertaking. All that mattered, obviously, was power, know-how, and resolve to rearrange things (!) in the world in such a way as to advance the commercial ambitions of the superior West.

Now recall that the habitual adoption of immoral positions will diminish the moral sense of those adopting them (cf. §136, 1, [c]; §140, 5), and it will become clear why the slave trade should have led to a genuine (if mostly unacknowledged) loss of humanity and moral sensitivity on the part of both the traders of black slaves and their owners. That is, it positively impaired their ability—their own and their descendants'—to recognize blacks and cultivate relations with them on a fully human and genuinely moral basis of equality. All this suggests, of course, that it impaired their religious sensibilities as well. No wonder attempts have been made to show scientifically and statistically that in the anti-abolitionist South, deep religious commitment and preparedness to join the abolitionist cause were positively correlated.[37]

[b] If there should be any truth in the hypothesis just elaborated, this would affect our interpretation of the interracial situation presently prevailing, say, in the United States. Here, our first observation has to be: the plight of the black community differs in one crucial regard from all other racially different groups, even of the most recent arrivals, the Hispanics and the East and South East Asians. Black people came not to improve their own condition; they were forcibly imported in order to improve the condition of those already in possession. The wide racial (as well as linguistic and cultural) chasm still prevailing between (on the one hand) blacks and (on the other hand) whites and other people of color coexisting today in one and the same society are a continuing, *present*, very ominous reminder of the historic inhumanity and violence of the slave trade (and thus, of the deep failure of intelligence and morality that inspired it). Today's racial situation in North America, in other words, remains to a large extent a *present* case of forced (and in that sense "unnatural") coexistence. No wonder the present-day encounter between two significantly different sub-cultures—one black, one non-black—remains, humanly speaking, very taxing. No wonder either that separatism both black and non-black continues

to bedevil us. No wonder, finally, that all of this continues to cry out for repentance and near-heroic attempts at reconciliation.

[9] Why would human beings want to reach out to other human beings across cultural divides? The proposed answer to this question is likely to be familiar by now. The cherished accomplishments of any culture or sub-culture are typically based on a sense of racial affinity, a broadly received common language or at least idiom, and shared manners. All of these facilitate a cultural tradition. All of them are also the fruit of successful past efforts to forge identity out of alienation. Still, in the last analysis neither the efforts nor the accomplishments are ever entirely self-authenticating, let alone definitive. For the impulse toward a civilized common culture, by which we forge a communal identity out of otherness, must draw upon something we do not control. It is (*pace* Sigmund Freud) rooted in humanity's native desire for self-transcendence, which is boundless because a transcendental *given*—that is, not of human devising (cf. §112, 2–3). Accordingly, not even the most meaningful or valuable and just structures of inclusion (or, for that matter, exclusion) can ever be definitive. Any *particular* search for just structures of inclusion and exclusion is an exercise in the dynamics of provisionality. Only by dint of continuous transition (cf. §76) and transformation can human traditions keep aspiring to the Infinite and thus stay alive.

Let us put this cultural truth in explicitly moral terms. Earlier, it was explained that only by continuous, conscientious refinement of its distinctive moral sense can any particular humane civilization give shape to its attentiveness to a shared sense of duty—that authoritative inner guide which demands that it be cherished and taken seriously, followed, not manipulated (cf. §105, 3; 5; cf. also GS 16; DH 4316; §134, 1). This typically happens is by way of a "hermeneutical circle": *cultures and sensibilities will become transparent to themselves only to the extent to which they open themselves to cultures and sensibilities other than their own.* The touchstone of human (*i.e., moral*) identity and authenticity, it turns out, is *the sustained search for the ever more truly common good*—a point made with great spiritual authority by the Catholic bishops of England and Wales in 1996, in a pastoral letter entitled *The Common Good and the Catholic Church's Social Teaching.*

This leads to conclusions. First of all, human beings do act responsibly and morally whenever and wherever they wrest viable and often splendid units of humane civilization from the multiplicity of sheer otherness—the welter of forces at work in the cosmos, both the productive and the counterproductive. Secondly, in doing so, they act morally only as long as they do so for the time being, and within the bounds of prevailing conditions of time and place. Particular cultures do indeed transform the world of time and place; thus they enable sizable segments of humanity to establish a genuine measure of personal and communal freedom and identity. They do so by including human beings in nations, societies, and communities held together by a sense of belonging, based on shared intuitions and on values embodied in common racial, linguistic, and cultural characteristics. Yet such cultures always remain limited, not only extensively, in that they succeed in turning only so much otherness into identity, but also intrinsically, inasmuch as the shared identity they achieve is never final, and thus, never wholly convincing.

The process of civilization, therefore, is not wholly self-authenticating or self-sustaining. While a key human (*i.e.,* moral) exercise, civilization keeps generating a steady supply of moral ambivalences and discontents. For, on the one hand, the native human thirst for truth, goodness, and worthiness of notice is boundless, and the sheer variety of otherness never stops beckoning. Yet on the other hand, the civilizing intellectual and moral impulses that foster the formation of common cultures and affirm them as positive goods are prone to decay; we tend to content ourselves so blithely with the limited forms of inclusion we have achieved that we become loath to attempt further ventures in communal self-transcendence. Not surprisingly, therefore, at times and in places, the analogical imagination will balk. For, while the dynamics of inclusion require that boldness and imagination conquer the prejudices bred by fear and fantasy, the latter often impersonate the former; prejudice can create the illusion of creativity and authenticity (§137, 5). And in any case, just how much exclusiveness can any cultural community legitimately claim in order to protect its identity? How much imagination and boldness can a cultural community afford without opening itself up to such an extent that it begins to dissipate its treasures, and thus, to squander itself and throw itself away? And *vice versa,* just at what point does legitimate concern with self-identity sink into self-absorption and fantasy?

These are rhetorical questions, of course, but they are raised to suggest some basic conclusions. First of all, the largely cosmic dynamics of power and influence cannot be trusted with the cause of justice, except in the sense that cosmic happenstance, personified in Dame Fortune or in the ministering angels (or depersonalized in the law of averages) tends to administer some kind of elementary justice under the aegis of God's Providence (§129, 4, c). However, anthropologically speaking, wherever and whenever possible, justice must be decided by careful discernment and sensitive negotiation. Inclusion and exclusion, association and disassociation, trust and healthy misgivings cannot and must not be left to the luck of the draw. Secondly, existing structures of inclusion and exclusion are often reinforced and idealized by myth and legend; imagination and justice, therefore, are often very hard to tell apart from fantasy and prejudice; communal discernment and negotiation is notoriously easier to commend than to practice (cf. §137, 6, d, [h]). Yet if a culture hopes to enjoy the wonderful blessings of justice, what is required is *prudence*, not only in persons and assemblies in positions of leadership (§135, 2, a), but in the culture at large as well. Such prudence as a public virtue implies: *culturally respected habits of pluralism*. But not any kind of culturally accepted pluralism will do, for prudence born out of of lack of civic interest is no more than lazy, apathetic tolerance—an attitude known to be prone to turning around and degenerating into aggressive forms of intolerance.

By contrast, prudence is a virtue both intellectual and practical; the word means "providence"; prudent persons and communities are oriented to what lies beyond the moral balance pursued within the limits of their systems of justice; they recognize the significance of more-than-local truth and more-than-local moral purpose; small wonder Aquinas can write that prudence is the *perfection* of moral virtue.[38] For prudence to become a public ("cultural") virtue, what is prerequired is a shared attitude of *appreciative, probing, quietly reasonable* openness, inspired by a vivid, responsible interest in otherness in all its forms, drawn toward an increasingly global purview, and capable of intercultural negotiation animated by modesty, patience, endurance, critical empathy, and a feel for kinships and analogies [s].

---

[s] Earlier, it was proposed that *temperance* is the cardinal virtue typically called for in the life of virtue insofar insofar as it involves the deliberate management of the impulse of *passion* (§131, 5). Here it is proposed that *prudence* is the counterpart of fortitude in the deliberate pursuit of *justice*. (cf. §§130–31). — Incidentally, we may have stumbled here upon the ethical significance of that explosive activity so typical of the affluent cultures: *cultural exchange* and *tourism*. Horizontal mobility of the recreational, exploratory, and educational kind *across societal stratifications* has changed the face, the economy and the cultural atmosphere of Europe in the past half century, and non-European countries have recently been following suit. I have met professional international tour-guides who interpret their work in this ethical perspective, in the teeth of too wide-spread a tendency in the tourism industry to turn recreational travel into an exercise in superficiality and even licence. — On a somewhat different subject, in light of today's demand for a cul-

Only on the basis of such prudence can cultures stand up for justice beyond its own boundaries. Provident care, therefore, must typify all those persons, communities, and entire cultures whose clear responsibility it is to act in behalf of that huge portion of humanity that continues to find itself excluded or on the brink of exclusion—all those who do not really count: the half-breeds, the inarticulate, the ill-mannered and the unmannered, the little people, the half-civilized, the plodding, the powerless, the disorganized who are in the grip of organized criminals, the marginal, the barely born and the unborn, the barely alive and the dying, the displaced—the countless who can only try, not to mention the countless who have given up trying? It is *patience*—the charism characteristic of the dedicated believers whom Maximus the Confessor compares with the stewards who were the mainstay of the ancient homesteads: securely working for a fixed wage, and *for that reason* entrusted with the care of the large number of dirt-poor day-laborers forced to live hand to mouth (cf. §53, 2, c):

The wage-earners [are] those who, out of desire for the goods that God has promised, patiently bear the weight of the day and its heat—that is to say, both the tribulation that has been implanted in, and forced upon, this present life as a result of our ancestor's sin, and the trials [naturallly] inherent in this life, so that we might acquire virtue. They are those who wisely, out of self-chosen conviction, trade in life for life—this present life for the life to come.[39]

[a] The undertaking here commended, if only in sketchy outlines, simply *must* become the inspiration of the affluent nations, of international political bodies like the United Nations, of multinational business corporations, of the great religious cultures, of the international Jewish community, of the Christian churches and communions. It certainly must become a vital part of the commitment of the Catholic Church, whose universality, always professed in the Creed as *an article of faith*, has, in our century, become *an em-*

---

ture of pluralism, Hegel's claim that the defeat of class privilege and slavery in his day was the culmination of *freedom,* which he viewed as Christianity's central theme (§133, 2, [*u*]), now looks premature. The self-transcendence involved in humanity's emancipation from the forces of cosmic alienation is only a first step toward the full liberation of the human spirit in history; it must be followed by the self-transcendence demanded by the distinctively anthropological acknowledgment of the unity of all of humanity. This transcultural imperative, conveyed (among many other things) by what we now rightly call "human rights," may very well turn out to be the chief moral imperative of the twenty-first century and beyond, just as freedom from slavery and oppression has been the chief moral imperative of the nineteenth, as Hegel was among the first to intuit.

pirical fact as well—a fact whose significance Karl Rahner has pointed out in a prophetic essay.[40] Since all these bodies are effectively transcultural in intent, they have an unprecedented opportunity as well as a clear moral responsibility on behalf of all of humanity—both enhanced by the potential of modern communications technology. For, in the wake of colonialism and decolonialization, revolutions of every kind, two devastating world wars, the Holocaust, two nuclear bombs and the continuing nuclear threat, we live in a world that is increasingly waking up to the limitations of influence, power, and the use of force as justifiable means to establish peace with justice. Henceforth, human persons and communities simply *must* learn the fine art of constructive inclusion and exclusion. Ever so patiently and deliberately, more and more of humanity will have to discover more and more that discovery of, and active encounter with, otherness is inseparable from self-discovery; familiarization with the unfamiliar other is a risky exercise in distortion of the other unless it is attended by the chastening (if often delightful) experience of familiarization with the yet-unfamiliar self [*t*].

[b] What has also been argued implies that the human knack for civilization, while a vital moral task, is no more self-authenticating and self-sustaining than the life of virtue (cf. §123). That is to say, like virtue, culture and morality are tremendous assets, yet they can turn into liabilities, in that they *can* become self-regarding and self-absorbed. This realization has immense theological significance—a theme to be elaborated in chapter 18.

[10] Let us sum up. In this section it has been argued that the dynamics of inclusion offer a formidable *moral* challenge. Humanity, relying on its capacity for appreciation, imagination, judgment, and deliberate action, must engage the knack for configuration and harmony resident in cosmic process. It must also deliberately add to

---

[*t*] It has already been suggested that this discussion is a transposition of Hans-Georg Gadamer's account of the "hermeneutical circle." In fact, Gadamer's philosophy, consistently hermeneutical as it is, is best viewed as a foundational moral philosophy of *culture*. For at the heart of Gadamer's anthropology lies a critique of the Enlightenment's rational, a-moral universalism, rooted in technological Reason, and enforced by means of "scientific method." In Gadamer's analysis, the aim of this method, with its spurious claims to objectivity and universality, was not appreciation and understanding, but control and mastery. Thus the Enlightenment was incapable of viewing distinctive cultural creations as anything but forms of prejudice—an inability it did its best to conceal. Small wonder Gadamer's writings are full of pleas for the need for *Bildung*—formation in *humanitas* and humane appreciation and virtue—as the road to truly universal knowledge and understanding.

and enhance it, by turning the forces of the cosmos as well as its own native potential to constructive, civilized ends. Only in this way can the world be humanized, and new, maturer forms of human identity and authenticity emerge.

But it has also been argued that the dynamics of inclusion are beset by fantasy. And fantasy's agenda is not moral development (that is, growth in human identity and authenticity), but its opposite, which is: inauthentic self-maintenance and self-assertion, both individual and communal. Consequently, the agenda of fantasy is also the opposite of commitment to the enhancement of the cosmos and humanity. For by fantasy we find ourselves, both individually and communally, pressured to seek ourselves. Not deliberate, responsible, measured, reasonable engagement *with* the other is fantasy's aim, but passionate endeavor to live *off* the other and *at the expense of* the other. Enslaved by fantasy, therefore, we will misperceive and mistreat the other; we will be unable to do justice to the other—other things and especially other persons, communities, and cultures. And in the process, we will misposition, misstate and mistreat ourselves as well; in our misengagement with otherness, we will find ourselves reinforcing the partial, unfinished, fantasy-based self-conceptions fantasy urges us to live by. In this way, we will be doing our true selves a serious injustice. That is, we will be sinning, at least indirectly, against God, whose image we both natively mirror and share with all that is other, especially human persons.

[11] The formulation of this general conclusion gives us an opportunity to take our leave of our theme: the effects of fantasy in the domain of *systemic* moral failure and sin. We must now return to investigations of a more personalist nature. We will do so by introducing and detailing a classical theme in ascetical theology, namely, the understanding of moral growth and development. However, by way of transition, let us consider two brief observations on that most characteristic component of the life of deliberation: *discernment.*

[a] First of all, in view of what has been explained, one conclusion should come as no surprise: individual persons need fearlessness, inner clarity, and resolve, all of them rooted in a conversion to a dependable inner sense of transcendence, if they are to take their distance from the crowd (*anachōrēsis* again: cf. §124, 13 and a–b) and to move beyond fantasy and prejudice. Persons and communities need the constant practice of discernment to discover and cultivate these crucial properties, if they are to move successfully in

the direction of virtue deliberately exercised, often in an environment marked by stagnation, intolerance, rumors of violence, actual violence, and other incentives to, and effects of, sin.

Something else becomes clear as well. Leaving aside infrequent
instances of strictly individual conversion, "personal" victories over
fantasy, prejudice, mystification, and "myth" are seldom solo performances. They are normally only within the reach of those who
are sustained by mature personal friendship and companionship
(cf. §95, 6–9; §137, 9, a). In fact, *personal* conversions usually occur in the setting of moral (and ultimately religious) *communities*
supported by narrative and liturgical traditions which, while acknowledging the anxiety inherent in the moral life, enshrine enduring experiences of both universalism and transcendence (cf.
§123, 7) [*u*].

[b] Secondly, let us recall a piece of ascetical advice, well-known
in the world of spiritual discernment. Christian saints and sages
have traditionally taught that evil spirits of every kind avail themselves of fantasies to tempt us (cf. §125, 5, g, [*xx*]). Now while fantasies are powerful encouragements to overt a-moral and immoral
action, *they operate covertly*; they shun the light of day; they derive
their power to tempt from being allowed to remain secret. This se-
crecy is of one piece with the fact that they are both habitual and
prejudicial. In fact, they are so much part of the accustomed interior world of individuals and communities that a peculiar "old-
shoe" familiarity attaches to them; we will tolerate them, and sometimes even cherish them, as regrettable parts of our little, private
circle of habit and intimacy. We let sleeping dogs lie. Accordingly,

---

[*u*] Let us draw a conclusion from this. Not *every* great myth and not *every* deliberate ("democratic") decision of human societies (or of smaller social units) carries
the guarantee of moral maturity. Social and societal dynamics are regularly torn
between the herd instinct (which encourages giving in to the pressure of momentary passion) and the sense of transcendence (which encourages both true community and inner freedom as a function of fortitude and patience). For this reason,
all mythologies and every social consensus must be *discerned:* not everything that is
immemorial, classic, socially accepted, or even accepted by vote is morally acceptable. One can hear this point frequently made in the United States, and rightly so;
one favorite way for North Americans to do so is to recall that the Third Reich had
its origin in the *legitimate* parliamentary moves that brought Hitler to power. But
we need not really look abroad to find instances of social dynamics of dubious
moral validity. To mention one example among many, a classic like Vance Packard's *The Hidden Persuaders* teems with evidence to the fact that American society is
very vulnerable to large-scale manipulation and self-manipulation by the intentional, deliberate creation of fantasy and rationalization. "Selling" is not always moral.
Neither are appeals to "freedom," as John Henry Newman observed (§136, 3).

the thought of bringing up individual and communal illusions and publicly casting doubts on them will occasion strong emotional resistance. Exposure is usually attended by much shame and passion.

Ignatius of Loyola likens these fantasies and temptations to a furious woman intimidating an irresolute man, to a suitor trying to charm a wife away from her husband, and to a wily robber captain designing a plan of attack. He adds that all who wish to advance in the life of the spirit are well advised to face these enemies down by breaking the spell they cast, by giving the secret away, ordinarily by manifesting hidden fantasies and temptations deriving from them to a discerning spiritual director.[41]

In our day this classical piece of ascetical advice, whose focus is strictly individual, would seem to invite a social application: the responsible pursuit of integral justice involves the unmasking of societal prejudices by careful social analysis (cf. §93, 9, b, [w]; cf. also DH 4730–41),[42] discerning explanation, and (at times) public, "prophetic" criticism and witness, both discerning and courageous.

[§139] THE CAPITAL SINS, THE ENNEAGRAM, AND SELF-ACCEPTANCE

[1] The classical ascetical tradition has deeply reflected on the life that is driven by self-serving fantasy and hence, lived on the strength of crippling basic attitudes. It has done so under the rubric of "the capital sins." Traditionally, they are listed as pride, avarice, lust, envy, gluttony, anger, and sloth [v]. In the English-speaking world, they are generally known as the "seven deadly sins."[43]

[a] The first systematic treatment of this vital theme in the pursuit of Christian perfection takes us back to the Christian Stoicism and Platonism of the final decades of the fourth century. Thus Evagrius Ponticus, in his collection of observations on the monastic life known as *Praktikos,* lists eight *logismoi* ("[bad] thoughts"); he regards them (not as *sins* but) as primal, habitual types of *temptation.* All of them take the concrete shape of *involuntary mental events* instigating actions that are apt to turn out sinful. He writes: "There are, all told, eight generic thoughts [*genikōtatoi logismoi*]; together, they account for all [bad] thoughts. The first is that of gluttony [*gastrimargia*], followed by that of fornication [*porneia*]; the third is of avarice [*philargyria*], the fourth of grief [in the sense of dejec-

---

[v] For a history of the idea, cf. Aimé Solignac's article *Péchés capitaux* in *DictSpir* XII, coll. 853–62. The present treatment is greatly indebted to this careful piece.

tion; *lypē*], the fifth of anger [*orgē*], the sixth of sloth [*akēdia*], the seventh of vainglory [*kenodoxia*], the eighth of pride [*hyperēphania*]. It is not for us to decide *whether* all of these will crowd in on the soul or not. What *is* for us to decide is whether they shall linger or not, or set off passionate reactions or not."[44] In several of his other writings, Evagrius exemplifies and details the fantasies and dreams involved in each of the eight "thoughts"; he also suggests strategies and practical remedies to contend with these interior enemies— the so-called *industriæ* of a later day.[45]

In the beginning of the fifth century, John Cassian brought Evagrius' teaching with him to the West, witness his treatment of the *octo principalia vitia* ("eight chief vices") in his *Institutes*[46] and in the *Conference of the Abbot Serapion* [*w*].[47]

[b] Leaving aside relatively insignificant variations in the order of enumeration, attempts were made at an early stage in the tradition to reduce the number from eight to *seven*, presumably under the pressure of numbers symbolism. This also started a tendency toward theological and conceptual systematization, somewhat at the expense of experiential subtlety. Thus, in the East, John Climacus (d. ± 650 A.D.) will merge pride and vainglory.

In the West, Gregory the Great (d. 604 A.D.) becomes the main conduit for the understanding of the capital sins. He adopts Augustine's theological position that pride (*superbia*) is the root of all sin. He then picks up the monastic notion of the spiritual combat: we must struggle with all the vices that lead us into temptation (*tentantia vitia*). Their number is legion, of course, but happily, most of them are minor—all they can succeed in doing is crowding in on the soul. However, there are seven major vices; while relatively few in number, they do weigh down the neglectful soul. Gregory also thinks of vices as *well-organized*. Each of the seven major vices is like the commander (*dux*) of an army (*exercitus*) of minor vices. The seven themselves in turn owe direct fealty to Pride, the Queen of Vices (*vitiorum regina superbia*), for, according to Scripture, pride is the beginning of sin (Sir 10, 15 Vg).

Gregory uses a different set of metaphors as well. Pride, he explains, is sin's poisonous root. From it spring its principal offshoots (*primae soboles*): vainglory, envy, anger, grief, avarice, "gluttony of the belly," and lechery. These unholy seven are doomed to meet

---

[*w*] The editors of the *Philokalia* included Cassian's treatment (*Philok* I, pp. 73–93)—a measure of its authority, also in the East.

their match in the Savior, who, fittingly, has come to the battle filled with the sevenfold gift of the Spirit.[48]

Oddly, in Gregory's arrangement, envy has been split off from grief, and sloth has disappeared altogether. (The latter just *may* be due to the fact that the dreaded state of *accidie*, or general malaise of the soul, is liable to occur in monastic settings rather than in Christian life in the world, to which Gregory's teaching about the capital sins is now increasingly geared.)

Another classic medieval account is found in the little treatise "The Five Sets of Seven" by Hugh of Saint Victor (d. 1141 A.D.). It lists pride (*superbia*), envy (*invidia*), anger (*ira*), grief (*tristitia*), avarice (*avaritia*), gluttony (*gula*), and lust (*luxuria*) [x]. By this time, Gregory's treatment has come to command almost universal respect, except that vainglory has once again been swallowed up by pride; more importantly, however, the Victorine treatment shows how, in typical twelfth-century style, revelry in ingenious systematization has replaced ascetical experience as principle of order.

Finally, in the *Summa theologiae*, Aquinas retrieves Gregory's military metaphor, and also joins him in treating the capital sins as the root causes of sin.[49] However, his full-scale treatment of the capital sins, each with its own assortment of minor vices, is found, not in the *Summa*, but in the *Disputed Questions on Evil*, in eight consecutive questions.[50] There, Aquinas once again follows Gregory in giving pride its position of preeminence, yet he also maintains that it is closely connected with vainglory.[51]

[c] These late classical and high medieval developments indicate a profound change in the understanding of the capital sins. Originally, they had been viewed as eight relatively well-established, recognizable forms of the *experience of concupiscence* powered by fantasy. Thus, the study of them had occupied a central place in the ascetical-mystical culture of self-knowledge in the service of the pursuit of self-denial and the contemplative love of God. Now they are being interpreted as actual, and indeed deadly, *sins*; accordingly, the study of them serves, and will serve for the foreseeable future, a dual purpose. First, theories about the capital sins and their

---

[x] *De Quinque Septenis* (*SC* 155, pp. 100–19). The four other, matching sets of seven are: (1) the seven petitions of the Lord's Prayer; (2) the seven gifts of the Holy Spirit; (3) the seven virtues drawn from the seven (!) beatitudes: poverty of spirit or humility, meekness, sorrow for sins, thirst for justice, compassion, purity of heart, and peace; (4) the beatitudes themselves: God's kingdom, possession of the land, consolation, abundance of justice, mercy, the vision of God, divine filiation.

retinue of ancillary vices now stimulate the *learned theological imagination*, with its delight in conceptuality. Secondly, and even more importantly, these theories now guide *penitential practice:* they now educate confessors and penitents alike in the elaborate varieties of immoral experience. Thus, in the late fourteenth century, when writing *The Canterbury Tales*, Geoffrey Chaucer can put on the poor Parson's lips a detailed account of the "sevene deedly synnes, this is to seyn, chieftaynes of synnes." But he will firmly set this account in the context of a long *penitential sermon*. After Pride, "the general roote of alle harmes," Chaucer's Parson treats "certein braunches, as Ire, Envye, Accidie or Slewthe, Avarice or Coveitise, . . . Glotonye, and Lecherye," each with "his braunches and his twigges."[52]

Interestingly, though, systematization never completely defeated experience. The well-read Flemish mystic Hadewijch, a contemporary of Aquinas, was very well aware of several of the Victorine writings, but in the matter of ascetical self-knowledge she remained independent. In her Twelfth Letter, under the rubric of the "affections" that obstruct Love, she examines a number of undesirable mental and practical habits. Interestingly, they bear a close resemblance to some of the deadly sins: self-will, false shame, unrighteous anger. But she treats all of them as "affections," not sins. Thus, conceivably without being aware of it, Hadewijch retrieved what Evagrius had in mind: predispositions, not sins.

[d] The early Christian ascetics were well aware that the battle with passion and its impact on the life of fantasy is not identical for everyone. In that sense, the ancient monastic traditions (like the Stoicism on which they drew) had rudimentary conceptions of "personality." For example, a master like Cassian can remind his monks: ". . . as we have said, we not are assailed in the same way, and it is up to each of us to direct the thrust of his battle against the kind of offensive that chiefly plagues him . . . And hence, we, for our part, must adjust our strategy depending on which vices are dominant in us, and how they are best tackled. In this way we will in due course conquer and be victorious, and attain to purity of heart and the fullness of perfection."[53]

Still, for all their awareness of the individual features that attach to the spiritual combat, the early ascetical traditions show no traces of theoretical personality typologies. Accordingly, Solignac is right in observing that "the classical doctrine of the capital sins would doubtless have to be revised today, in light of the contributions of the human sciences."[54] Let us briefly study one intriguing recent attempt at retrieving the "eight generic thoughts" tradition in a psychologically sophisticated manner: the *enneagram*.

[2] The enneagram (from Gk. *ennea*, "nine") is an arrangement of nine personality types. Pioneered in the first half of the twentieth century by the esoteric Russian writer Georges Ivanovitch Gurdjieff and detailed by Peter Demianovich Ouspensky, it was (independently?) rediscovered and elaborated around 1960 by the Bolivian seeker Oscar Ichazo, on the basis of deep personal experiences and appeals (partly fanciful, it would seem) to Sufi notions and esoteric sources.[55]

The form in which the enneagram is now widely known was developed and introduced to North America by the Chilean psychotherapist Claudio Naranjo. Eventually, in 1990, Naranjo came to explain the enneagram's fundamental features in a small book entitled *Ennea-Type Structures;* but full-size theoretical treatments had preceded him in print.[56] This came about because Naranjo's teaching had been gaining favor in informal ways since the late nineteen-sixties, initially through the Jesuit theologian Robert Ochs.[57] At the time, many Catholic religious in North America were seeking interior self-renewal as well as relief from, and insight into, their inner weaknesses and compulsions. For better for worse, self-articulation and self-discovery by means of the enneagram became widespread in the early nineteen-seventies, mainly by oral tradition and with the (sometimes dubious) help of pages upon pages of photocopied materials passed along among friends and associates, especially in Jesuit houses of formation and related circles in North America. This made it possible, as early as 1981 (*i.e.,* before any serious psychological, let alone theological, literature on the enneagram had appeared), for Jerome P. Wagner to find enough subjects to make the enneagram the object of a skillful doctoral dissertation in clinical psychology. In it, Wagner showed that the enneagram is substantially coherent and reliable as a system of personality typology.[58]

Theological acceptance of the enneagram first surfaced in 1982, when Bernard Tyrrell, in his book *Christotherapy II,* argued the enneagram's relevance to the understanding of capital sins.[59] Its potential as a practical guide to self-discovery, self-acceptance, and growth in the prayerful pursuit of Christian perfection was rather more fully demonstrated in the rest of the decade, when a few helpful as well as insightful books on the subject were published.[60]

The following diagram shows the nine types (in capital letters and with the standard number designations), the ideal self-images (with the underlying ego-fixations in parenthesis), the typifying passions (in italics), the areas of avoidance (in small capitals), and, respectively, Palmer's and Naranjo's quick characterizations of each type:

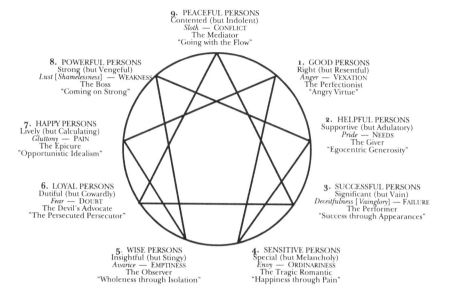

9. PEACEFUL PERSONS
Contented (but Indolent)
Sloth — CONFLICT
The Mediator
"Going with the Flow"

8. POWERFUL PERSONS
Strong (but Vengeful)
Lust [*Shamelessness*] — WEAKNESS
The Boss
"Coming on Strong"

1. GOOD PERSONS
Right (but Resentful)
Anger — VEXATION
The Perfectionist
"Angry Virtue"

7. HAPPY PERSONS
Lively (but Calculating)
Gluttony — PAIN
The Epicure
"Opportunistic Idealism"

2. HELPFUL PERSONS
Supportive (but Adulatory)
Pride — NEEDS
The Giver
"Egocentric Generosity"

6. LOYAL PERSONS
Dutiful (but Cowardly)
Fear — DOUBT
The Devil's Advocate
"The Persecuted Persecutor"

3. SUCCESSFUL PERSONS
Significant (but Vain)
Deceitfulness [*Vainglory*] — FAILURE
The Performer
"Success through Appearances"

5. WISE PERSONS
Insightful (but Stingy)
Avarice — EMPTINESS
The Observer
"Wholeness through Isolation"

4. SENSITIVE PERSONS
Special (but Melancholy)
Envy — ORDINARINESS
The Tragic Romantic
"Happiness through Pain"

[3] Wagner and Walker provide a articulate summary of the theory behind the enneagram viewed as a psychological theory, as follows:

. . . each individual is disposed inherently to experience and respond to reality in one of nine styles. This base is one's essence or *genuine self,* the locus of one's inner resources and strengths. . . . In the course of development, due mainly to socio-environmental pressures, this core disposition may become rigid and distorted such that it becomes *a caricature of the real self.* The person becomes fixated in his or her strategy and engages in *repetitious patterns of thinking, feeling, and behaving.* This fixation or compulsive strategy is called the ego, a manipulating, defensive mechanism oriented toward survival. Each of the nine ego fixations has: a characteristic *idealized self-image,* an attitudinal-emotional response set (a *passion*) that accompanies this image; an *area of avoidance antithetical to the self-concept,* an appropriate *mechanism of defense* to isolate the ego from the avoided area. In freely surrendering to his essence or genuine style, the person will realize his full potential and live in harmony with the world. By compulsively operating from his ego defense system, the individual narrows himself and lives outside the laws of his own being and those of reality [y].

---

[y] Cf. "Reliability and Validity Study of a Sufi Personality Typology: The Enneagram," p. 712 (italics added). From a philosophical and theological point of view

[4]   Leaving aside the interesting addition of Fear (6), the correspondence between Evagrius' eight generic thoughts and the enneagram's remaining eight ego-fixations along with their corresponding
passions is striking.   More importantly, however, the two systems
have *assumptions and purposes* in common. They both treat the fixations and self-limitations caused by both passion and fantasy as *obstacles to a mature sense of both self and reality.*

[a]   For Evagrius, the goal of the ascetical life (*praktikē*) is *integration*: he explains that the passions and the spirit must become mutually enhancing rather than mutually estranging. The ordering of
the passions will restore them to their natural function, which is: to
support the life of the mind rather than to mix it up. This will advance the life of *gnōsis*: the person will come to "the true knowledge of the things that are." "Setting about the contemplation of
things the way they are" will in turn open the mind to "the truth
hidden in all things that are," and the latter will, finally, ready the
mind for *theologia*: the superior, wholly spiritual, ineffable knowledge and love of God.[61]

[b]   The enneagram has a analogous developmental-ascetical purpose. By enlightening persons about the distinctive shape of finitude in themselves (as well as in others), it helps them get a sense
both of the typical shape of their self-limitations and self-distor-
tions and of their distorted and distorting relationships with otherness. It also offers them guidance toward surmounting these debilitating fantasies and postures, which are self-defeating as well as
unrealistic.

But the enneagram also lends itself to the attainment of Evagrius' mystical goal. In pointing the way to growth in the direction of
a true self, it fosters the kind of integration that gives people access, not only to the benefits of personality types other than their
own,[62] and hence, to realistic love of others, but also to the kind of
personal integrity that is apt to lead to union with God [z].

---

the phrase "essence or genuine self" claims a bit much. It is best taken to refer not
to people's *essence*, but to their *identity experience* and to their *awareness of personality*.
The latter are particular and thus limited, but precisely for that reason they provide individual persons with basic dispositions and directions for growth and development. They enable them to develop as healthy individual persons and thus to
approximate their deeper, authentic identity; it also enables them to have a sound
access to "reality," and especially to other persons, across differences in personality
structure and life experience, and thus to approximate truly other-regarding love.
[z] On this theme, cf. especially R. Rohr and A. Ebert, *Discovering the Enneagram*,
pp. 179–231, *Experiencing the Enneagram, passim*, and Robert J. Nogosek, *Nine Por-*

[5] This, finally, leads to a theme emphasized neither by the early ascetics nor in the modern psychological treatments of the enneagram, but very conspicuous in the recent literature that places the enneagram in the context of the life of prayer religious and dedication. That theme is *self-acceptance*—of the kind that specifically includes *the acceptance of one's characteristic, persistent natural flaws and of the afflictions they cause*. The theme of self-acceptance has acquired great prominence in the modern era, with its enhanced appreciation of the distinctiveness of the individual person's experience of self and hence, of God. No wonder Romano Guardini wrote a touching little tract on the subject, *Die Annahme seiner selbst*. But even an early Jesuit who enjoyed the confidence of St. Ignatius of Loyola, Jerome Nadal, while visiting Jesuit houses in Portugal in 1555, can explain how natural flaws, if duly acknowledged, can preserve virtue. A Portuguese Jesuit present at one of Father Nadal's conferences reports:

Father Nadal did not want to say more, except this: *from our natural imperfections, which we conquer only with difficulty, we can draw humility and self-knowledge*, and in this way, solid virtue is sustained. Nor was this opinion of his contrary to the practice of our Father Ignatius, [namely, to say] that everyone should strive to mortify his natural and overt imperfections. For it would appear that those who carefully watch the course of their natural imperfections (which rarely involve sin) are bound to stay away from the [imperfections] that are by nature sinful.[63]

This genuinely modern piece of spiritual direction (though not entirely without precedent in early Christian asceticism: cf. §54, 5, d, [o]) is still very pertinent today. Dissociation of sensibility and exaggerated self-consciousness (§99, 5; cf. §120, 3, a) are cultural facts in the West, wearisome if also potentially productive (§28, 6, d). While they have affected us all, the more sophisticated and the more highly motivated among us are more conscious of them. Accordingly, many of us now experience ourselves as somehow divided and at odds with ourselves, and (since it is frequently pointless and self-defeating to fight cultural phenomena) we have come to consider this modern experience of identity an ordinary complication of modern life (cf. §120, 3, a). As a matter of fact, complete integration now tends to strike us as so remote a possibility that we regard the experience of ourselves as incomplete, anxious, and inwardly divided as representative and normative, and indeed, as an occasion for personal growth.

---

traits of Jesus. A careful study of some of the books listed above (Rohr and Ebert being especially useful) will reveal further convergences between the enneagram and Evagrius' *Praktikos.*

At the same time, the human thirst for an affective sense of inner identity and harmony is too deep-seated to be entirely abandoned, especially since this sense is the precondition of genuine union with God as well as its fruit. Thus we moderns are liable to find ourselves caught between the cultural acceptance of the divided self and our persistent inner desire for integration and unity.

[6] In such a situation of fundamental ambiguity, true relief is to be expected from patient discernment alone. For without it, we may find ourselves settling for a very unsatisfactory alternative. This requires a brief explanation.

Under the pressure of trepidation and anxiety (cf. §113, 1), we are liable to think that the attainment of at least *some* sense of identity (even if it should consist in the adoption of a mostly artificial *persona*) is preferable to the wearisome (and probably endless) wait for full personal integrity (cf. §120, 3, a). After all, in our culture wholehearted self-acceptance is so taxing that we may find ourselves taking short cuts to forms of *inauthentic self-acceptance*, resulting in a counterfeit sense of identity.

[a] One such short cut is the canonization of one's own *limitations*. Defeated in advance by the realization that authentic identity and genuine openness are a matter of interminable struggle, individuals and communities will run for cover in particularity and prejudice. They will make a habit of entertaining fantasies about the blessings of the stable state—their own. Unfortunately, such fantasies will hold their deeper, more authentic desires in check; as a result, they will settle for mere placidity and call it contentment. If they are Christians, they will settle for mere certainties and abandon the search for the peace the world cannot give; they will get stuck in the pistic stance (§54, 3, a–d). As a result, moral responsibility will yield to timidity; need for authoritative assurance will win out over generosity and thirst for truth; worst of all, estrangement from otherness will prevent bold human growth and development. In the theological arena, this option has clear affinities with integralism (§19).

[b] The opposite solution (and the one more likely to find favor among the motivated and the charismatic: cf. §54, 4, a–d) has already been touched on (cf. §64, 3–7). Unlike the one portrayed in the previous paragraph, it is self-aware and sophisticated. The problem is that it has affinities with modernism (§20). Many contemporary Christians expect to gain personal integration and a

deep sense of identity from the cultivation of unconditional openness and unqualified tolerance. They will relativize all that is particular and definite, and adopt consistently universalist positions instead [*aa*]. The theological problem with this is the dwindling of any discernible Christian identity (and indeed, of any specific profession of faith). As a result, they will be virtually incapable of communicating, from a real, identifiable position, with real, tangible others—people who live by, and operate from, equally real, identifiable positions. But this suggests that the posture of high-minded detachment they cultivate is apt to disguise a deep moral arrogance. Members of a substantially self-engrossed cultural elite here permit themselves, in the interest of their own fine sense of presumed identity, to sit in implicit judgment on others, and thus to rationalize their indifference to the predicament of struggling humanity around them. In other words, they are unwittingly falling victim to a fantasy—one different from the one treated before but no less likely to foster estrangement. In this way, very much like those who canonize limitation, they, too, end up cutting their incomplete selves off from the very otherness they must engage in order to find their authentic, complete selves.

[7] The truly humane and theologically sound resolution of this impasse is conversion to the Jewish and Christian tradition of *self-acceptance at the hand of God*. Only to the extent we wholly accept our entire *given*, precarious, painfully limited, and hence, never wholly undivided selves, beset by *propatheia*, concupiscence, and the effects of sin (cf. §113, 3, a), can we bid farewell to fantasy and open ourselves to the awareness of our native attunement to God (cf. §112, 2–4). Thus, too, we will be able to predispose ourselves, *in the weakness of our deficient sense of identity* (§137, 1), to the ultimate discovery of that authentic identity which coincides with complete faith-abandon to God. In this way, too, we will find ourselves enabled to bid farewell to prejudice and open ourselves to all forms of otherness, with the humble, disciplined, discerning realism that is the soul of all integrity and love of truth. In doing so, we will find ourselves maturing in qualified acts of engagement, and thus approximatng our true identity (whose foretaste, we discover, we quite frequently get to experience, in moments of inner relief and unspeakable comfort and joy).

[*aa*] Paul Tillich's theology remains an impressive monument to this type of religious quest for the reconstitution of human integrity. Cf. F. J. van Beeck, *Christ Proclaimed*, pp. 202–17.

And in all of this, Christians may find a new vision of the historical Jesus, as he enacts and embodies total abandon to God and unconditional love of all persons (and indeed of all that is), in a life of struggling human individuality as painfully limited as ours and in circumstances and encounters at least as trying.

[§140] SUMMARY: ALIENATION TURNED INTO ESTRANGEMENT

[1] Our analyses of the deliberate life—its potentialities and its hazards—have taken us back to a theme broached long ago: self-acceptance and its precariousness (§112). We are situated—essentially and not just incidentally (§122, 3)—in a cosmos intrinsically marked by incompletion and provisionality, so much so that a modern scientist can write, for good *scientific* reasons:

It is wrong to think of the past as "already existing" in full detail. . . . What we have the right to say about past space-time and past events, is decided by choices—of what measurements to carry out—made in the near past and now. The phenomena called into being by these decisions reach backward in time in their consequences . . . , back even to the earliest days of the universe. Registering equipment operating in the here and now has an undeniable part in bringing about that which appears to have happened. Useful as it is under everyday circumstances to say that the world exists "out there" independent of us, that view can no longer be upheld. There is a strange sense in which this is a "participatory" universe.[64]

But it is not just humanity's *understanding of the cosmos* that participates in this essential provisionality. *Humanity itself participates in it.* Even those who are now dead continue, through their past actions, to change the world in new and unanticipated ways [*bb*]. No wonder that it was argued, in an earlier chapter, that death is the human individual's transition to a state *both provisional and definitive.* And by way of explanation it was added (§124, 12, c–d):

[*bb*] This leads to a suggestion that is a few removes away from the matter in hand, but nonetheless interesting. The proposition that the moral record of those who have died remains open this side of the eschaton implies that there may be individuals whose saintliness becomes apparent and real by signs and marvels of a *moral* nature that were not established nor even establishable when they died or shortly thereafter. John Henry Newman is a case in point. More than a century after his death, Newman, through his writings, is still bringing countless persons to intellectual and moral conversion and to the Christian Church. In other words, he is turning out to be a prophetical figure of considerable significance—something he was not widely judged to be in his life, nor even shortly after his death. This is a "moral miracle," and it should therefore become an integral part of the record of the process of his beatification and canonization.

As long as humanity and the cosmos are running their course in time and space, the actions of human beings, both individually and communally, are and remain part of a spatial and temporal network of moral (and immoral) endeavor which remains unfinished (and *a fortiori*, unrevealed). In that sense and to that extent, the moral status of all particular individuals and communities remains unrevealed, too. . . . Any *full* revelation of each and every person's given and acquired identity must include the whole network of the *relationships* that has contributed to their personal being. For that reason, this full revelation can only be eschatological—*i.e.*, ultimately the work of divine grace. Not until all of humanity, along with the entire cosmos, reaches its definitive destiny can Christ be complete and fully revealed. Only in that revelation, too, can the holiness of individual persons and their place in God's Kingdom become fully manifest.

This radical lack of definition is apt to put our capacity for endurance to a painful test. For we are part of a humanity that is as often troubled by its incompleteness as it is encouraged by it; regarding indeterminacy as a source of hope never comes easy. We sense we are caught in the middle, yet we must act. No wonder we find ourselves regularly betraying our transcendence, forsaking discernment and reason, and having recourse to fantasy instead, both individually or communally. We forge caricatures, antagonists, rivals, and even enemies out of forms of otherness we hardly know, let alone understand. In the immediacy of self-interest, we will capitulate, fail to engage, fail to respond, compromise. As frequently, however, we will find ourselves *forcing* things. Anxiously as well as impatiently, we will misdefine ourselves both by setting ourselves apart from the other and by "putting the other in its place." But once, uncertain of our transcendence as we are, we have put otherness out there, we find ourselves dreading engagement with it; fearful of being inadequate to the other, we prefer separation; we even reinforce it. In this way, otherness will turn into strangeness; miserably, alienation becomes estrangement.

It is a case of forced, self-defeating *reculer pour mieux sauter*—balking in order to jump forward all the more forcefully. For, sooner or later, the distance from otherness we have established by (mis-)defining ourselves will become too much for us. So, in order to bridge the gap we have engineered for ourselves, we simply *have* to come back. But to get ourselves to do so, we now have to *force ourselves*; no wonder we come back at otherness with a vengeance. That is, instead of encountering the other discerningly and carefully, we seek to charge, attack, gain possession, envelop, annex, ingest; at the very least we seek to avert surmised attempts on the part of the other at charging, attacking, possessing, enveloping, annexing, ingesting. In order to avoid being taken advantage of for all we are worth, we will try to take advantage of otherness for all it is worth. In order to avoid being taken advantage of and exploited, we will use and exploit. In order to avoid being devoured, we will devour. *Homo homini lupus.*[65] In sum, instead of exercising transcendence and *humanitas* by cultivating appropriate, *measured* encounters with otherness, we will allow ourselves to be moved by anxiety; we will act on fantasy and ego. In doing so, we sadly forget two things.

[2] First of all, our attempts are *self-defeating.* Inasmuch as we seek to identify ourselves by (mis-)definition, we forget that the very otherness we attack or take our distance from is our own kith and kin— it will involve us no matter what. The world of otherness, and especially the world of other human beings, may be an troublesome relative, but it alone can draw us out of our limited individual, social, and cultural selves, in pursuit of an identity at once more profound and more encompassing (§122, 1, e). Whatever we do to put that world in its place (as a mere means to our ends at best, and as an obstacle to our self-fulfillment at worst), it keeps inviting us to befriend it, for its own sake as well as in the interest of our own growth in humanity. To the extent that we keep turning down this invitation, we will, undiscerningly, find ourselves implicitly turning all otherness into a rival power. This habit will in turn become a self-fulfilling prophecy: since otherness is against us (or so we fantasize), we have no option but to turn down its every invitation to engage ourselves. In the mean time, what in actual fact we end up doing is embracing the false friends that *really* leave us no option: our characteristic patterns of self-maintenance and self-assertion—the delusions, illusions, and misconceptions of fantasy, whether individual, communal, or cultural. In this way, miserably, in the very act of seeking to establish ourselves we are merely entrenching ourselves; in the act of seeking to expand ourselves, we are confining and diminishing ourselves. For in treating otherness solely as as an adversary, or at best, as a means to bolster our narrow self-interest, we implicitly debase *ourselves.* We will ignore that otherness is *our own* otherness (cf. §122, 1, b); that we participate in it; that it is the very stuff of our own emergence, enhancement, and growth. In taking our distance from otherness, we become the prisoners of self-maintenance and self-assertion. That is to say, in the last resort we are being untrue to our authentic selves. And thus, we are involving ourselves in the self-contradiction

that is at the heart of sinfulness and outright sin, and perhaps even beyond it (§113, 3).

[3] But, secondly and far more fatefully, the attempt is *spiritually suicidal* even as we live. For what ensues when we understand all otherness as alien, merely instrumental, antagonistic, and always potentially hostile, and even more when we go on to treat it that way?

We will fall victim to a vague disgust. Wretchedly, it may occur to us that life in alienation is *in itself* a condition in which the menace of death eclipses the promise of life. Habitual worry, fear, and anxiety about ourselves will obstruct clarity and freedom in our engagements with otherness; even worse, we will stop gaining the inner maturity that is the fruit of appropriating and integrating such engagements. Preoccupation with our isolated selves and our self-interest will infest our options as well as our notions about life, well-being, meaning, and indeed, ourselves. Standardized images of ourselves and routine ways of handling otherness will inhibit discernment and choice, especially when we are ill, under stress, frustrated, or discontented. Life will turn into a wearisome, self-centered struggle, and eventually, we will find ourselves living (if that is the right word) by mere habit, stale certainty, and banal assurance, not by vision and venture, let alone by faith, hope, and self-abandoning love. *Tædium vitæ*, in which deep-seated depression and impotent rage are apt to coincide, will supplant life.

Gerard Manley Hopkins had first-hand knowledge of this deep desolation *and* of the temptation to desperate self-impoundment encouraged by it. He escaped defeat in the end, but not without giving himself a brutally honest account of his experience. This is illustrated by a sonnet "written in blood," in which the one ray of light is the acknowledgment, at the very end of the poem, that he is still living this side of everlasting death. Yet otherwise, turned in on our desolate selves, Hopkins knows, we become our own poison:

> I am gall, I am heartburn. God's most deep decree
> Bitter would have me taste: my taste was me;
> Bones built in me, flesh filled, blood brimmed the curse.
>
> Selfyeast of spirit a dull dough sours. I see
> The lost are like this, and their scourge to be
> as I am mine, their sweating selves; but worse.[66]

Living by exclusion and fantasy, therefore, means living life against the horizon of a hidden consternation, unthematic but for that very reason all-pervasive. The cause of the consternation is the specter of an undying death—a spiritual death that looms at the far end of the dark passageway into biophysical and psychophysical death. To the extent we fall a prey to this consternation, fantasies of death will invade the life of deliberation and dominate it. Consumed by worry about self-maintenance and self-worth and at the same time determined to assert ourselves in such a way as to force recognition and survival, we will insist on exercising, at the expense of our authentic, lasting selves, an incomplete, mistaken, *defensive* self; we may even make attempts, as brave as they are futile, at asserting this self as definitive. But in that very effort the only thing we reveal is how deeply we understand, if only residually, just what we as well as all other human beings are like, namely, incomplete and never completely autonomous (cf. §121, 4):

Creatures endowed with reason are unable to be unto themselves the good by virtue of which they can become happy.[67]

Insisting on defending a mistaken individual or communal identity has a foil in our dealings with the world of otherness: we will engage in acts and develop habits of mis-positioning ourselves. That is to say, we will mis-identify ourselves by inappropriate association with *particular things and persons* of our own preference, as if they could be a match for the measureless human desire for fullness of life and happiness to which we are natively called. In this way, we will combine loss of human identity and authenticity with (in Augustine's idiom) over-association with "changing goods," or (in Martin Buber's) with things and persons treated largely (or even exclusively) by way of mere "It's."

[a] Incidentally, reflections like these can help us take the measure of *our own* preparedness for biophysical and psychophysical death. To have come to accept death is tantamount to having substantially moved, for one's sense of self, beyond both the limited security and the incidental consternations proffered by the world of otherness. That is, being ready for death means having come to depend, for one's sense of identity and purpose, no longer on passion and on self-regarding fantasies arising from passion, but on vision inspired by reason, imagination, and positive regard for otherness. For to be prepared to die is, in the last analysis, to have come to love the other for the sake of the other, and not just for one's own benefit. Those among us are truly prepared to die and perhaps even ready for God (cf. §124, 1) who are prepared, not only to let the other be, but also to let go of the other, and even to give

up one's own life for the sake of the other. Needless to say, it takes forms of *paideusis* inspired by faith-commitment to arrive at this state of loving abandonment of self (cf. §115, 5 and a–b).

[4] By now, the self-defeating contradictions involved in sin as the disease of the deliberate life must be obvious. Individually and communally, *we sin whenever, with appreciable deliberation, we maintain, assert, and even embrace ourselves at the expense of otherness in all its forms.* That is, we sin when we actively settle for, and try to save, our selves as *we*, incomplete as we are, have come to know and shape them and acknowledge them and depend on them. For in so doing we find ourselves among those, who, in the words of Jesus, will lose their lives by dint of endeavoring to save them (cf. Mk 8, 35 parr.; Mt 10, 39 par. Lk 17, 33; Jn 12, 25). We make this endeavor, of course, to keep death at bay. But ironically, the selves we thus endeavor to save are the very selves which death will force us to abandon (§124, 4).

Similar things can be said of all the particular things, both material and mental, on which we rely in the interest of sustaining such limited lives and identities. That is, *we sin whenever we endeavor to secure our own life by clinging to the very things we know death will require us to leave behind,* instead of availing ourselves of them only insofar as they support life, enhance the pursuit of happiness, and prepare us for the discovery of our true selves—the selves that are meant to last forever. Thus, we sin to the extent that, living by fantasy, we use the world of otherness as an excuse to settle for present, very limited advantage, rather than cherishing it as a standing invitation to seek unlimited growth and development in authentic human creativity and identity.

[5] To the extent that this happens, something far more dreadful happens as well: we gradually lose interest in the moral (that is, the human) life. But even worse, we lose the *capacity* for such a life. For as we are first dulled, then diminished, and finally engulfed by stubborn habits of sinful self-absorption, conscience—that true impulse for deliberation in us—will move in the direction of effective moral and spiritual non-existence (§136, 1, [c]). When this happens, we become more and more liable to lose our openness to the appeals that still come to us from otherness. That is to say, we will lose our capacity for conversion and penitence. For conscience subdued will first elude, then overlook, and finally resist each and every move in the direction of *exitus* and engagement with otherness. And in the wake of this, we lose our appetite for reflection and self-examination, of the kind that could lead to moral recovery.

In this way, the distinctively human project—the life of conscious-ness and freedom stimulated and enriched by engagement with eve-ry form of otherness—will deteriorate into a life in which free and open deliberation sours into self-willed intractability. Communities and persons blighted by this disease of the mind and the soul will anxiously hang on to what they take to be their identity; yet all they are holding on to is a stagnant yet transitory, limited, forged, and ul-timately unreal identity. And in due course, they will be captives of fantastic, mostly self-regarding *false ideals* (cf. §138, 8; cf. §114, 4).

[6] In the Jewish and Christian traditions, sin has an inseparable rel-ative: death. This raises a question. At this distinctively anthropolog-ical level, what shape does death take? Clearly, sin here no longer consists in living instinctually, by the power of passion. And so, for its part, death can no longer be the end of sensuality—that is, the death which the worldly and the carnal passionately and indeed des-perately labor to delay, defy, and deny (§133, 9).

For in the life of deliberation, both sin and death are more insidi-ous. Sin now disguises itself; it becomes the willful pursuit of *false ideals*. Accordingly, when the deliberate life degenerates, the death sinners must both face and dread is no longer just biophysical and psychophysical, but death by self-impaction of mind and desire, pro-duced by inability to understand and discern what is really real. This lack of realism makes the prospect of psychophysical death as unset-tling as it makes it pointless; to the estranged and the self-absorbed death means: moving from less and less to nothing in particular. In-creasing weary of life, they will run from death by shrugging it off. No wonder they will defend themselves, unconsciously or deliberate-ly, against *enjoyment* of life, never mind of hope for life beyond death, sometimes with a noble resignation, sometimes spitefully. But they will, unconsciously or deliberately, defraud others of the light of life by encouraging loss of nerve. But in such a context, life itself will turn cheap, and violence will seize its opportunity.

Albert Camus intuited this when he wrote:

The evil that exists in the world almost always comes from unawareness, and good intentions, if they are not enlightened, can cause as much dam-age as wickedness. People are more good than evil, so that is not really the issue. But they *are* more or less unaware, and this we call virtue or vice; and the vice that drives one to despair most of all is this: unawareness that pre-sumes it knows everything, and on that score confers upon itself the au-thority to kill. The souls of the murderous are blind, and there is neither true goodness nor loyal love without the greatest possible clear-sightedness.[68]

Or, to quote William Frazier once again (cf. §116, 5, b),

> ... life itself works malignantly beneath the surface ... whenever running from death reaches destructive proportions. *Life in this sense, given to defeating death by escaping death, is the engine of our fallen world.*[69]

Not surprisingly, therefore, the prejudiced and the estranged, hardened in conscious or deliberate self-defense, are apt to interpret the prospect of death as par for the course, and so, as a perverse encouragement to resort to violence if and as needed. *Taedium vitae* turns into a practical license to defeat and kill. Compared to *this* breakdown of humanity, enslavement to sensuality and immorality of the passionate kind looks, at times, insipid and almost innocuous [*cc*].

Why is this so? The Jewish and Christian traditions answer, *noblesse oblige.* The cosmos is cherished as noble and "good." Still, Jews and Christians cherish humanity as nobler—as *"very* good" (Gen 1, 31). How could those who are formed in this school, being alert to the extent to which anthropology transcends cosmology, tire of living by the standards inherent in humanity? And, accordingly, how could they *not* be aware that the nobler the promise, the more dismal the failure? Throughout, the reflections and explorations of this chapter have been devoted to the consciousness of *human dignity* as the root of the demand for humane—*i.e.*, moral—living.

[7] Yet this consciousness has deeper consequences. Gregory of Nazianzus reminds us that being mindful of our human dignity means: being "mindful of the nobility [we] have from on high."[70] This conviction, too, is ineradicably etched in the Jewish and Christian traditions: it is humanity's distinctive glory to be made in the image and likeness of the living God. Now only the Living God is *God*—that is, the One apart from whom nothing, whether cosmic or human, can mean anything or amount to anything. This theme, as forbidding as it is life-giving, will have to be the focus of the reflections and explorations of the next installment of *God Encountered.*

[*cc*] The Great Tradition has been unflagging in its determination to oppose every form of *dualism*, especially dualism of the kind that would identify matter with evil (cf. §79, 6, and [*ff*]; §121, 5, and [*ii*]). This explains why in Dante's *Inferno* those damned for deliberate fraudulence are further down in the Pit (and hence, closer to Satan) than the willfully violent, and the latter in turn deeper down than those who in life were guilty of the passionate and sensual sins of anger and self-indulgence. For the same reason, in the *Purgatorio,* those being purified of the sins of pride, envy, and resentment must labor harder to climb the Mountain of Purgatory than those who have sins of the flesh and its impulses to repent of. Cf. especially *Inferno* XI, 16–90 and *Purgatorio* IV, 88–96.

Notes

Retrospect and Prospect

1. Cf. *S. Th.* I, 78, 3, *in c.* Aquinas defines "sense" as *quædam potentia passiva, quæ nata est immutari ab exteriori sensibili* ("a passive faculty whose nature it is to be affected by something outside us that is capable of being sensed"). The five senses, he adds, are hierarchically ordered. Touch and taste mediate perception by being affected (*immutari*) by immediate contact (*medium coniunctum*); smell and hearing combine contact with distance—*i.e.*, they operate by being both naturally and "spiritually" affected. The eye, so Aquinas thought, worked by being affected only "spiritually"; it was, therefore, the highest of the senses.
2. On this subject, my former physics and philosophy teacher J. J. W. Berghuys has written a lucid and compelling monograph: *Mens en Kosmos—een groots geheel: Uitweg uit de crisis in rationeel denken.* Berghuys shows that the notion that cosmic process is wholly deterministic is the result of the mistaken idea that the "exactness" of mathematically-based knowledge insures realism.
3. Virginia Woolf, *The Waves*, pp. 126–27.
4. *Gregory the Great*, p. 41.

Chapter 15

1. Cf. *Phaedrus* 237d; cf. *PlatoCDia*, p. 485.
2. This description is inspired by one of Hadewijch's letters (XVIII, 24–25; cf. *De brieven van Hadewijch*, pp. 136–39; ET *The Complete Works*, p. 85).
3. Cf. Christopher Moss, "Extraterrestrials and the love of God." He writes: ". . . the number of galaxies required before we find a single instance of life spontaneously emerging is staggering. The number of these galaxies, if written down, would be one followed by over thirty-nine thousand zeros, in face of which the number of galaxies in the visible universe, a mere hundred billion, fades into utter insignificance. It means that the possibility of life spontaneously emerging is practically nil." Moss' position, while intellectually respectable is not shared by a great many of his colleagues; what matters for our argument is not the probability of the actual existence, but the *moral* consequences of the exceedingly small margin of probability.
4. Joseph Butler, *The Analogy of Religion,* Introduction.
5. On these themes, cf. P. Schoonenberg, *Man and Sin*, pp. 111–18.
6. Arthur J. Vidich and Joseph Bensman, *Small Town in Mass Society: Class, Power and Religion in a Rural Community.*
7. William Shakespeare, *Macbeth*, III, iv, 136–40.
8. For a partly frivolous, partly insightful exploration of these phenomena in mid-twentieth century British English, cf. *Noblesse Oblige*, by Alan S. C. Ross, Nancy Mitford, and others.
9. H. L. Mencken, *The American Language.*, pp. 90–103, 271–84, 311–18.
10. Cf. Paulo Freire, *Pedagogy of the Oppressed.*
11. Cf. Walter J. Ong's *Fighting for Life*, esp. pp. 51–115.
12. Again, cf. Walter J. Ong's *Fighting for Life.*
13. Cf. Iiro Karjanto, "Fortuna," esp. pp. 553–57.
14. Giovanni Boccaccio's work was imitated in short compass by Geoffrey Chaucer in the *Monk's Tale* (*Works*, ed. Robinson, pp. 189–98; cf. the commentary, pp. 746–500). Cf. also some of the songs in the medieval collection known as *Car-*

mina Burana (marvelously set to music by Carl Orff, with the appropriate subtitle *Cantiones Profanae*), as well as Howard R. Patch's monograph *The Goddess Fortuna in Mediaeval Literature.*

15. *Inferno,* VII, 22–96.

16. *Si vis pacem para bellum:* freely quoted after Flavius Vegetius Renatus, who actually wrote *Qui desiderat pacem præparet bellum* ("Let the one who wants peace prepare for war": *Epitoma rei militaris,* 3).

17. I recall a stunning example of failure to realize this. In the course of an election campaign, the late Spiro Agnew, then Vice-President of the United States, tried to justify an idiotically expensive space program by exclaiming: "Let it never be said there was something Americans *could* do, and they didn't do it!"

18. Cf., *e.g.,* Jörg Klima, "Instinkt und Moral."

19. The original meaning of "spoon" is "chip of wood" (used for stirring).

20. On this subject, cf. J.W.M. Verhaar, *Some Reflections on Perception, Speech and Thought.*

21. Motto of William of Wykeham (1324–1404), bishop of Winchester. Also of New College, Oxford, which he founded in 1379.

22. Cf. Frank McConnell, "What Hath Phil Wrought?"

23. Stephen J. Pope, *The Evolution of Altruism and the Ordering of Love,* p. 57. Pope is rendering *S. Th.* I–II, 24, 1.

24. Cf. Aquinas' treatment in *S.Th.* II–II, 123, 1, *in c.*

25. "Give to each what is due to them": Cicero, *De legibus* 1, 16, 19.

26. Cf. George Aschenbrenner's important essay "Consciousness Examen."

27. Cf., for instance, Lewin's *Field Theory in Social Science.*

28. See his *La vie affective des groupes.*

29. Cf., *e.g.,* William Meissner's *Group Dynamics in the Religious Life,* Charles Curran's *Psychological Dynamics in Religious Living,* and John Futrell's *Making an Apostolic Community of Love.*

30. Examples are Theodore Mills, *The Sociology of Small Groups,* and Joseph Luft, *Group Processes: An Introduction to Group Dynamics,* and W. G., Bennis and H. A. Shepard, "A Theory of Group Development." Stewart Tubbs's *A Systems Approach to Small Group Interaction* (1988) gives a good retrospect.

31. Cf. *The Johari Window: A Graphic Model for Interpersonal Relations.*

32. Virginia Woolf's expression: §124, 7, [*aa*].

33. Cf. Dylan Thomas *(Collected Poems 1934–1952,* p. vi): "I read somewhere of a shepherd who, when asked why he made, from within fairy rings, ritual observances to the moon to protect his flocks, replied 'I'd be a damn' fool if I didn't!' These poems, with all their crudities, doubts, and confusions, are written for the love of Man and in praise of God, and I'd be a damn' fool if they weren't."

34. Cf. esp. Annotations 7–8, 14–15, 17 in the *Spiritual Exercises* of St. Ignatius Loyola [7–8, 14–15, 17].

35. On noticing, resistance, and contemplative attitude, cf. W. Barry and W. Connolly, *The Practice of Spiritual Direction,* pp. 65–100, 46–64.

36. Cf. Latin *legere:* to collect, to pick, to choose, to read; Greek *anagignōskein:* to know once again, to recognize, to read out loud; etymological equivalents of *read* in various Germanic languages (*e.g.,* Dutch *raden*): to make sense of something obscure, to guess.

37. *The House of Fame,* ll. 765–69 (*Works,* ed. Robinson, p. 289; for the references to the sources, cf. p. 783).

38. *S. Th.* II–II, 1, 2, *ad 2:* "Actus ... credentis non terminatur ad enuntiable, sed ad rem. Non enim formamus enuntiabilia, nisi ut per ea de rebus cognitionem habeamus, sicut in scientia, ita et in fide."

39. For the following, cf.. Plato's Seventh Letter (esp. 341^b– 345^c): *PlatoCDia,* pp. 1574–98 (esp. 1588–92).

40. *Quæstiones ad Thalassium*, LXIII; *PG* 90, 669C: *Oukoun ho monōi tōi grammati tēs Graphēs parakathēmenos, monēn echei tēn aisthēsin kratousan tēs physeōs; kath'ēn hē pros sarka tēs psychēs schesis monē diaphainesthai pephyke. To gar gramma mē nooumenon pneumatikōs, monēn echei tēn aisthēsin perigraphousan autou tēn ekphōnēsin, kai mē synchōrousan pros ton noun diabēnai tōn gegrammenōn tēn dynamin.* (Italics added for emphasis.)

41. Cf. Paulo Freire, *Pedagogy of the Oppressed*, pp. 57–74.

42. Cf. *The Two Cultures and the Scientific Revolution* and *The Two Cultures: And a Second Look*.

43. Authors, respectively, of the broadly based *Der Untergang des Abendlandes* [1918–22] and the narrowly based *The Closing of the American Mind* [1987].

44. Marshall McLuhan, *The Gutenberg Galaxy* (1962); Walter Ong, *The Presence of the Word: Some Prolegomena for Cultural and Religious History* (1970), *Rhetoric, Romance, and Technology* (1971), *Interfaces of the Word: Studies in the Evolution of Consciousness and Culture* (1977), *Ramus, Method and the Decay of Dialogue* (1983), *Orality and Literacy: The Technologizing of the Word* (1985).

45. "Histoire des mentalités, histoire de la lenteur dans l'histoire": J. Le Goff, "Les mentalités," p. 82.

46. "Ainsi ce qui semble dénué de racines, né de l'improvisation et du réflexe, gestes machinaux, paroles irréfléchies, vient de loin et témoigne du long retentissement des systèmes de pensée": J. Le Goff, "Les mentalités," p. 81.

47. ". . . les nébuleuses d'où cristallisent les mentalités": J. Le Goff, "Les mentalités," p. 88.

48. " . . . au deçà de la galaxie Gutenberg": J. Le Goff, "Les mentalités," p. 88. Cf. Marshall McLuhan, *The Gutenberg Galaxy.*

49 *Ethik*, pp. 112–13 (cf. ET p. 102). The editors of the latest German edition note that in all probablity Bonhoeffer knew Hermann Rauschning's *Die Revolution des Nihilismus*, which appeared in Zürich in 1938 and interpreted national socialism as nihilism.

50. Cf., *e.g.*, Gerth and Mills, *From Max Weber*, pp. 228–31.

51. I am not social scientist any more than a historian (cf. §23, 5, b), so I can only refer to what little I have read and understood about this problem. I have found extremely enlightening a report entitled *Grande pauvreté et précarité économique et sociale*, drawn up by the saintly Père Joseph Wresinski on behalf of the French Council on Economic and Social Affairs, and submitted to the Government of the Republic.

52. *After Virtue*, p. 245 (italics added).

53. Alwine de Vos van Steenwijk, *Pour combattre la pauvreté et l'exclusion, repenser l'activité humaine.* Again, I can only refer to what little I have read and understood about this problem.

54. One spectacular instance explained by Froehlich is the 12th century ceiling in the Romanesque parish church in Zillis, a village in South-East Switzerland straddling the ancient Alpine pass route to Como and Milan. Its 153 panels form a *mappa mundi* replete with numerological and pictorial symbolisms.

55. Cf. esp. pp. 131–54.

56. Cf. *The Illustrations from the Works of Andreas Vesalius*, pp. 84–89, 216–18.

57. Cf., for instance, Arthur Henkel and Albrecht Schone, *Emblemata.*

58. Cf. F.J. van Beeck, *Christ Proclaimed*, pp. 54–55, 548–51.

59. Cf. his *Über die Verborgenheit der Gesundheit, passim.*

60. This is the central issue explored in Douglas McGregor's classic *The Human Side of Enterprise.*

61. William Shakespeare, sonnet CXXIX ("The expense of spirit in a waste of shame"), ll. 13–14; Shakespeare's sonnet is a thumbnail analysis of the syndrome just described.

52. Cf., *e.g.*, *S. Th.* I-II, 74, 1, *ad* 2.

Chapter 16

1. On these concepts, cf. Abraham H. Maslow, *Religions, Values, and Peak-Experiences* and *Toward a Psychology of Being.*
2. *S. Th.* I–II, 61, 1, *in c.*
3. Cf. question 56, articles 4–5, and especially the dazzling question 60, art. 5.
4. *S. Th.* I–II, 58.
5. *S. Th.* II–II, 168, 2 (cf. Aristotle, *Nicomachean Ethics* IV, 8, 1127ᵇ34–1128ᵃ17; *AristBWks*, p. 1000); 160, 2, *in c.*; cf. also 72, 2, *ad 1*, and I–II, 60, 5, *in c.*
6. "Eutrapelie, eine vergessene Tugend" (ET in *Man at Play*, pp. 91–105); cf. also art. Eutrapélie, *DictSpir* 4, 1726–29.
7. Cf. *Phaedrus* 246b, 247b, and esp. 253c–254e (*PlatoCDia*, pp. 493–94, 499–500).
8. Max Scheler, *Der Formalismus in der Ethik und die materiale Wertethik* (ET *Formalism in Ethics and Non-Formal Ethics of Values*).
9. "Augustine on the Unity and the Interconnection of the Virtues."
10. *Ibid.*, pp. 94–95.
11. Cf. his "Caritas en humanitas"; cf. also his *Theologia moralis*, vol. I, pp. 239–53, nrs. 259–72.
12. "Justice driven to extremes is extreme injustice"—the simplified version of Terence's line *ius summum sæpe summast malitia* ("justice driven to extremes is often extreme malice": *Heauton Timorumenos*, line 796).
13. Cf. *S. Th.* II–II, 120. *Epikeia* is a corruption of Gk. *epieikeia*; cf. Aristotle, *Top.* 141ᵃ16; *Eth. Nic.* VI, 10, 1137ᵃ32 –1138ᵃ3 (*AristBWks*, pp. 1019–20).
14. *Systematic Theology*, I, p. 240.
15. Plato, *Socrates' Defense (Apology)* XXVIII, 38·1–5: *hekasts hēmeras peri aretēs tous logous poieisthai kai tōn allōn, peri hōn hymeis emou akouete dialegomenou kai emauton kai allous exetazontos* (cf. *PlatoCDia*, p. 23).
16. Cf. Plato, *Socrates' Defense (Apology)*, 40·4–5 (*hē ... eiōthyia moi mantikē hē tou daimoniou*); 40·1 (*to tou theou sēmeion*); 37 5–7 (*hēsychian agein, tōi theōi apeithein*); cf. *PlatoCDia*, pp. 22–24.
17. From the *Letter to the Duke of Norfolk*, in *Certain Difficulties Felt by Anglicans*, vol. II, pp. 249–50 (passage in italics quoted in Pope John II, *Veritatis Splendor*, 34).
18. Cf. "Those who sit in the sty of contentment, meaning Death": T. S. Eliot, "Marina" (*Collected Poems 1909–1962*, p. 115).
19. William Shakespeare, *Hamlet, the Prince of Denmark*, III, I, 58.
20. For these conceptions, cf. S. T. Coleridge's *Biographia Literaria*, vol. I, chap. 13 and vol. II, chap. 14 (ed. Shawcross, I, pp. 195–202; II, pp. 12–13). On the subject, cf. J. A. Appleyard, *Coleridge's Philosophy of Literature*, pp. 197–208.
21. On this subject, cf. Ray L. Hart, *Unfinished Man and the Imagination.*
22. Cf. *The Collected Stories*, pp. 58–85; quotation p. 74.
23. On prejudice and conformity, cf. Gordon W. Allport's classic *The Nature of Prejudice.*
24. Gerard Manley Hopkins, "Pied Beauty."
25. On scotosis and mythic consciousness, cf. Bernard Lonergan, *Insight*, pp. 191–92, 536–42. Both concepts are productively used by Mary Frohlich, "From Mystification to Mystery," pp. 176–77, 179–81. Incidentally, Lonergan's understanding of myth and mythology differs from some more positive conceptions of *myth* used thus far in this systematic theology; cf. esp. §41; §98, 5. But cf. also §98, 5 and [*ee*].
26. *The Unicorn*, p. 116; cf. §110, 4, b, [*hh*].
27. From World War II, I remember the expression *faktisch vorgehen*: to squelch resistance, the German occupying forces were encouraged or ordered simply to do *something*. "Something," that is, *anything*, appropriate or inappropriate.
28. "Nature does not proceed by leaps"—an early seventeenth-century maxim favored by (among others) the great Swedish botanist and zoologist Carolus Linnaeus (Carl von Linné, 1707–1778).

29. On this topic, cf. my *Catholic Identity after Vatican II*, pp. 1–34.
30. "Mastery does not show itself till it sets limits."
31. *Irrequietum est cor nostrum donec requiescat in te:* Augustine, *Confessions* I, i (1).
32. "Toute institution raisonnable est déracinement. La constitution d'une véritable société est déracinement — le terme d'une existence où le «chez soi» est absolu, où tout vient de l'intérieur" ("Simone Weil contre la Bible," in *Difficile liberté*, p. 183). Cf. §98, 5, [*ee*].
33. Cf. F. J. van Beeck, "Christian Faith and Theology in Encounter with Non-Christians: Profession? Protestation? Self-maintenance? Abandon?", esp. pp. 52–63.
34. *limos, loimos, abrochia, nosoi, polemoi:* Dorotheus of Gaza, *Instructions* XIV, §155 (*SC* 92, pp. 436–37).
35. Cf. Gerard Manley Hopkins' sonnet *God's Grandeur:* "And for all this, nature is never spent; . . ."
35. Burton Stevenson's *Home Book of Proverbs, Maxims, and Familiar Phrases* (New York: Macmillan, 1948), following Purchas' *Pilgrims*, erroneously cites Aquinas' "*Summa Theologica*" (I–II, 1, 5) as the source of this oft-quoted phrase. The maxim is, in fact, a simplification of Aquinas' comment on Aristotle's observation in the *Nicomachean Ethics: kakiston gar to enantion tōi beltistōi* ("for the worst is the contrary of the best": VIII, 10; 1160ᵇ8–9; *AristBWks*, p. 1069). Aquinas writes: *... patet quod ipsa corruptio est pessima. Pessimum enim est contrarium optimo* (*"*... it is obvious that this corruption is the worst. For the worst is what is contrary to the best": *In Eth. Arist. ad Nic. Expositio*, ed. Marietti [1677]).
37. Cf., for instance, John Auping, *Religion and Social Justice*—a re-working of his earlier, rather ambitious *The Relative Efficiency of Evangelical Non-Violence.*
38. Cf. *S. Th.* II-II, 49, 6, *ad 1.*
39. *Myst.* XXIV (*PG* 91, 709D–712A).
40. "Towards a Fundamental Theological Interpretation of Vatican II."
41. Cf. *Spiritual Exercises*, nrs. 325–27.
42. Cf. Pedro Arrupe, "Sobre el «análisis marxista»."
43. Cf., *e.g.*, Cross, pp. 1264–65, where, incidentally, "covetousness" stands for avarice.
44. *Praktikos* 6 (*SC 171*, pp. 506–09; ET, pp. 16–17); cf. *PG* 40, 1271–78.
45. *Praktikos*, chaps. 7–14, 15–39, and the tract *Peri tōn oktō pneumatōn tēs ponērias* ("On the Eight Spirits of Malice"). The latter has come down under the name of Nilus (*PG* 79, 1145–64; Cross, along with many others, confuses this treatise with a seventh-century anthology on the same subject drawn from writings by Evagrius, John Climacus, and John Cassian: *Peri tōn oktō tēs kakias logismōn* ["On the Eight Thoughts of Evil"], also attributed to Nilus [*PG* 79, 1435–72]).
46. *Inst. coen.* V, 1 (*SC* 109, pp. 190–91).
47. *Conlationes*, V (*SC* 42, pp. 188–217).
48. *Mor. in Job*, XXXI, 45, 87 (*PL* 76, 620–21).
49. *De causa peccati: S. Th.* I–II, q. 84.
50. *Quæstiones disputatæ de Malo*, qq. 8–15.
51. Cf. *Q. D. de Malo*, 8, 1, *in c.* (*Unde oportet*).
52. Cf. *The Parson's Tale* (*The Works of Geoffrey Chaucer* [ed. Robinson], pp. 229–64; quotations p. 239, ll. 386–88).
53. *Conferences*, V, 27 (*SC* 42, p. 216–17): "... sicut diximus non uno modo inpugnamur omnes, et oportet unumquemque nostrum secundum qualitatem belli quo principaliter infestatur concertationum luctamen adripere, ... Et ita prout ipsa uitia in nobis obtinent principatum atque inpugnationis exigit modus, nos quoque oportet ordinem instituere proeliorum, secundum quem prouentus quoque uictoriae triumphique succedens faciet nos ad puritatem cordis et perfectionis plenitudinem peruenire."
54. Art. "Péchés capitaux," *DictSpir* XII, col. 859.
55. Cf. Sam Keen, "We have no desire to strengthen the ego or make it happy."

Also, Helen Palmer, *The Enneagram*, pp. 3–25; Don Richard Riso, *Personality Types*, pp. 11–19.

56. Cf. Don Richard Riso, *Personality Types* (1987); Helen Palmer, *The Enneagram* (1988). Fully seven years before Naranjo's book, in 1983, J. G. Bennett's rather more esoteric little book *Enneagram Studies* had appeared.

57. Cf. Don Richard Riso, *Personality Types*, p. 15–17; Richard Rohr and Andreas Ebert, *Discovering the Enneagram*, p. 9.

58. For a summary of the findings, cf. Jerome P. Wagner and Ronald E. Walker, "Reliability and Validity Study of a Sufi Personality Typology: The Enneagram."

59. Pp. 177–80.

60 In 1984, three religious, Maria Beesing, Robert J. Nogosek, and Patrick H. O'Leary, published *The Enneagram: A Journey of Self Discovery*. This was followed, three years later, by *The Enneagram and Prayer*, by Barbara Metz and John Burchill. In the same category belongs Richard Rohr and Andreas Ebert, *Das Enneagram: Die 9 Gesichter der Seele* (1989; ET *Discovering the Enneagram*, 1990) and his later *Experiencing the Enneagram* (1994), both of which very thematically put the enneagram in the context of religious development.

61. *Praktikos* 2 (*[meta] gnōseōs tōn ontōn alēthōs*); 86 (*epiballein tēi theōriai tōn gegonotōn*); 84 (*peras gnōseōs theologia*); *Gnostikos* 49 (*la vérité cachée dans tous les êtres*); cf. also *Praktikos* 92 (*SC* 171, pp. 498–99, 674–77, 694–95; ET ed. Bamberger, pp. 15, 37, 39).

62. Jerome P. Wagner and Ronald E. Walker, "Reliability and Validity Study," p. 712: "The assets of the other types are available to and utilized by the integrated individual."

63. "Não queria o P. Nadal dizer mays, senão que los defeitos naturais, que com dificuldade vencemos, podemos tirar humildade e conhecimento proprio, com que la virtude solida se conserve. Nem era esta sua opinião contraria ao costume, que N. P. Ignacio tinha de trabalhar por mortificar os defeitos naturays e exteriores de cada hum; porque quem se occupa com diligencia em perseguir os defeitos naturais, que poucas vezes tem culpa, parece que deve estar longe dos que de sua natureza são culpaveis." Cf. *MHSI* 66 (2nd edition, 1943, vol. 1), pp. 621–23, nrs. 152–53; quotation nr. 153, ll. 85–93 (italics added; also partly quoted by Solignac).

64. John Archibald Wheeler, "Delayed Choice Experiments and the Bohr–Einstein Dialog." I owe this reference to my friend Denis Sardella, professor of chemistry at Boston College.

65. "Human beings are wolves to human beings"—the popular version of *lupus est homo homini, non homo* ("wolves—that's what human beings are to human beings, not human beings": Plautus, *Asinaria*, l. 495).

66. Sonnet: 'I wake and feel', p. 166 in Catherine Phillips' edition, which also contains some illuminating remarks on the subject on pp. 372–73.

67. ". . . rationalis creatura . . . ita facta est, ut sibi ipsi bonum, quo beata fiat, esse non possit": *Ep.* 140 (*Liber de gratia Novi Testamenti ad Honoratum*) XXIII, 56 (*CSEL* 44, p. 202; *PL* 33, 561).

68. *La Peste*, p. 1324 (cf. *The Plague*, p. 124): "Le mal qui est dans le monde vient presque toujours de l'ignorance, et la bonne volonté peut faire autant dégâts que la méchanceté, si elle n'est pas éclairée. Les hommes sont plutôt bons que mauvais, et en vérité ce n'est pas la question. Mais ils ignorent plus ou moins, et c'est ce qu'on appelle vertue ou vice, le vice le plus désespérant étant celui de l'ignorance qui croit tout savoir et qui s'autorise alors à tuer. L'âme du meurtrier est aveugle et il n'y a pas de vraie bonté ni de bel amour sans toute la clairvoyance possible."

69. "The Incredible Christian Capacity For Missing the Christian Point," p. 400.

70. "*memnēmenoi tēs anōthen eugeneias*": Gregory Nazianzen, *Oration* XXVII (= *Or. theol.* I), 7, 16–17 (*SC* 250, p. 88–89; *PG* 36, 20C [49–50]).

Bibliography

Allport, Gordon W. *The Nature of Prejudice.* Cambridge, MA: Addison Wesley, 1954.

Appleyard, J. A. *Coleridge's Philosophy of Literature: The Development of a Concept of Poetry 1791–1819.* Cambridge, MA: Harvard University Press, 1965.

Arrupe, Pedro. "Sobre el «análisis marxista»." *Acta Romana Societatis Jesu* 18 (1980–83): 331–38 (ET "On Marxist Analysis," 347–54).

Aschenbrenner, George. "Consciousness Examen." *Review for Religious* 31 (1972): 621–24.

Augustine, Saint. *Confessions.* Translated with an Introduction and Notes by Henry Chadwick. Oxford: Oxford University Press, 1991.

Auping, John. *The Relative Efficiency of Evangelical Non-Violence: The Influence of a Revival of Religion on the Abolition of Slavery in North America.* Rome: Pontificia Università Gregoriana, 1977.

———. *Religion and Social Justice: The Case of Christianity and the Abolition of Slavery in America.* Mexico D.F.: Universitad Iberoamericana, [1994].

Barry, William A. and Connolly, William J. *The Practice of Spiritual Direction.* San Francisco: Harper & Row, 1982.

Baum, Gregory. *The Priority of Labor: A Commentary on* Laborem Exercens, *Encyclical Letter of Pope John Paul II.* New York and Ramsey, NJ: Paulist Press, 1982.

Beeck, Frans Jozef van. *Catholic Identity after Vatican II: Three Types of Faith in the One Church.* Chicago: Loyola University Press, 1985.

———. "Christian Faith and Theology in Encounter with Non-Christians: Profession? Protestation? Self-maintenance? Abandon?" *Theological Studies* 55 (1994): 46–65.

———. *Christ Proclaimed: Christology as Rhetoric.* New York, Ramsey, NJ, and Toronto: Paulist Press, 1979.

Beesing, Maria, Nogosek, Robert J., and O'Leary, Patrick H. *The Enneagram: A Journey of Self Discovery.* Denville, NJ: Dimension Books, 1984.

Bennett, J. G. *Enneagram Studies.* York Beach, ME: Samuel Weiser, 1983.

Bennis, W. G., and Shepard, H. A. "A Theory of Group Development." *Human Relations* 9 (1956): 415–37.

Bensman, Joseph. See Vidich, Arthur J.

Berghuis, J. J. W. *Mens en Kosmos—een groots geheel: Uitweg uit de crisis in rationeel denken.* Kampen: Kok Agora, 1995.

Bergson, Henri. *Les deux sources de la morale et de la religion.* Bibliothèque de philosophie contemporaine. Paris: Presses universitaires de France, 1948 (ET *The Two Sources of Morality and Religion.* Notre Dame, IN: University of Notre Dame Press, 1977).

Bernardin, Joseph Cardinal, and others. *Consistent Ethic of Life.* Edited by Thomas G. Fuechtmann. Kansas City, MO: Sheed & Ward, 1988.

Biernatzki, William E. *Roots of Acceptance: The Intercultural Communication of Religious Meaning. Inculturation: Working Papers on Living Faith and Culture,* 13. Rome: Pontificia Università Gregoriana, 1991.

Bloom, Allan. *The Closing of the American Mind.* New York: Simon and Schuster, 1987.

Bonhoeffer, Dietrich. *Ethik.* Edited by Ilse Tödt, Heinz Eduard Tödt, Ernst Feil, and Clifford Green. *Dietrich Bonhoeffer Werke,* 6. München: Chr. Kaiser Verlag, 1992 (ET [of the sixth German edition, 1963] *Ethics.* New York: Macmillan, 1965).

Buber, Martin. *Ich und Du.* Second edition. Köln: Verlag Jakob Hegner, 1966 (ET *I and Thou.* Translated by Walter Kaufmann. New York: Charles Scribner's Sons, 1970).

Burchill, John. See Metz, Barbara.

Butler, Joseph. *The Analogy of Religion, Natural and Revealed. Works,* vol. i. Oxford: Oxford University Press, 1849.

Buytendijk, F. J. J. *Algemene theorie der menselijke houding en beweging.* Aulaboeken, 175. Utrecht/Antwerpen: Het Spectrum, 1964 (FrT *Attitudes et mouvements: Étude fonctionelle du mouvement humain.* [Paris]: Desclée De Brouwer, 1957. GmT: *Allgemeine Theorie der menschlichen Haltung und Bewegung, als Verbindung und Gegenüberstellung von physiologischer und psychologischer Betrachtungsweise.* Berlin: Springer, 1956).

Camus, Albert. *La Peste.* Collection Folio. [Paris:] Gallimard, 1972 (ET *The Plague.* Vintage Books. New York: Random House, 1972).

Carmina Burana. Edited by Alfons Hilka and Otto Schumann. Second edition. 2 vols. Heidelberg: Carl Winter Universitätsverlag, 1970.

———. See Orff, Carl.

Catholic Social Thought: The Documentary Heritage. Edited by David J. O'Brien and Thomas A. Shannon. Maryknoll, NY: Orbis, 1992.

[Chaucer, Geoffrey.] *The Works of Geoffrey Chaucer.* Edited by F. H. Robinson. Second Edition. London: Oxford University Press, 1957.

Chenu, M.-D. *La théologie au douzième siècle.* Paris: Vrin, 1957 (Partial ET *Nature, Man, and Society in the Twelfth Century: Essays on New Theological Perspectives in the Latin West.* Chicago: University of Chicago Press, 1968).

The Cloud of Unknowing and the Book of Privy Counselling. Edited by Phyllis Hodgson. *Early English Text Society,* 218. Revised 1958. Reprinted 1981. London, New York, and Toronto: Oxford University Press, 1944 (for 1943).

Coleridge, Samuel Taylor. *Biographia Literaria.* Edited by J. Shawcross. Revised edition. 2 vols. London: Oxford University Press, 1954.

Connolly, William J. See Barry, William A.

Cotter, Wendy. "Our *Politeuma* is in Heaven: The Meaning of Philippians 3. 17–21." In *Origins and Method: Towards a New Understanding of Judaism and Christianity.* [*Festschrift* John C. Hurd.] Journal for the Study of the

New Testament Series, 86. Sheffield: Sheffield Academic Press, 1993, pp. 92–104.

Daniélou, Jean. *Les anges et leur mission.* Chevetogne: Éditions de Chevetogne, 1953 (ET *The Angels and Their Mission.* Westminster, MD: Newman Press, 1957).

Dante Alighieri. *La divina commedia.* Milano: Ulricho Hoepli, 1987.

———. *Tutte le opere.* Edited by Fredi Chiappelli. Milano: U. Mursia & C., 1965.

D'Arcy, Martin C. *The Mind and Heart of Love, Lion and Unicorn: A Study in Eros and Agape.* London: Faber, 1953.

Dulles, Avery. *Models of Revelation.* Garden City, NJ: Doubleday, 1983.

Dupré, Louis K. *Transcendent Selfhood: The Loss and Rediscovery of the Inner Life.* New York: Seabury, 1976.

Eliot, T. S. *Collected Poems 1909–1962.* London: Faber and Faber, 1963.

Emblemata: Handbuch zur Sinnbildkunst des XVI. und XVII. Jahrhunderts. Edited by Arthur Henkel und Albrecht Schöne. Stuttgart: J.B. Metzlersche Verlagsbuchhandlung, 1967.

Evagrius Ponticus. See Guillaumont, Antoine.

———. *The Praktikos* and *Chapters on Prayer.* Edited by John Eudes Bamberger. Spencer, MA: Cistercian Publications, 1970.

Fingarette, Herbert. *The Self in Transformation: Psychoanalysis, Philosophy, and the Life of the Spirit.* New York–London: Basic Books, 1963.

Ford, John C. "The Morality of Obliteration Bombing." *Theological Studies* 5(1944): 261–309.

Frazier, William B. "The Incredible Christian Capacity For Missing the Christian Point." *America* 167(1992): 398–400.

Freire, Paulo. *Pedagogy of the Oppressed.* Revised edition. New York: Continuum, 1993.

Froehlich, Karlfried. "Cultivating a Symbolic Mentality." Unpublished paper, 1995.

Frohlich, Mary. "From Mystification to Mystery: Lonergan and the Theological Significance of Sexuality." In *Lonergan and Feminism.* Edited by Cynthia S. W. Crysdale. Toronto: University of Toronto Press, 1994, pp. 175–98.

Futrell, John C. *Making an Apostolic Community of Love.* St. Louis, Institute of Jesuit Sources, 1970.

Gadamer, Hans-Georg. *Das Erbe Europas: Beiträge.* Bibliothek Suhrkamp, 1004. Frankfurt am Main: Suhrkamp, 1989.

———. *Über die Verborgenheit der Gesundheit: Aufsätze und Vorträge.* Bibliothek Suhrkamp, 1135. Frankfurt am Main: Suhrkamp, 1993.

Gerth, H.H. See Weber, Max.

Golding, William. *The Inheritors.* New York: Harcourt, Brace & World, 1955.

Guardini, Romano. *Die Annahme seiner selbst.* Würzburg: Werkbund Verlag, 1965.

Hadewijch. *The Complete Works.* Translated and introduced by Mother Columba Hart. The Classics of Western Spirituality. New York: Paulist Press, 1980.

―――. See Mommaers, Paul.

Hart, Ray L. *Unfinished Man and the Imagination: Toward an Ontology and a Rhetoric of Revelation.* New York: Herder and Herder, 1968.

Hegel, Georg Wilhelm Friedrich. *Vorlesungen über die Philosophie der Geschichte. Werke in zwanzig Bänden,* 12. Frankfurt am Main: Suhrkamp Verlag, 1970.

Hengel, Martin. *Crucifixion in the Ancient World and the Folly of the Message of the Cross.* Philadelphia: Fortress, 1977.

Henkel, Arthur. See *Emblemata.*

Hollenbach, David. *Justice, Peace, and Human Rights: American Catholic Social Ethics in a Pluralistic Context.* New York: Crossroad, 1988.

[Ignatius of Loyola, Saint.] *The Spiritual Exercises of Saint Ignatius.* Translated by Thomas Corbishley. London: Burns and Oates, 1963.

Ingram, H. See Luft, Joseph.

Ishiguro, Kazuo. *The Remains of the Day.* London: Faber & Faber, 1989.

John Paul II, Pope [Karol Wojtyla]. Encyclical *Veritatis Splendor.* ET in *Origins* 23(1993): 297. 298–334.

Karjanto, Iiro. "Fortuna." In *Aufstieg und Niedergang der Römischen Welt: Geschichte und Kultur Roms im Spiegel der neueren Forschung.* XVII. Band (1. Teilband). *Prinzipat.* Berlin and New York: Walter de Gruyter, 1981, pp. 502–58.

Keen, Sam. "We have no desire to strengthen the ego or make it happy: A conversation about ego destruction with Oscar Ichazo." *Psychology Today,* July 1973, pp. 64–72.

Keller, Hagen. "Vom 'heiligen Buch' zur 'Buchführung': Lebensfunktionen der Schrift in Mittelalter." *Frühmittelalterliche Studien* 26(1992): 1–31.

Klima, Jörg. "Instinkt und Moral." *Wort und Wahrheit* 28(1973): 333–337.

Kol, Alphonse van. "Caritas en humanitas." *Bijdragen* 16(1955): 69–90.

―――. *Theologia moralis.* Two vols. Barcelona: Herder, 1968.

Langan, John P. "Augustine on the Unity and the Interconnection of the Virtues." *Harvard Theological Review* 72(1979): 91–95.

Le Goff, Jacques. *La naissance du Purgatoire.* Paris: Gallimard, 1981 (ET *The Birth of Purgatory.* Chicago: University of Chicago Press, 1983).

Le Goff, Jacques. "Les mentalités: Une histoire ambiguë." In *Faire de l'histoire.* Edited by Jacques Le Goff and Pierre Nora. Volume 3: *Nouveaux objets.* Paris: Gallimard, 1974, pp. 76–94.

Lévinas, Emmanuel. *Difficile liberté: Essais sur le judaïsme.* Second edition. Paris: Albin Michel, 1976.

Lewin, Kurt. *Field Theory in Social Science: Selected Theoretical Papers.* Edited by Dorwin Cartwright. New York: Harper, 1951.

Lewis, C. S. *That Hideous Strength.* London: Bodley Head, 1945.

————. *Out of the Silent Planet.* London: Bodley Head, 1938.

————. *Perelandra.* London: Bodley Head, 1943.

Luft, Joseph. *Group Processes: An Introduction to Group Dynamics.* Palo Alto, CA: National Press, 1963.

————. "The Johari Window." In *Selections from Human Relations Training News.* Washington, DC: NTL Institute for Applied Behavioral Science, 1969.

———— and Ingram, H. *The Johari Window: A Graphic Model for Interpersonal Relations.* Western Training Laboratory for Group Development. Los Angeles: University of California at Los Angeles Extension Office, August, 1955.

MacIntyre, Alasdair. *After Virtue: A Study in Moral Theory.* Notre Dame, IN: University of Notre Dame Press, 1981.

Mann, Thomas. *Der Zauberberg.* Frankfurt: S. Fischer Verlag, 1924 (ET *The Magic Mountain.* Harmondsworth: Penguin, 1960).

Markus, Robert A. *Gregory the Great and his world.* Cambridge: Cambridge University Press, 1997.

Martz, Louis L. *The Poetry of Meditation: A Study in English Religious Literature.* Revised edition. New Haven: Yale University Press, 1974.

Maslow, Abraham H. *Religions, Values, and Peak-Experiences.* Columbus, OH: Ohio State University Press, 1964.

————. *Toward a Psychology of Being.* Second edition. New York, Cincinnati, Toronto, London, and Melbourne: Van Nostrand Reinhold, 1968.

McConnell, Frank. "What Hath Phil Wrought? A Coarsening of Culture." *Commonweal* 123, Number 6 (March 22, 1996): 20–1.

McGregor, Douglas. *The Human Side of Enterprise.* New York: McGraw-Hill, 1960.

McLuhan, Marshall. *The Gutenberg Galaxy: The Making of Typographic Man.* Toronto: University of Totonto Press, 1962.

Meissner, William W. *Group Dynamics in the Religious Life.* Notre Dame, IN: Notre Dame University Press, 1965.

Metz, Barbara, and Burchill, John. *The Enneagram and Prayer.* Denville, NJ: Dimension Books, 1987.

Mills, Theodore. *The Sociology of Small Groups.* Englewood Cliffs, NJ: Prentice Hall, 1967.

Mitford, Nancy. See Ross, Alan S. C.

Mommaers, Paul. *De brieven van Hadewijch.* Averbode: Altiora, 1990.

————. *Hadewijch: Schrijfster–Begijn–Mystica.* Averbode: Altiora, 1989.

Moss, Christopher. "Extraterrestrials and the Love of God." *The Tablet* 250 (1996): 100–02.

Murdoch, Iris. *Metaphysics as a Guide to Morals.* London: Chatto & Windus, 1992.

————. *The Sovereignty of Good.* London and Henley: Routledge and Kegan Paul, 1970.

————. *The Unicorn*. London: Chatto & Windus, 1963.

Naranjo, Claudio. *Ennea-Type Structures: Self-Analysis for the Seeker*. Nevada City, CA: Gateways/IDHHB, Inc., 1990.

[Neville, Henry.] *The Isle of Pines; or, A late Discovery of a fourth Island near Terra Australis, Incognita, by Henry Cornelius Van Sloetten*. In Worthington Chauncey Ford. *The Isle of Pines 1668: An Essay in Bibliography*. Boston: The Club of Odd Volumes, 1920, pp. 51–87. Also in Onofrio Nicastro. *Henry Neville e l'isola di Pines*. Pisa: SEU, 1988, pp. 67–119.

Newman, John Henry. *Certain Difficulties Felt by Anglicans in Catholic Teaching*. Vol. II. London: Longmans, Green, and Co., 1885.

Nogosek, Robert J. See Beesing, Maria.

————. *Nine Portraits of Jesus: Discovering Jesus through the Enneagram*. Denville, NJ: Dimension Books, 1987.

O'Connor, Flannery. *Collected Works*. Edited by Sally Fitzgerald. *The Library of America*, 39. New York: Literary Classics of the United States, Inc., 1988.

————. *The Habit of Being: Letters of Flannery O'Connor*. Selected and edited by Sally Fitzgerald. New York: The Noonday Press, 1988.

O'Leary, Patrick H. See Beesing, Maria.

Ong, Walter J. *Fighting for Life: Contest, Sexuality, and Consciousness*. Ithaca and London: Cornell University Press, 1981.

————. *Interfaces of the Word: Studies in the Evolution of Consciousness and Culture*. Ithaca, NY and London: Cornell University Press, 1977.

————. *Orality and Literacy: The Technologizing of the Word*. Reprint. London and New York: Methuen, 1985.

————. *The Presence of the Word: Some Prolegomena for Cultural and Religious History*. New York: Simon and Schuster, 1970.

————. *Ramus, Method and the Decay of Dialogue*. Cambridge, MA and London: Harvard University Press, 1983.

————. *Rhetoric, Romance, and Technology: Studies in the Interaction of Expression and Culture*. Ithaca, NY and London: Cornell University Press, 1971.

Orff, Carl. *Carmina Burana: Cantiones Profanae*. Chicago: Bolchazy-Carducci Publishers, 1984.

Packard, Vance Oakley. *The Hidden Persuaders*. New York: D. McKay, 1957

Pagès, Max. *La vie affective des groupes: Esquisse d'une théorie de la relation humaine*. Paris: Dunod, 1968.

Palmer, Helen. *The Enneagram: Understanding Yourself and the Others in Your Life*. San Francisco: Harper & Row, 1988.

Patch, Howard R. *The Goddess Fortuna in Mediaeval Literature*. Cambridge: Harvard University Press, 1927.

Pope, Stephen J. *The Evolution of Altruism and the Ordering of Love*. Washington, DC: Georgetown University Press, 1994.

Rahner, Hugo. "Eutrapelie, eine vergessene Tugend." *Geist und Leben* 27 (1954): 246–53.

Rahner, Karl. "Towards a Fundamental Theological Interpretation of Vatican II." *Theological Studies* 40(1979):716–27 (GmT "Theologische Grundinterpretation des II. Vatikanischen Konzils. In *SchrzTh* 14, pp. 287–302).

Riesman, David. *The Lonely Crowd: A Study of the Changing American Character*. New Haven and London: Yale University Press and Oxford University Press, 1970.

Riso, Don Richard. *Personality Types: Using the Enneagram for Self-Discovery*. Boston: Houghton Mifflin Company, 1987.

Rohr, Richard and Ebert, Andreas. *Das Enneagram: Die 9 Gesichter der Seele*. München: Claudius Verlag, 1989 (ET *Discovering the Enneagram: An Ancient Tool for a New Spiritual Journey*. New York: Crossroad, 1990).

Rohr, Richard and Ebert, Andreas, and others. *Experiencing the Enneagram*. New York: Crossroad, 1994.

Ross, Alan S. C., and Mitford, Nancy, and others. *Noblesse Oblige: An Enquiry into the Identifiable Characteristics of the English Aristocracy*. London: Hamish Hamilton, 1956.

Scheler, Max. *Der Formalismus in der Ethik und die materiale Wertethik: Neuer Versuch der Grundlegung eines ethischen Personalismus. Gesammelte Werke, 2.* Bern and München: Francke Verlag, 1954 (ET *Formalism in Ethics and Non-Formal Ethics of Values: A New Attempt Toward the Foundation of an Ethical Personalism*. Evanston: Northwestern University Press, 1973).

Schenk, Erich. *Mozart: Eine Biographie*. München: Wilhelm Goldmann Verlag, 1983.

Schoonenberg, P. J. A. M. *Man and Sin: A Theological View*. [Notre Dame, IN]: University of Notre Dame Press, 1965.

Schöne, Albrecht. See *Emblemata*.

Schumacher, E.F. *Small is Beautiful: A Study of Economics as if People Mattered*. London: Sphere Books, 1974.

Schutz, William C. *The Interpersonal Underworld (FIRO: A Three-Dimensional Theory of Interpersonal Behavior)*. Palo Alto, CA: Science and Behavior Books, 1966.

Shepard, H. A. See Bennis, W. G.

Snow, C. P. *The Two Cultures and the Scientific Revolution*. New York: Cambridge University Press, 1959 (Expanded edition: *The Two Cultures: And a Second Look*. Cambridge: Cambridge University Press, 1963).

Spark, Muriel. *The Collected Stories*. Harmondsworth, Middlesex: Penguin Books, 1994.

Spengler, Oswald. *Der Untergang des Abendlandes: Umrisse einer Morphologie der Weltgeschichte*. Two vols. München: C. H. Beck, 1927.

[Sullivan, Harry Stack.] *The Collected Works of Harry Stack Sullivan, M. D.* Edited by Helen Swick Perry and others. 2 vols. New York, W. W. Norton and Co., [no yr.].

Thomas, Dylan. *Collected Poems 1934-1952*. London: J.M.Dent & Sons, 1952.

Tillich, Paul. *Systematic Theology.* Three volumes in one. Chicago: University of Chicago Press, 1967.

Tubbs, Stewart. *A Systems Approach to Small Group Interaction.* Third edition. New York: Random House, 1988.

Tyrrell, Bernard J. *Christotherapy II: The Fasting and Feasting Heart.* Ramsey NJ: Paulist, 1982.

Verhaar, J. W. M. *Some Reflections on Perception, Speech and Thought.* Assen: van Gorcum, 1963.

[Vesalius, Andreas.] *The Illustrations from the Works of Andreas Vesalius.* Edited by J. B. deC. M. Sauders and Charles D. O'Malley. New York: Dover Publications, 1973.

Vidich, Arthur J., and Bensman, Joseph. *Small Town in Mass Society: Class, Power and Religion in a Rural Community.* Revised edition. Princeton Paperbacks, 131. Princeton, NJ: Princeton University Press, 1968.

Vos van Steenwijk, Alwine de. *Pour combattre la pauvreté et l'exclusion, repenser l'activité humaine: Contribution au Sommet mondial pour le développement social, Copenhagen, March, 1995.* (Mouvement international ATD Quart Monde, 107, Avenue du Général Leclerc, 95480 Pierrelaye, France).

Wagner, Jerome P. and Walker, Ronald E. "Reliability and Validity Study of a Sufi Personality Typology: The Enneagram." *Journal of Clinical Psychology* 39(1983): 712–17.

Walker, Ronald E. See Wagner, Jerome P.

Walser, Martin. *Finks Krieg.* Frankfurt am Main: Suhrkamp, 1996.

———. *Seelenarbeit.* Frankfurt am Main: Suhrkamp, 1983.

[Weber, Max.] *From Max Weber: Essays in Sociology.* Edited by H.H.Gerth and C. Wright Mills. New York: Oxford University Press, 1946.

Woolf, Virginia. *The Waves.* Reprint of the 1931 edition. A Harvest/HBJ Book. New York and London: Harcourt Brace Jovanovich, 1978.

Wresinski, Joseph. *Grande pauvreté et précarité économique et sociale. Journal officiel de la Républque Française: Avis et rapports du conseil économique et social.* 1987 — No 6, February 28, 1987.

Subject Index

Name Index

Scripture Index

CORRIGENDA in Volume II/3

On page 78, cancel the top line, and add the following line at the bottom:

jectivity and geometrical method as they have typically been (cf. §7,

p. 18 footnote, line 1: §136, 5–6	read §139, 5–6
p. 27 footnote, line 3: §140, 1–2	read §141, 1; §146, 13
p. 31 line 6: §310, 10	read §133, 8
line 10: §318, 4	read §138, 8; §140, 5
line 14: §142, 14, a	read §148, 15, a; §163, 6; 10, b
p. 51 line 13: §130, 7	read §130, 1; §131, 1–2
p. 66 line 39: §130, 8–9	read §133, 5–6
p. 72 footnote, line 9: §§127–130	read §§127–133
line 15: §§131–137	read §§134–140
p. 74 line 12: §130, 6, [n]	read §133, 2, [v]
§134, 10; 12–14	read §137, 10; 12–14; §138, 4
p. 96 line 25: §129, 7 and [j]	read §129, 6, a and [l]
p. 119 line 2: §134, 1	read §137, 1
p. 121 line 19: §139, 7–8	read §146, 6–7
line 22: §139, 1, b–d	read §146, 1, b–d
p. 128 line 11: §138, 2–3	read §146, 6–8
p. 129 line 29: §132, 1; §134, 1, [e]	read §135, 1; §137, 1 [e]; §138, 11, a
§142, 4 and a–b	read §124, 10, a–b
p. 130 footnote, line 18: §131, 2, c	read §134, 2, c
line 22: §141, 3–4	read §142, 3, a; §155, 4, a
p. 151 line 28: §138, 2	read §140, 1

Frans Jozef van Beeck, S.J., is the author of twelve books and about sixty essays and articles. In the area of theology, examples are "Towards an Ecumenical Understanding of the Sacraments" (1966); "Sacraments, Church Order, and Secular Responsibility" (1969); *Christ Proclaimed: Christology as Rhetoric* (1979); *Fifty Psalms: An Attempt at a New Translation* (with Huub Oosterhuis and others; 1969); *Grounded in Love: Sacramental Theology in an Ecumenical Perspective* (1981); "Professing the Uniqueness of Christ" (1985); *Catholic Identity after Vatican II: Three Types of Faith in the One Church* (1985); "The Worship of Christians in Pliny's Letter" (1988); *Loving the Torah More than God? Toward a Catholic Appreciation of Judaism* (1989); "Tradition and Interpretation" (1990); "Divine Revelation: Intervention or Self-Communication?" (1991); "Professing Christianity Among the World's Religions" (1991); "Two Kind Jewish Men: A Sermon in Commemoration of the Shoa" (1992); "The Quest of the Historical Jesus: Origins, Achievements, and the Specter of Diminishing Returns" (1994) "Christian Faith and Theology in Encounter with Non-Christians: Profession? Protestation? Self-maintenance? Abandon?" (1994); "Fantasy, the Capital Sins, the Enneagram, and Self-Acceptance: An Essay in Ascetical Theology" (1994); "My Encounter with Yossel Rakover" (1995). In the area of literature, there are pieces like *The Poems and Translations of Sir Edward Sherburne (1616-1702)* (1961); "Hopkins: *Cor ad Cor*" (1975); "A Note on *Ther* in Curses and Blessings in Chaucer" (1985); "The Choices of Two Anthologists: Understanding Hopkins' Catholic Idiom" (1989). The following installments of *God Encountered: A Contemporary Catholic Systematic Theology* are in print: Vol. One, *Understanding the Christian Faith* (1989; 2nd revised edition 1997); Vol. Two/1, *The Revelation of the Glory: Introduction and Fundamental Theology* (1993); Vol. Two/2, *The Revelation of the Glory: One God, Creator of All That Is* (1994); and Vol. Two/3, *The Revelation of the Glory: Finitude and Fall* (1996). The balance of Volume Two/4 is close to completion, and will shortly appear as *The Revelation of the Glory: The Genealogy of Depravity: Living Alive to the Living God* (Two/4B). Volume Two/5, to be subtitled *The Revelation of the Glory: The Glory of God in the Face of Christ,* has been in process for some time. The third and final volume, with the tentative subtitle *A World Brought Home,* is still in the planning stage. Father van Beeck's personal predilections include liturgy, preaching, teaching, spiritual direction, good conversation, and music (he used to be a decent violinist), and even a little bird watching.